UPDATE CULTURE AND
THE AFTERLIFE OF
DIGITAL WRITING

T0308970

UPDATE CULTURE AND THE AFTERLIFE OF DIGITAL WRITING

JOHN R. GALLAGHER

UTAH STATE UNIVERSITY PRESS
Logan

© 2019 by University Press of Colorado

Published by Utah State University Press
An imprint of University Press of Colorado
245 Century Circle, Suite 202
Louisville, Colorado 80027

All rights reserved
Printed in the United States of America

The University Press of Colorado is a proud member of
the Association of University Presses.

The University Press of Colorado is a cooperative publishing enterprise supported,
in part, by Adams State University, Colorado State University, Fort Lewis College,
Metropolitan State University of Denver, University of Colorado, University of Northern
Colorado, University of Wyoming, Utah State University, and Western Colorado
University.

∞ This paper meets the requirements of the ANSI/NISO Z39.48–1992 (Permanence of
Paper).

ISBN: 978-1-60732-973-2 (paperback)
ISBN: 978-1-60732-974-9 (ebook)
DOI: https://doi.org/10.7330/9781607329749

Library of Congress Cataloging-in-Publication Data

Names: Gallagher, John R., 1983– author.
Title: Update culture and the afterlife of digital writing / John R. Gallagher.
Description: Logan : Utah State University Press, [2019] | Includes bibliographical refer-
    ences and index.
Identifiers: LCCN 2019033219 (print) | LCCN 2019033218 (ebook) | ISBN
    9781607329732 (paperback) | ISBN 9781607329749 (ebook)
Subjects: LCSH: Electronic publishing. | Authors and publishers.
Classification: LCC Z286.E43 G35 2019 (ebook) | LCC Z286.E43 (print) | DDC
    070.5/797—dc23
LC record available at https://lccn.loc.gov/2019033219

The University Press of Colorado gratefully acknowledges the generous support of the
University of Illinois toward the publication of this book.

Parts (but not much) of this manuscript have appeared in previous publications. Some
of the ideas related to templates in chapter 2 appeared in "Challenging the Monetized
Template," *Enculturation* 24 (2017): n.p. A small section in chapter 4 appeared in "Five
Strategies Internet Writers Use to 'Continue the Conversation,'" in *Written Communication*
32 (4): 396–425. A small section of chapter 5 appeared in "Monitoring and Managing
Online Comments in Science Journalism," in *Citizenship and Advocacy in Technical
Communication: Scholarly and Pedagogical Perspectives*, edited by Godwin Agboka and
Natalia Matveeva (New Yovrk: Routledge), 137–52. However, most of the ideas have been
updated and edited.

Duty Calls, courtesy of XKCD

CONTENTS

ACKNOWLEDGMENTS

The people most responsible for this project are its participants. I did not pay any of them. They graciously volunteered their time, often when it was convenient for me. Interviewing them was a pleasure. I consider talking with writers to be the best part of my job. To all the bloggers, journalists, redditors, and reviewers: thank you for making this project possible.

In terms of scholarly support, Steve Holmes offered me in-depth guidance throughout this project while keeping a sense of humor along the way. I acknowledge that my spouse, Shelby Hutchens, tolerated interviews at random times of the day and listened to me drone on about the project, especially toward the end. There are many people in the computers and writing community I am grateful for knowing and friending; while I cannot name all of them, thanks to Kristin Arola, Kevin Brock, Jim Brown Jr., Aaron Beveridge, Dànielle Nicole DeVoss, Dustin Edwards, Harley Ferris, and Rebecca Tarsa. Because this project was largely conceived as a new project, it holds little relationship to my dissertation. Nevertheless, the seeds of this project started in my dissertation, and I wish to thank Donna LeCourt and Anne Herrington for giving me the methodology that made this book possible. I am indebted to Paul Prior's and Catherine Prendergast's career advice, humor, and grace during my career at UIUC. Thanks to Maria Gillombardo for suggesting *Afterlife* as a possible title of this manuscript. Thank you to Rachael Lussos for copyediting this manuscript. Thank you to the University Press of Colorado and my editor, Rachael Levay, for support throughout the publication process. Thank you to the University of Illinois at Urbana-Champaign, which provided a subvention grant to help increase the circulation of this book.

Family, and the values family represents, is the most important thing in life, something my participants reminded me of during our interviews. I dedicate this book to my family, especially my father (John E. Gallagher), Quentin, Landry, and Shelby. My sister (Michelle Carr) and mother (Karen Holmes) were enthusiastic about my writing throughout many years, and I thank them for their support over the long arc of a life. Andy Potts listened to me read terrible undergrad papers late at night—thank you for your support, good sir. My friends, Greg Sargent and Michael Gormley, have stood by me for over a decade—thank you and I love you guys. I lost my good friend, Tucker Harpin, and mother-in-law, Lynn Wenig, while finishing this book. I think they would be proud of this book. Family are the ones who stand behind you when things are tough.

UPDATE CULTURE AND THE AFTERLIFE OF DIGITAL WRITING

INTRODUCTION

Update Culture

This book evolved from an unusual phenomenon that occurred while I was interviewing a blogger as part of a project about participatory audiences. The project investigated how digital writers consider their audiences who write back to them, often via comments. In 2013, I interviewed the blogger Kelly Salasin over the phone. I sat in my mother's home in Philadelphia, and Kelly sat in her home in Vermont. While we were talking about a blog post of hers that was spotlighted by the *New York Times*, we both had her blog open on our respective computers. Kelly sat in her home, reading through her blog posts as I asked her questions about the local tragedy she had blogged about. A funny thing began to happen. As I asked her questions about her blog posts and writing processes, she would say, "I need to update that." And then she would.

As soon as I'd leave the webpage and return, new changes would appear without any indication the blog post had been different moments before. I asked Kelly if she changed her texts based on the comments she received. "All the time," she said. "If the comments are any good, I'll change my posts." At one point, Kelly even remarked, "My own perception of a post can change depending on the comment." She pointed me to a series of her blog posts that had received numerous comments and thousands of pageviews.[1] "I went back and read each post again and again," she said, "because I heard from all sorts of [commenters]." Kelly talked at length about the work and time she put into her writing *after* it was already floating around on the internet, that is, after it was published to the internet and circulating on social media. As her writing was circulating, sometimes due to her actions and sometimes due to the actions of others, such as the *New York Times*, she found herself attending to the comments.

Years later, and after continuing to interview dozens more digital writers, I realized participants made changes to their texts based on audience comments. Even more frequently, those writers attended to their feedback and made savvy decisions based on comments and other

DOI: 10.7330/9781607329749.c000

indicators of reception, such as Facebook Likes or Twitter Retweets. My interview data demonstrate that as digital writing circulates, it does not do so statically or without making a claim on those who initially wrote it. These data illustrate a fundamental shift in the analytic and inventive focus from an end product of writing to the emergent responses to online commenters. To be clear, print writers deal with editors, and newspapers print letters to the editor. However, social media is different from this response due to the scale of response and the real-time responsivity. Due to these factors, digital writers make a variety of decisions and engage in a remarkable range of activities after they initially complete a digital text.

This book argues that these decisions and activities are not only important considerations but are perhaps even more important than the analysis of the first text a digital writer produces. While most scholarship in writing studies continues to examine the end product, even as that end product circulates and changes, I suggest we examine how digital writers' processes and strategies change over the course of time as they experience their audiences' reactions and responses. In other words, this book documents and analyzes digital writers' decisions *after* a text has been composed and *during* its delivery. While print writers have in some ways always dealt with the afterlife of their texts, such as novelists going on book tours or journalists going on television to discuss an article, the internet and social media have greatly intensified this afterlife, as well as made the activities of this afterlife extremely heterogeneous. In an age of participatory audiences and audience comments on a "published" piece of writing, digital writers can now see how audience interaction impacts the reception of their texts—in real time and over long periods of time. Seeing and reading this audience reception influence the way digital writers *write during the circulation of their texts*, which is not possible for print-based writing. It is an outgrowth of real-time social media writing, wherein changes made to a "published" text can be read by internet audiences almost instantaneously. And in rhetorical terms, digital writers' new *topoi* (commonplaces) don't just inform their primary creative act. Rather, online audiences pose new *topoi* and change *doxa* (common beliefs) that beg for additional inventive possibilities and interactions.

To be sure, writing studies scholars have started to attend to the ecological and circulatory elements of writing, a conversation distilled in Laurie Gries and Collin Brooke's edited collection *Circulation, Writing, and Rhetoric* (2018), as well as in Gries's individual work (2013, 2015) and Dustin Edwards's work (2017, 2018). Circulation has engendered an extensive conversation in writing studies that includes rethinking and critiquing the canons in light of seismic changes in semiotic resources and modalities (Brooke 2009; Prior et al. 2007), as well as moving beyond classroom practices of writing (Dobrin 2011). This diverse conversation on circulation—or more accurately, conversations—includes remodeling delivery (Porter 2009; Ridolfo 2012; Ridolfo and DeVoss 2009; Trimbur 2000; Yancey 2004), distant reading and thin description (D. Mueller 2018), addressing the economies of circulations (Chaput 2010; Eyman 2015; Johnson-Eilola 1995; LeCourt 2017), algorithms, bots, and propaganda (Laquintano and Vee 2017), multimodality and remixing (Dubisar and Palmeri 2010), fandom (DeLuca 2018), self-publishing (Laquintano 2016), and the effects of circulation on digital tools and researchers (Solberg 2012). Moreover, new media researchers have addressed circulation in the context of metrics (Beer 2016) and neoliberalism (Dean 2005). Writing studies theory on circulation has also bled into the digital humanities, addressing feminist historiography (Enoch and Bessette 2013), virality (Wuebben 2016), and attention (Horn, Beveridge, and Morey 2016). At the intersection of circulation, writing studies, and the digital humanities lies Jim Ridolfo's work on textual diaspora, or the idea that the existence and circulation of manuscripts communicate the existence of a people (Ridolfo 2013, 2015).

While this body of work is productive and certainly an improvement on older static models, such as Lloyd Bitzer's rhetorical situation (1968), these conversations trace the evolution of texts, conversations, and discourse as they circulate rather than what writers or speakers are doing as that discourse evolves. These conversations on circulation focus intently on content rather than on the processes of those who wrote or initiated that content.

In terms of circulation, writing studies considers the life of documents, texts, and other discourse as they move outside the control of the initial writer or content creator. James Porter (2009) has even gone so far as to posit, "Circulation refers to the potential for [a] message to have a document life of its own and be re-distributed without your direct intervention" (213). This approach, while an important and necessary element to address, has left largely unattended the circulatory activity of writers who initiate discourse, leaving circulatory writing processes ripe for study. By studying these neglected circulatory writing processes, we can better learn about what digital writers do after they've published a text and delivered an argument. We can learn about the ways digital writers create audiences and attract attention for their texts to increase circulation. We can also learn how digital writers develop novel inventive strategies for selecting which comments to respond to as a primary inventive act that grows their digital *ethos* or brand. Opening up these processes assists us in seeing all the various activities and responsibilities writers have *after* they've written—and in turn, the ways those activities shape how they write.[2]

For example, in Gries's highly useful concept of iconographic tracking (2013, 2015), Shepard Fairey's image of Obama remixes rapidly, spreading into sometimes shocking contexts and purposes. The images themselves, rather than those who composed them or edited them, are of primary concern for researchers engaged in iconographic tracking. Circulation here seems to focus upon the *results* of the circulation, not necessarily on the writerly processes of circulation. I propose an alternative view of circulation: what if circulation in writing studies focused on how writers or discourse producers alter their activities in response to audience input? An analogy here might be a scenario in which Shepherd Fairey decided to change the color or aesthetic style of his image in response to critical tweets or perhaps created a new image in response to a critical mass of suggestions.

Thus, as its subject matter, this book asks, *What are writers doing once their writing is in circulation?* This book responds to this broad question about circulation by extending this concern to digital writing and rhetoric. It asks the following: What are writers doing during the circulation of their *digital* texts and how are they doing it? Furthermore, how do their writing styles change and adapt over time as they learn how to predict or negotiate their audiences' public praise, criticism, or myriad forms of online interaction? My short answer is that, due to the speed, frequency, scale, and access of audience participation on the internet, writers attend to the afterlife of their texts through a variety of strategies that fuse oralities and literacies through what I call *textual timing*, *textual attention*, and *textual management* (chapters 3, 4, and 5 of this book).

The speed, frequency, scale, and accessibility of circulating discourse have inaugurated what I label an *update culture*, one in which writers like Kelly attend to comments on their writing, write continuously in response, and contend with emergent audiences at extreme intensity. And, potentially, digital writers can never cease responding to these readers, especially if these writers are committed to answering their commenters' questions. More precisely, update culture is an ongoing expectation to reread, edit, and update texts in digital environments mediated by interactive internet interfaces—think here of social media applications wherein average users do not need to know how to program or use markup language. Update culture describes a type of digital semiosis in which audiences and writers are engaged in discursive exchanges with one another. To rethink Roland Barthes's claim about the death of the author, the digital writer is often alive, answering questions and responding to comments from the audience—along with a variety of other activities. This call and response enables digital writing and rhetoric to exist in a state of flux and fluidity. Boundaries between texts, words, conversations, and digital activity become fluid and changeable—ideas I turn to in the conclusion of this book. As legal scholar Peter Tiersma (2010) notes in *Parchment, Paper, Pixels,* "The distinction between speech and writing is not as clear-cut as it once was. Modern technologies have made it possible to preserve speech for long periods of time as well as to transmit it over long distances" (13–14).

While writing studies and rhetoric scholars understand speech and writing were never entirely separate, update culture extends and reorients this description because it emerges from a particular technology: interactive and participatory internet (IPI) templates. This book consequently offers the claim that an important part of studying update culture lies in assessing how templates influence both the comments audiences leave as well as how digital writers negotiate these comments. These templates are structures that provide decorum and, following James Brown Jr.'s *Ethical Programs: Hospitality and the Rhetorics of Software* (2015), Wendy Chun's *Updating to Remain the Same: Habitual New Media* (2016), and Steve Holmes's *The Rhetoric of Videogames as Embodied Practice: Procedural Habits* (2017), habits for users, thereby providing *expectations* about how to write and communicate. I use *decorum,* following Robert Hariman (1992), to mean "a dynamic practice of social composition for rhetorical effect" (150). More simply, templates provide conventions and expectations about how to write digitally, and templates prefigure the writer-audience relationship. Although I say more about templates in chapter 2, for now, you might think of an empty Facebook profile or a content-management system such as WordPress. An everyday person can communicate with these templates without any specialized computer expertise. By providing decorum, habits, and expectations of continuous communication, these templates provide the technological capability previous technologies such as the cuneiform tablet, the scroll, the codex, and the book did not enable. These templates enable the slide among reading, writing, talking, and listening to become easier—and confirm that the digital rhetoric theories of the 1990s and early 2000s have been borne out (Gurak 2003; Lanham 1993; Welch 1999). Templates enable users to talk through, around, and with text. They allow, as many new media theorists have argued, communication similar to the speed of talking but through writing. In the context of these templates, writing and digital communication can be updated, edited, and revised. The *expectation* in update culture is that texts circulate rapidly, words mutate, and images become modified—what Jim Ridolfo and Dànielle Nicole DeVoss (2009) call "rhetorical velocity," with respect to the movement of texts, and what Gries's *Still Life with Rhetoric* (2015) has documented as the changing evolution of images through iconographic tracking.

This book thus makes two overall claims. First, update culture is a contemporary phenomenon related to internet interfaces that I call *interactive and participatory internet (IPI) templates.* These templates, as structures for everyday users, encourage a continuous process of rewriting and rereading texts with the expectation that digital texts will be different at subsequent times (Gallagher 2017). As Katelyn Burton (2015) has observed in an analysis of various digital media, the digital world is not as permanent as we might think. We now *expect* digital writing and rhetoric to be mutable in ways simply not possible with previous forms of media and interfaces. It's tempting, then, to focus on how rhetoric flows, as many circulation theories have. By contrast, templates show where procedural rhetorics produce constraints, such as creative constraints like procedural enthymemes (Brock and Shepherd 2016). While many prior forms of media and interfaces enabled certain aspects similar to update culture, IPI templates have encouraged an expectation of rapid and scaled exchange.

Second, writers cope with and react to update culture in ways that result in departures from writing processes that do not account for these rapid expectations. I aim to *document* the ways individual writers do this by identifying and analyzing the decisions writers make and execute given their impressions of their participatory audiences. I am not simply arguing that writers employ strategies to contend with rapid audience response. I document *how* they do so. While I reference some theoretical contexts such as habitus or new materialism in the context of circulation work, I also bolster these approaches with qualitative data. Methodologically, rather than taking a theoretical approach to update culture, I take a descriptive, empirical approach of forty case studies of digital writers, and I attempt to extrapolate some of the broader implications of these descriptions. Very broadly, I find that writers use oral modes of communication to describe their own writing tactics.[3] The three primary strategies my participants reported and demonstrated were timing, attention, and management. I focus primarily on these writers because they cope with update culture *taken to its highest intensity* in that they actively consider their audience participation.

THE INTERVENTION OF THIS BOOK

To describe the intervention of this book, I offer context about the relationship between writers and their audiences. In the fields of writing studies and rhetoric, researchers have frequently investigated how writers, speakers, and rhetors produce discourse. Less frequently but still regularly, they study how audiences receive discourse, that is, texts, visuals, videos, and GIFs. As Jens Kjeldsen (2016) reminds us, "If we really want to understand rhetoric and argumentation we have to understand audiences, we have to study how people receive, interpret, and respond to instances of rhetoric" (138). While some research, particularly marketing-oriented studies as well as fandom studies (see, for example, Barnes 2015; DeLuca 2018; Jenkins 2008, 2013; Potts et al. 2018; Reagle 2010), has engaged in empirical study of the reception of television shows, films, and texts, the study of audience reception occurs less frequently because it is expensive and time-consuming and does not necessarily yield new insights (the null case). Even less studied is the topic of this book: how writers, speakers, and rhetors respond to audience reception. Methodological and technological considerations confront this third type of research. Do writers and communicators even have audience reception? How often and in what ways? Can they respond to audience reception? Will they? How is this different from the role of an editor in the postproduction inventional process?

While these questions could have been posed in the past, answers would have been found less frequently and with more difficulty before the rise of IPI templates because, as I noted at the outset of this introduction, these templates enable real-time, synchronous audience reception to be reacted and responded to on the part of writers. These templates open digital communication to nonspecialists who cannot author their own websites. With these templates, digital writers can see part of their audience reception by reading through digital comments and tracking analytical data. Due to web-scraping techniques that can make use of templates and application programming interfaces (APIs) that record input data, we can effectively document audience reception at scales never before possible (with profoundly new ethical considerations, too).

While reaction to editorial feedback has been well documented, reaction to the participatory audiences' reception has not been well established. There are a few examples of television audiences affecting the storyline of a television show, but they are rare. Netflix and other algorithmically driven services have harnessed reactions to certain shows, directors, and actors. For example, the 2013 show *House of Cards* was algorithmically developed based on audience behaviors (Hallinan and Striphas 2016, 128). Nevertheless, editors are often present and function to serve as intermediaries.

Participatory audiences, via their comments, are different from editors for five reasons. First, participatory audiences are not offering feedback meant for a draft or revision. They are reading a text they perceive as published, or the internet equivalent of published. Second, participatory audiences are often literally much closer to a writer's text. I often label this latter individual the *initial writer*. That is, participatory audiences often have a writing space designed on or near an initial writer's text, such as a comment function. We might even label commenters *responding writers*. Third, because they have a readily accessible space designated for commenting and reacting, participatory audiences can respond much faster and in greater numbers than editors. Fourth, participatory audiences are not acting as mediators between readers and writers. They *are* the readers. Finally, participatory audiences are heterogeneous. Whereas a writer might have at most a few official editors, digital writers can have innumerable participatory audiences, many of whom are unexpected and, quite often, unwanted. The contribution of this book is primarily to document and analyze how digital writers communicate *after* the production of a text and *during* its circulation. Writing has an afterlife those in writing studies, I believe, should attend. My claim here gives rise to the title of this book: *Update Culture and the Afterlife of Digital Writing*.

THE TERM *UPDATE*

At the outset of this book, I need to explain the phrase *update culture*. I use the word *update* for three reasons. First, *update* echoes the print notions of *update*, such as when a newspaper issues a correction to a story in subsequent issues. This use of the word *update* invokes not an entire break from prior media but a *remediated* connection (Bolter and Grusin 2000). Digital updates can be made to the same article, in rapid succession, over the course of a few hours, days, or weeks. Second, *update* folds in the language of software updates. Because we encounter updates in our smartphones, mobile devices, and computer software, I locate update culture as part of digital culture and digital rhetoric. Third, *update* implies not only that new information can appear but also that information may be recycled or rewritten based on new input. Entire texts are not always entirely rewritten—parts and segments of them are revised or edited at a high intensity. It is a more granular process than Ridolfo and DeVoss's (2009) concept of rhetorical velocity. In update culture, then, an expectation of updating is accepted and acceptable. Writers must contend with this expectation.

HISTORICAL FORMS OF UPDATE CULTURE

It's important to note that update culture is not a radical break or emergence from the past. My approach hopefully avoids, following the example of other researchers and public critics, positing the present as radically new. If update culture is not radically new, then it is more a dramatic intensification of historical antecedents and precedence. While print writers had to attend to the afterlife of their writing, the scale, scope, and frequency of that afterlife exceed print analogues. Update culture in this sense extends three historical concerns: (1) frequency and overload, (2) marginalia and comment culture, and (3) a movement from mass literacy and authorship to mass revision.

Digital writing often faces charges from authors such as Nicolas Carr (2010) and Sherry Turkle (2011) of force-feeding readers and writers too much information. Frequency and overload are assumed in update culture, notably the intense frequency of producing text and reengaging texts after the initial production of discourse. Frequency and overload do not appear ex nihilo because of technology, however. They are historically bound and imbricated with past uses of writing.

Frequent writing has played an important role since at least Julius Caesar's initiation of the *acta diurna* in the Roman Republic. The *acta diurna* ("daily acts"), or the *acta diurna populi Romani* ("daily acts of the Roman people"), was a daily gazette—a sort of newspaper without the paper—of official acts carved into stone or metal in public places or forums. The *acta diurna*, which continued "publication" from 59 BCE to the third century CE, is a very old example of what some critics identify as a new problem: writing is a frequent occurrence. While critics like Carr and Turkle maintain that twenty-first-century reading and writing are too frequent and rapid to allow readers to maintain focus and attention, the *acta diurnal* is just one historical example of the increased frequency of writing. Jeremiads that argue digital writing is too frequent and overloads readers miss the histories of reading and writing.

The view that writing is too frequent and rapid is contestable, particularly in light of Ann Blair's *Too Much to Know* (2011). Blair argues convincingly against the "decline narrative" offered by academic and public technocritics who see the present as an ineffective era for maintaining attention and, in my view, want to refocus readers to appropriate topics worthy of study. As Blair writes, "The decline narrative has been used for centuries and continues to appeal today, often fueled by general anxieties rather than specific changes. But given the long history of the trope, it seems no more appropriate to our context than it does to the Renaissance or the Middle Ages when it was used so extensively" (267). While Blair's aim is to document the ways Renaissance writers, scholars, and readers managed an unprecedented (for that time) scale of information, the broad goal in *Too Much to Know* is to offer "some historical perspective on our current concerns" of information overload (5).

Blair's text offers context for this book: update culture is part of a long trajectory of the increasing speed, scope, and intensity of writing. The extreme frequency and overload of social media and digital exchanges are part of the historical evolution of reading and writing and the technologies of both. *Too Much to Know* presents an account of the fear of overload in the time of the Renaissance, offering a corrective for contemporary critics of digital reading, writing, and user habits. I specifically bring up Blair's argument because it helps frame this book as part of a long history, one that precedes and will continue after *Update Culture and the Afterlife of Digital Writing.*

Working under the assumption that audiences are participatory, writers expect audience response when communicating in IPI template environments. While digital cultures assume participatory cultures, as argued notably by Henry Jenkins's *Convergence Culture* (2008) and *Spreadable Media* (2013), writing has a long history of audience participation. Recordings of everyday minutiae, via digital comments, frequent emails, and digital forums, have tendrils throughout our recorded history, as H. J. Jackson's *Marginalia* (2001) argues. Reader response, marginalia, and comment culture offer us antecedents of update culture and the afterlife of digital writing.

Using evidence from Renaissance manuscripts, William Sherman's *Used Books* (2008) helpfully reframes the act of reading as inherently an act of participation. Sherman claims, "Reading is just part of the process that makes for fruitful interaction with books. Only with marking and practice can books lead us to the kind of understanding needed to make them speak to our present needs" (4). If we replace books with digital texts in the preceding passage, then Sherman's words become relevant to studies of the internet and digital culture. The act of reading a text is only a small part of its value. Discussion, dissection, and responding to texts are a vital part of why we write and read—a fact proven by the rise of digital forums and literally trillions of digital texts made since the turn of the millennium.

Sherman's *Used Books* (2008) serves as a reminder, and perhaps corrective, to the idea that only recently have readers responded to writing and made comments. Sherman notes that a number of Renaissance manuscripts have extensive reader notes, many of which don't simply summarize an author's statement but extend and reorient it to the thoughts of the reader: "A large percentage of the notes produced by readers had no obvious connection with the text they accompanied—but nonetheless testified to the place of that book in the reader's social life, family history, professional practices, political commitment, and devotional rituals" (xiii). While other readers could not have seen these comments immediately, manuscripts were circulated and readers could think about and process what other readers wrote, possibly even responding to other commenters. In fact, Phil Palmer's "'The Progress of Thy Glorious Book': Material Reading and the Play of Paratext in *Coryats Crudities*" (2014) offers a particularly penetrating example of the ways readers can respond in "print and manuscript marginalia" (339). Palmer analyzes *Coryats Crudities* in terms of reader comments, mining it for "distinct modes of reading and interpretation" (338). *Coryats Crudities* has, as a text, numerous comments that function as evidence of comment culture before the internet. Similarly, Matteo Pangallo's *Playwriting Playgoers in Shakespeare's Theater* (2017) argues that participatory culture has been alive and well since at least the 1600s, with "fandom" leading those in the audience to create and comment on the plays of famous playwrights. In *The Ethics of Reading in Manuscript Culture* (1994), John Dagenais reflects Sherman's, Palmer's, and Pangallo's approaches. Dagenais recounts the following about reading manuscripts that contained reader response and reaction in manuscripts:

> I found that the medieval literature I had been studying till then—the medieval literature based on "texts" and an established canon of authors—was not the same medieval literature I encountered in the manuscripts. The medieval literature I found was far more fluid and dynamic. It had rough edges, not the clean, carefully pruned lines of critical editions; and these edges were filled with dialogue about the text—glosses, marginal notes, pointing hands, illuminations. (xvi)

My point in bringing up these authors and their work is that readers have a long history of participating with texts, making the texts heteroglossic. We even have records of ancient Sumerian scribes adding comments to the decrees of those dictating words on cuneiform tablets and clay tokens—comments that sometimes contradict or poke fun at those dictating. Comments and writer-reader participation have likely been around for as long as writing has existed.

IPI templates extend these dynamic writer-audience relationships by enabling everyday writers to revise their texts even as the text is in circulation. This ability means that not only are everyday people reading and writing, but they are also editing, a notion that extends Deborah Brandt's *The Rise of Writing* (2014) and Tim Laquintano's *Mass Authorship and the Rise of Self-Publishing* (2016). Brandt argues in *The Rise of Writing* that North American society is in the process of moving from mass literacy to mass writing: the general populace reads and can also write. Laquintano's work extends Brandt's claims by arguing that writers no longer need to be authorized by an official venue, such as a publishing house; instead, they can become authors through nontraditional means, such as publishing their books directly as ebooks. In short, we no longer have only everyday writers but also everyday authors. Together, Brandt's and Laquintano's arguments prompt us to think about reading, writing, and publishing as tasks that are quickly becoming common for the majority of the (US) population. People of various classes, races, and genders have greater access to writing technologies and develop wider ranges of reading and writing skills.

This book extends these arguments about increased reading and writing to revision and editing en masse, or mass revision. We don't just write and communicate at a rapid pace and on a staggering scale in update culture. IPI templates encourage a fluid view of writing, which in turn prompts us to see our writing as tremendously flexible. I dwell on this metaphor of fluidity in the conclusion of this book because it helps describe the writing that occurs with the digital writers I present in this project.

OUTLINE

To make my argument, I divide this book into eight chapters. Chapter 1 introduces my methods and participants. Chapter 2 lays out the technological foundation of update culture: IPI templates and their rhetoric. Chapters 3, 4, and 5 empirically investigate how writers contend with update culture. These chapters discuss three broad oral concepts as they occur in text-based internet venues: timing, attention, and management. Chapters 6 (ethics), 7 (learning and pedagogy), and 8 (theoretical implications) tease out the implications of the data chapters. The appendix offers a methodology narrative to clarify the origins and development of this project.

After introducing my methods and participants in chapter 1, chapter 2 examines what I call *template rhetoric*. Template rhetoric provides the technical capability for update culture to form, thereby supplying the ability of digital writing to have an afterlife. Interactive templates dominate contemporary networked communication; users do not need specialized web-development skills but can use click-based interfaces to communicate. This functionality has a democratizing effect upon users. Everyone can more easily communicate in a networked fashion, thus creating the intensity of update culture and the expectation for writing to change from moment to moment.

Chapter 3, "Textual Timing," recuperates the rhetorical concept of *chronos* by fusing it with *kairos*, thereby arguing for the importance of clock time and quantitative time when contending with environments that have the endless possibility for *kairotic* moments. This chapter thus asks, *When* do writers respond to participatory audiences? I describe three models of digital time in this chapter: *kairos-chronos* fusion, template timing, and algorithmic timing.

Chapter 4, "Textual Attention," explores the ways participants decide on *what* audience reception should receive attention and how to give that attention. Attention describes the way my participants contend with their participatory audiences. While giving attention to their audience reception, my participants create an emergent mental understanding (often referred to as a *hive mind*, *groupthink*, or the *writing police*) different from their original understanding of the audience. Participants, after reading and carefully thinking about their comments in a holistic sense, decided which comments to ignore, which ones to remain silent about, and which ones to refute. I then discuss textual attention as a three-part act in which writers attend to their audiences by offering some sense of thanks after searching for sincere or genuine responses and questions. While classical rhetoric prefigures speakers and writers as already having attention, new forms of persuasion and identification require *creating*, *keeping*, and *filtering audiences*.

Chapter 5, "Textual Management," argues that contending with update culture means that some participants decided to communicate back to audiences in ways that reflect managing audiences, literally through text and in broader ways that echo speakers managing listeners. Drawing on impression-management theory and Krista Kennedy's *Textual Curation: Authorship, Agency, and Technology in Wikipedia and Chambers's* Cyclopædia (2016), I identify a heterogeneous variety of tactics participants employed, including macromanagement, indirect management, direct management, and responsive management. These techniques help writers engage in branding their unpaid content, a type of branding I label *aspirational.*

In chapter 6, "Ethics in Update Culture," I discuss ethical implications of digital writing's afterlife and what happens when writers take on the circulation of their texts. I address the pitfalls of update culture as reported to me. I then address the issue of change and that we may not be able to look at writing itself to determine what is ethical. I suggest virtue ethics as a viable alternative for ethical writing in update culture because a virtue-ethics framework emphasizes writerly habits and dispositions, that is, *virtues*, over ethical rules or outcomes.

Chapter 7, "Learning and Pedagogy in Update Culture," teases out educational implications for general digital writers, as well as for teachers of digital writing. For the former, I discuss the issue of inadvertent attention. While this book focuses on writers who already have a participatory audience, its strategies remain useful for those without audiences because anyone on the internet can suddenly attract hordes of commenters. I use a case study to demonstrate the power of inadvertent attention. I examine how a faculty member at the University of Nebraska, Amanda Gailey, wrote an Amazon review and subsequently became the target of gun zealots. I discuss how Gailey's case offers us a reason for using timing, attention, and management, even for people who don't aim to inculcate participatory audiences. In the second half of this chapter, I examine pedagogical questions and implications.

In chapter 8, "An Epistemology of Change," I offer theoretical remarks about the strategies I present in the preceding data chapters. I argue that approaching writing as something malleable might enable us to better understand emergent types of literacy and writing practices that coalesce on various digital platforms. In synthesizing textual timing, attention, and management, I argue that digital writers generally view their writing as changeable.

1

METHODS AND PARTICIPANTS

This book is based on forty case studies of digital writers. The scope of this book is restricted to three principles of selection: (1) individuals (2) who write and communicate within IPI-templated environments while (3) actively considering responses from their audiences. I choose these three principles of selection for specific reasons related to the goal of this book, which is to identify writing strategies for negotiating with the rapid audience feedback that occurs in update culture. I choose individuals rather than groups of people, institutions, or autotelic communities because identifiable strategies that individuals use to contend with their participatory audiences may be more easily transferred to other individuals than from group to group due to the complexity of collaboration. Other studies, notably Krista Kennedy's *Textual Curation: Authorship, Agency, and Technology in* Wikipedia *and Chambers's* Cyclopædia (2016), examine how organizations, communities, or groups contend with participatory audiences.

While the three main strategies I present in this book—timing, attention, management—may be applied to groups, organizations, or institutions, I can neither confirm nor deny their effectiveness and, therefore, make no claims about this act of transfer. While this individualistic approach does not fully account for the medley of activities and institutional structures that my participants are embedded within, individuals still make choices when reading their comments, reacting to interface affordances (e.g., Likes, Shares, Retweets), and communicating with interactive websites. In other words, individual writers remain actors and can speak directly to writing within a medley of social pressures and expectations.

I also restrict my claims to contexts of IPI templates. In broad terms, I don't investigate people who design, code, or program their own websites from scratch. I investigate people who write and communicate through the portals and prestructured designs of a company or corporation. IPI templates are immensely important to this project because my claims are couched in what I call *template rhetoric*, something my previous work has investigated (Gallagher 2015a, 2015b, 2017).

DOI: 10.7330/9781607329749.c001

While the next chapter lays out template rhetoric in depth, I briefly explain it here: users communicate with each other on the social web through interactive templates that structure the available means of communication. Users frequently invent new ways of using the means given to them, such as creative hashtags on Twitter or quirky uses of photographs on Instagram, but users act within these structures due primarily to a lack of coding access. Even expert computer programmers are often forced to use templates because the vast majority of users have chosen the corporate-based social web rather than designing their own websites. Explicit examples of templates include Facebook, Twitter, and Instagram. More subtle examples of templates include the review system of Amazon and even WordPress's preformatted toolkits.

Last, I restrict my claims to individuals *who consider audience response*. I use *"consider"* here generously. Users who respond explicitly to their audiences fall into my scope but so do users who read and ignore their comments, users who block trolls, and users who have enough experience with audience response to form an imagined, generalized reader, such as a hivemind or lurker. I examine and investigate people who contend, explicitly or implicitly, with audience response. Consequently, this selection criterion means that my participants already have audience participation.

CONTEXT

This study is situated in the template-standardized interactions of internet cultures that emerged in the mid-2000s. While business models refer to this as Web 2.0 (O'Reilly 2005), I use the phrase *interactive and participatory internet (IPI)* to emphasize users' motivations, purposes, and goals. As IPI environments and templates proliferate, textual participation has grown along with them in the form of commenting cultures. While online comments have only been briefly touched upon or mentioned tangentially by writing studies (Gallagher 2018; Sparby 2017; Tarsa 2015), a vast body of research exists on commenting and commenters in communication and media studies. For a comprehensive review of empirical studies, see Malinen (2015) and for a taxonomy of comments, see Joseph Reagle (2015). This previous research, in very broad terms, focuses on IPI environments, the commenters, and the functions of digital comments. First, researchers have investigated the discussion factors that make an IPI environment interactive (Ziegele, Breiner, and Quiring 2014) and how the nature of the forum influences the civility of that interaction (Rowe 2015; Santana 2016), touching on issues of race and racism (Loke 2012), as well as gender and sexism (Moss-Racusin, Molenda, and Cramer 2015). Second, researchers have studied the parameters that impact a commenter's credibility (Kareklas, Muehling, and Weber 2015), which is often intertwined with issues of anonymity (Reader 2012; Santana 2013) and motivation (or perceived motivation) given that motivation appears to be social (Springer, Engelmann, and Pfaffinger 2015). It has been noted that trolling can negatively impact credibility (Phillips 2015), including the credibility of the text, by influencing reader trust (Marchionni 2015). Finally, digital comments themselves can perform a variety of functions, including reviewing (Chevalier and Mayzlin 2006), interpreting and questioning scientific arguments (Len-Rios, Bhandari, and Medvedeva 2014), recording reader reactions to journalistic information (Ürper and Çevikel 2016), editing ebooks (Laquintano 2010, 2016), peer reviewing and community building in digital classrooms (Molinari 2004), and encouraging democratic discourse at the local (Canter 2013) and national (Dashti, Al-Kandari, and Al-Abdullah 2015) levels. These studies demonstrate mechanisms by which a wide variety of comment cultures can evolve and the effects these cultures have on both commenters and original texts.

This study extends our understanding of digital comment culture(s) by examining ways initial writers respond to comments. While researchers have assessed how digital comments shape attitudes of other commenters (Sung and Lee 2015), to my knowledge no researchers have focused on how initial writers react to comments after their initial discourse, aside from my past work (Gallagher 2015a, 2018). This study provides a look at the impact comment culture has on the production and producers of IPI texts as those texts circulate around the internet. To put it less formally, this study examines how writers revise, tweak, and rethink their writing strategies as their texts move about the internet accumulating comments and other types of reception (Likes, etc.).

INTRODUCTION TO PARTICIPANTS

I studied writers in these participatory environments because they are significantly more likely to be everyday writers, thus giving this study more utility to everyday users, such as students and other aspirational writers who want to know more about the world digital writers encounter. While I say more about some of the economics in chapter 5, "Textual Management," the writers I studied were either not paid or contingent labor. Those who did make money from their writing often contended with the gig economy, that is, temporary work outside traditional organizational structures, in some form or another. In light of these economic considerations, their goal was often to be read widely, which meant they engaged their audiences via comments in an attempt to build a digital *ethos*.

I found that internet writers who actively considered their participatory audiences exhibited interesting similarities, despite having disparate purposes. They tended to share similar strategies for contending with participatory audiences; in other words, it was the interaction with audiences that generally united these writers. Whether it was Amazon reviewers, digital journalists, bloggers, or redditors, I found participants took on the language of their particular template while trying to establish their own writing style and voice. While searching for a writing style is nothing new, my participants searched for ways to engage, quite literally, readers in the participants' own style and voice. They were not just imagining the audience. They read comments and thought about how to engage readers, using the affordances of their templates and their own personal style. As I'll discuss in chapter 5, even dealing with trolls might be a way to demonstrate personal style. They often considered algorithms in complex ways, sometimes rising to the level of an audience.

I draw on case studies of forty writers who contend with participatory audiences. It is incidental that this number turned out evenly. I studied three main groups of writers: redditors, Amazon reviewers, and digital journalists or bloggers. What they all have in common is that they generally have broad audiences on the basis of being top-level redditors (top fifty based on comment karma, an indication of audience visibility based on audience voting), top-level Amazon reviewers (top one hundred based on Amazon's ranking system), and journalists or bloggers who actively consider their audiences (self-reported and with sizable Twitter followings). Many journalists in my study kept their own blogs, which makes this distinction often murky. I also allowed the more well-known participants to make contacts for me (snowball sampling) and thus expand my pool to interested and qualified participants. I determined all rankings during my initial contact with participants (and they have since changed, ranking higher and lower depending quite literally on the day). I also interviewed multiple participants who withdrew from the study because they were fearful of reprisals from their employers, corporations (Amazon), or the public (being doxxed).

I conducted a total of sixty-eight official interviews, along with numerous message interviews, emails, message exchanges, and text messages conducted along the way. All but four participants lived in the United

States (two lived in Canada, and two lived in the United Kingdom). Ages ranged from nineteen to sixty-four at the time of our initial interviews. Redditors were between nineteen and fifty years old, reviewers between twenty-seven and sixty-four years old, journalists between twenty-three and fifty-four years old, and bloggers in their thirties and forties (they chose to give me an age range to avoid being identified). Twenty-two were men, and eighteen were women. Nearly all the redditors happened to be men, and most of the journalists I contacted happened to be women. While some interested participants on reddit were under eighteen, I could not study these individuals because I did not have approval from my institution to interview minors. I therefore did not interview anyone under eighteen. With most participants, I conducted two interviews, but some participants were too busy for a second interview or simply chose not to do a second interview. I conducted three interviews each with Kelly Salasin and StickleyMan, and I conducted four interviews with Tracy Monroe. I interviewed people at their convenience and with IRB approval. In addition to interviews, I draw on field notes of digital interfaces, comments from participatory audiences, and texts writers produced.

Most interviews lasted between 40 and 120 minutes. The shortest interview was 35 minutes, and the longest was Seymour O'Reilly's interview (three hours and 20 minutes; this however was an extreme outlier). Some participants chose to be interviewed over email or message function for the sake of privacy (of the sixty-eight interviews, eight were extensive-message or email interviews, while the rest were phone or videochat). I respected this request for privacy, particularly in light of the prominent positions these writers hold in their respective communities or platforms. I offered participants the option to use their real names, use a pseudonym, or be anonymous. Table 1.1 briefly describes the participants.

I found a tension between everyday writers' desire for personal style when engaging audiences and the restrictive template rhetoric of their respective platforms and websites. The writers I studied paid close attention to what they were writing. Readers did not, as my participants told me. For instance, the reviewers I studied were explicit about being helpful because that is the designated purposed of reviews, according to Amazon. They reported that readers did not always reward the explicit purpose of a review; amusing reviews were often rewarded, much to the consternation of my participants. Redditors paid close attention to tone and style, often in the hopes of either accruing karma or to be entertaining or engaging. Journalists and bloggers focused on accuracy because

Table 1.1. List of participants, their roles, and descriptions

Name of participant	Role	Description
Way_Fairer (screenname) Scott Steffens (real name)	Top-10 redditor	Way_Fairer held the top position as a reddit commenter for several years. He is known as a witty replier, being able to respond quickly and with a variety of discourses, including emoticons, GIFs, and clever phrases. Way_Fairer reined in his activity after a newspaper ran a story on him, revealing his identity. He replies to all comments by mirroring that comment's punctuation and style.
StickleyMan (screenname)	Top-10 redditor	The fourth-rated redditor, StickleyMan, aims to orient members of reddit toward taking an attitude of learning while looking for a random but constructive experience for himself within his texts. It is important to note two facets of his persona: (1) StickleyMan is an extensive producer of GIFs, aiming to be humorous in his non-alphabetic-based texts, and (2) he has garnered a reputation as an insightful commenter. These two features, I believe, are what give him the online authority to have "meaningful" and "productive" conversations on reddit. The purpose of his conversations (texts) is fundamentally dialogic: other redditors help him learn and gain insight, and he hopes other redditors learn from him and each other.
Ramses-ThePigeon (screenname) Max Patrick Schlienger (real name)	Top-10 redditor	RamsesThePigeon describes himself as reddit's jokester. Other redditors I interviewed have described him as one of the "hardest working" redditors out there, even if sometimes his jokes miss in their timing. As one random redditor wrote, RamsesThePigeon "writes amazing stories, writes hilarious screenplays, master of obscure trivia, explains things in funny ways, 4,000,000 karma from OC [original content], 50+ years of reddit Gold." RamsesThePigeon liked this description, so I therefore include it in his description. He reposts his longer writing because he spends a lot of time on it and believes it deserves to be recirculated (or in reddit's terms, "copypasta"). RamsesThePigeon recently started a YouTube channel to expand his brand.
AndrewSmith1986 (screenname)	Top-60 redditor (formerly top 2)	AndrewSmith1986 is the first redditor to reach 300,000 and one million comment karma. Having been around reddit for many years, he has an institutional sort of memory and was often able to make metacomments about reddit. He has been banned and unbanned more than once. He explicitly can recall large patterns of reddit's discourse and met his significant other on reddit. While he sometimes loathes reddit (as many redditors do), AndrewSmith1986 also recognizes that reddit's hivemind can bring perspective about the current moment of news and events. He is a Pisces.
Kijafa (screenname)	Top-25 redditor	Kijafa views his writing as both pattern matching and standing out ("having a schtick"). While not well known outside high-karma user circles, he runs the fantasy football league in the Century Club (an exclusive subreddit for redditors with 100,000 karma). This gives him many personal connections to high-level redditors, as well as an ability to think in metaterms about reddit. He was formerly known as a "reddit storyteller" during his peak years, 2013–14.

continued on next page

Table 1.1—*continued*

Name of participant	Role	Description
Omnipo-tent_Goose (screenname)	Top-30 redditor	Omnipotent_Goose told me, "I consider myself to have a pretty good sense of humor, and just pretend like I'm talking amongst friends, and make the comment I would make if we were sitting around looking at the same thing. Oh, and puns. Reddit loves puns and wordplay. A bunch of my top comments where I've gotten gilded [given 'gold,' a reddit currency] numerous times have been puns." He has another account that isn't about karma; as he writes in an email, "I have an alternate account that I don't really care how much karma I get on it. I use it to help people out and ask and answer questions on topics that I'd like to learn more about, or know the answers to."
Mattreyu (screenname)	Top-30 redditor	Mattreyu doesn't consider himself a writer but does enjoy the exchange reddit affords. He has reduced his political activity because he was receiving harassing comments. As he told me, "I've had people harass me and tell me to die/get cancer/etc. I also moderated a subreddit a year or so ago that would point out accounts that were botted in political subreddits during the election. I got a lot of grief there in particular, with some other subreddits calling me out specifically. That actually made me step back from political activities online in general, and I wiped a good part of my account history just to avoid getting harassed." As he describes himself, "I'm first and foremost a commenter, and that's mostly a mix of making jokes and trying to provide context for other submissions. My successful posts are mainly from /r/trippinthroughtime. All of the stuff I post there is original content. I have a background in art/art history so I have an idea of what artists/movements to look for."
DiegoJones4 (screenname)	Top-30 redditor	DiegoJones4 is an outlier in terms of how he sees his writing: he views all exchanges like "exchanges in [a] bar." Since he views reddit as his hobby, accessing it often after work, he simply likes to have interesting conversations. In this sense, he describes his high-level position as much more about quantity (he makes a lot of posts) than quality. He actively considers his audiences because of this dialogic approach and aims to inculcate a good "bar-like" conversation.
thehealeroftri	Top-40 redditor	Thehealeroftri, outside reddit, writes short stories. Inside reddit, he mainly participates in sports discussions, especially about professional basketball. He thinks carefully about timing his writing as it coincides with various basketball games. He reads his notifications carefully, looking for various responses that appear genuine.
toxicbox	Top-40 redditor	Toxicbox considers himself a "karma farmer," which is a nicer term than the more caustic "karmawhoring" for people who try to accrue karma. He prefers "karma farmer" because rather than pander to his audiences, he tries to engage them and garner a lot of "engagement." He advises avoiding taking the "bait" with a troll although he still actively reads his notifications. He argues that trolls always have an "out" for claiming they did not mean to troll.

continued on next page

Table 1.1—*continued*

Name of participant	Role	Description
Just1morefix (screenname)	Top-50 redditor	Just1morefix considers himself a writer in general, most often journaling and writing poetry occasionally. He hopes there is a "deeper level" of engagement with his writing than one might expect from reddit. He understands reddit is for joking but also hopes other users will come away satisfied with their interactions with him. He hopes "we've learned a little bit." A successful post for Just1morefix is when a "real" exchange occurs. He is not "looking for a transcendent moment" but is looking for human-to-human connection.
LandLubber77 (screenname)	Top-50 redditor	LandLubber77 says, "I don't have a job that gives me the opportunity to write, so though I'd like to, I don't often write outside of my contributions to reddit." Although he readily admits that accruing karma is a goal of his, he has more important goals: "Trying to tell a good story or craft a clever pun or piece of wordplay is an oddly satisfying thing, like doing your morning crossword puzzle."
Portarossa (screenname)	Top-50 redditor	Portarossa is the only self-identified woman redditor who responded to my message. She writes fiction for a living and finds reddit a good way to get rid of writer's block (writing in the subreddit "WritingPrompts" was how she first got introduced to reddit). As she told me over email, "I consider a post successful if it seems to resonate with people. That's not necessarily the same as it being popular. Taking a look at my most upvoted posts—and boy, isn't *that* just an exercise in narcissism—the majority of the absolute top-rated are (usually pretty dopey) one-liners. That's not to say I don't love the fact that I managed to give thousands of people a bit of a laugh, but I think generally they're quite fleeting."
Roboticide (screenname)	Top350 redditor	Roboticide is one of the "marathon" redditors. That is his term for a redditor who has not accumulated karma rapidly but has instead accumulated it over the course of many years (seven in his case). He is deeply reflective about his activity in the subreddit about World of Warcraft and actively corrals different redditors on that subreddit. He also sets rules and establishes decorum for this subreddit.
DevasoHouse (screenname)	redditor with over 500,000 karma on multiple accounts	DevasoHouse is a jokester redditor who isn't necessarily after extensive conversations. Rather, he considers his writing much more akin to improvisational comedy, which mimics his background. However, he does answer commenters who ask him genuine and sincere questions (not trolling questions). In this sense, even though he does not always *consider* audience, he does in fact attend to their queries.
HitchhikersPie (screenname)	redditor with over 100,000 karma	HitchhikersPie is active on various sports subreddits and contributes actively to various communities (including the New England Patriots). He actively reads through all his responses, even though he clearly does not reply to them all. He often tries to rescue comments if they are downvoted, meaning he tries to respond and offer better context for the "poor performing" comment.

continued on next page

Table 1.1—*continued*

Name of participant	Role	Description
Kelly Salasin (real name)	Blogger	Salasin is a well-known blogger in Vermont who has received attention from the *New York Times* and has been blogging since 2009. She constructs her role as a writer by inviting an open readership while simultaneously including herself as an implicit participant; she thanks her readers and makes remarks within the comment function of her blog posts. She often produces texts using the textual participation of her audience.
Penelope Trunk (real name)	Blogger	Penelope Trunk is a well-known mommy blogger and self-help blogger who offers career advice to young professional women. Since I first interviewed her in 2013, she has attracted some controversy for writing inflammatory posts about mental health. She reads her comments and is an advocate for the "having haters" mentality; in other words, knowing that some people may dislike her style. She finds that this attention still plays an important role in her writing. As a writer, she talked most about having a digital style and advised novices to develop a personal relationship with participatory audiences.
Heather Armstrong (real name)	Blogger	Heather Armstrong is formerly the number-one mommy blogger on the internet. She now calls herself an "influencer." As her most recent entertaining bio reads, "When I first wrote a bio for this site I called myself a SAHM—a Stay At Home Mom, or, Shit Ass Ho Motherfucker. More than a decade later I am now what's referred to as a FTSWM—a Full-Time Single Working Mom, or, Fuck That Shit Where's Marijuana. This used to be called mommy blogging. But then they started calling it Influencer Marketing: hashtag ad, hashtag sponsored, hashtag you know you want me to slap your product on my kid and exploit her for millions and millions of dollars. That's how this shit works." Armstrong told me she reads all her comments and ardently manages her audiences in a variety of ways.
Anonymous Blogger (ABL)	Blogger	This anonymous blogger runs a well-known website about science and actively manages commenters to keep the science accurately represented.
Tracy Monroe (pseudonym chosen by participant)	Online journalist/ blogger	Monroe is a journalist and educator about science writing. She writes regularly about health sciences, including childrearing, childbirth, and vaccinations. She teaches journalism. She maintains a regular blog and professional advice column. To combat the myth of a vaccine-autism connection, she has developed strategies for engaging commenters who do not believe her work. With respect to antivaccine readers and commenters, Monroe told me, "You really need to listen to their argument so you can deconstruct it." She has developed forums for refuting standard arguments of antivaccine readers and commenters. Monroe believes her acumen as a question-posing journalist helps her contend with and monitor deleterious comments.

continued on next page

Table 1.1—*continued*

Name of participant	Role	Description
Matt Grimes (pseudonym chosen by Gallagher)	Online journalist/ blogger	Grimes is a Canadian medical doctor who writes for an award-winning blog and a variety of well-known news organizations. Grimes told me, "I've been blogging for ten years and writing for various media outlets." About comments, he remarked that they are "generally only incredibly on-board or the opposite. It's very polarizing. Effusive praise or calling people names." He sees value in the comments for his readers ("I do see value for my readers") but recently turned off comments (within six months from the time of our interview) on his personal blog, although comments on some of his more public work are still functional. He did so because "the negative comment will skew interpretation," despite feeling "guilty about turning off the comments." He still encourages readers to engage in discussion but reroutes them to an online forum such as Facebook. He views venues off his personal website as productive sites of engagement: "Facebook is different from the comment section. People tend to engage one another there." These views demonstrate a vexed relationship to comments, one that reflects recent shifts in eliminating comment sections on scientific writing on the web. As a result of this work, Grimes acquired several trolls. He brought this to the attention of his place of work in case there were attempts to get him fired. Instead, this initiated a promotion because it brought attention to the value of his online activity.
Lola Upton (pseudonym chosen by Gallagher)	Online journalist	Upton is a science writer who mainly tries to inform and secondarily aims to educate. When I asked her about the distinction between these ideas, she told me informing was "providing information" whereas education was "taking the next step." She elaborated on this "next step" by telling me educating means the reader "understands information," "why it is important," and what "readers can do right now." She explained educated readers would "react" in some way, which could mean a range of activity from donating money to "talking about the issue over coffee." As a science writer who sees herself as situated within a "print model," she wants to keep the conversation surrounding comments on topic and focused on "the science." For this reason, she believes "comments are too personal" and too frequently attack journalists. Her ideal goal with respect to comments is "to have an online conversation" about the topic, but she has not experienced that ideal very often. Upton believes that writing on the internet, like print writing, is "goal-oriented and always seeks to engage readers in some way." Engagement takes many forms for her, and thus "context is important." For Upton, "Comments make you forget there is a lost art to not giving a shit about what people think about you." She believes individuals need to have their own view of themselves and "not view themselves through the lens of others."

continued on next page

Table 1.1—*continued*

Name of participant	Role	Description
Christy McKenzie (pseudonym chosen by Gallagher)	Online journalist/ blogger	Christy McKenzie is a blogger at a variety of well-known aggregation websites. She writes on politics, fashion, and current events. When I first interviewed her in 2015, she was somewhat scared of comments and avoided engaging with them. Over the course of the past three years (2015–18), she became bolder and began to take on commenters, turning her fear into outrage and productive anger. Like many other participants, she learned to take on commenters rather than avoid them.
Rosa Kennedy (pseudonym chosen by Gallagher)	Online journalist	Kennedy is a committed environmental journalist and writes for a variety of online news organizations and blogs. She told me, "I started writing online in 2003 when I signed on to work on [presidential candidate John] Kerry's [2004] campaign." This was her first experience with participatory audiences, via comments, because, as she recalled, "I had to figure out who was an anarchist and who was a real commenter and who was a concern troll." A concern troll is someone who feigns interest, typically by asking a question, only to attack an online exchange or derail an ongoing debate. Kennedy is "always writing toward the lurkers rather than the commenters" because "they greatly outnumber the commenters." She tends to conceive of her audience as "people reading the comments but not asking questions." Kennedy tries to avoid overt influence by commenters and "being pulled in one direction by the commenters."
Maggie Skinner (pseudonym chosen by Gallagher)	Online journalist	Skinner started out as an independent blogger in 2004 and eventually wrote for multiple professional science societies. For various science websites, Skinner is "required to monitor" her comments, a labor that is uncompensated even though it is an "expectation that probably falls under the category of 'duties as assigned.'" This is because there is a "fairly substantial literature about the effects of comments." She "almost quit over comments" at a major online news magazine. However, according to Skinner, comments are not as vitriolic as emails: "Email commenters show a scarier side of commenters because it takes time and effort to send that email." She has been compared to "the whore of Babylon" by a commenter. It's never one comment that bothers Skinner; it's the accumulation of them over time because, for her, "they chip away at you." Skinner has a two-tiered system that involves a yellow card and a red card, although she admits there is a third category of comment she labels "completely batshit crazy with no connection to reality." This third type of comment, which is generally incoherent or off topic, she ignores and deletes if she can. This two-tiered system acts as a warning system and is her way of "making a public statement about comments" that are "over the line." The system "really seems to help," although she warns that writers must be "really clear about consequences," that is, reader response, when choosing to delete comments.

continued on next page

Table 1.1—*continued*

Name of participant	Role	Description
Liza Margulies (real name)	Amazon reviewer (top 100), blogger, and general internet writer	Liza Margulies is a photographer, blogger, and reviewer. She has published an academic chapter too. Margulies, like many other bloggers and reviewers, takes on many roles online. Her blog and reviews are intimately connected, as people comment on the blog about her reviews. Margulies answers every comment ("all," she told me) that asks her a question, even if the questions are sometimes snarky.
Michael Edelman (real name)	Amazon reviewer (top 100)	Michael Edelman describes himself on his Amazon "About Me" page as "a former quality assurance analyst and project manager, part time web consultant (who isn't?), free lance writer and photographer, and former student and researcher in the neurosciences." Statistically, Edelman writes the second-longest reviews in this study (the first being Seymour O'Reilly). As he told me in an email, "I try, first and foremost, to be interesting, and then to be informative. How much effort I put into both depends on the length of the review and how interested I am in the subject of the book, or the usefulness of the item." With commodities, he returns to the review in the following months to answer questions and rethink his own perspectives. As he told me, "In the case of goods, I often return to a review after a month, several months, or even several years if I find something notable to comment on. This might be a product that suddenly failed in use, or something that lasted longer than I expected. I recently updated an expensive cooking pot that I initially liked, but which lost its nonstick coating in short order. In the case of books, I might reread a book and change my opinion of it, or find some additional insight, or correct a factual error that I discovered or that I made in my review."
Mike W (screenname)	Amazon reviewer (top 100)	Mike W is a well-established reviewer who recently developed an awareness of the economic implications of his work. He has grown "a bit cynical" since I first interviewed him in 2015 and, in 2018, told me he reined in his reviewing. However, he learned to argue well in online "sports, politics, entertainment forums" before he started reviewing. As a result, he learned how to speak "to people in that [online] world and there's people I've been communicating with in those forums for years and years that I feel like I know better than the people I see every day in real life." He considers himself a good writer and, like Trunk, thinks style is "really important to develop online." He reads all the comments he receives and responds to the "sincere" ones.
Ciaran (screenname)	Amazon reviewer (top 100)	Ciaran considers himself a writer and quit his job to be a writer. While he couldn't make a living on his writing alone, he does have a successful writing project. "Reviewing," said Ciaran, "has been quite pervasive in many aspects of my life." He also had to contend with the "fake review" epidemic, which he compares to the 2016 "fake news" epidemic. He considers himself to be an honest reviewer who refused to take money but was lumped in with many of the paid reviewers. As a result, Ciaran dealt with a lot of customers who didn't believe his reviews. Consequently, he searches for genuine questions from readers of his reviews while ignoring accusations of being a paid company shill.

continued on next page

Table 1.1—*continued*

Name of participant	Role	Description
Jason Rob (pseudonym chosen by Gallagher)	Amazon reviewer (top 100)	Having written reviews since 2001, Jason Rob is a prominent reviewer, reaching the top ten. He reviews frequently but with the goal of quality over quantity. He is aware of style and tries to write reviews with an eye toward developing style depending on the product. (Humor, he told me, goes well "when reviewing dog poop bags.") Rob recently started a YouTube channel, reflecting a larger trajectory of online writers delving into other content areas besides a narrow definition of writing. He is the only reviewer who writes his reviews in a word-processing document and then copies and pastes them into the review template.
Seymour O'Reilly (pseudonym chosen by Gallagher)	Amazon reviewer (top 100)	Seymour O'Reilly reviews online supplements, among a wide variety of other products. Interestingly, he aggregates his reviews as commenters ask questions. In other words, he continues to update and edit reviews to include questions and queries. His reviews are the longest of any participant in this study. During our interviews, he admitted to taking down unsuccessful reviews and reposting them, a strategy not uncommon although still not frequent. As he told me, "Sometimes you misjudge the timing of reviews."
Dennis Nielsen (pseudonym chosen by Gallagher)	Amazon reviewer (top 100)	Dennis Nielsen considers himself a writer and considers reviewing to be somewhere between a "hobby and a job." He told me he goes "overboard" and sometimes thinks about writing reviews all day. He said, "I try to be concise. I think that's probably one of my first goals, although some of my reviews are very long. I try to be concise and organized. I try to imagine that the reader is a very busy person whose time is valuable. I go through and polish up the reviews to try to get rid of wasted words, try to get it so that someone could just glance. . . . I try to use headers and things, bullets and so forth so that people could very quickly get to the part of the review that they care about." He struggles with audiences who expect "review inflation" and tries to address comments from readers who do not like his ratings.
Bretty (pseudonym chosen by participant)	Amazon reviewer (top 100)	A reviewer in the United Kingdom, Bretty writes reviews on a variety of products but mostly focuses on books. Bretty explicitly enjoys taking on trolls and "taking the piss out of them."
Bill Elijah (pseudonym chosen by Gallagher)	Amazon reviewer (top 100)	Bill Elijah writes for fun and considers reviewing a hobby. As a former top-10 reviewer, he pays close attention to his audience. He told me, "I will always correct factual errors. I don't have a process for deciding which reviews to update. It's usually following comments or when something I remember I reviewed turns out to be different from what I thought it was." He is a little sad he is no longer a top-10 reviewer.
Sandy Winston (pseudonym chosen by Gallagher)	Amazon reviewer (top 100)	Sandy Winston is a reviewer who broke into the top 100 completely by accident after writing reviews of products she bought. Sandy Winston was not part of the Vine program and stopped reviewing after receiving too many "sketchy" offers for reviewing. She did enjoy the attention but found reviewing took too much time away from her family.

continued on next page

Table 1.1—*continued*

Name of participant	Role	Description
Sheila Thomas (pseudonym chosen by Gallagher)	Amazon reviewer (top 100)	Sheila Thomas uses writing reviews as a way to keep her mind sharp after having a family and career. Now in her "late fifties and sixties," she views reviewing as a hobby, although she wishes she would be paid. She answers every question and query from her commenters early in the morning.
Anonymous reviewer (AR1)	Amazon reviewer (top 100)	This reviewer is from the US Northeast and is now a well-known influencer. Once she became well known on other platforms, she asked to be anonymous (and not use her screenname).
Anonymous reviewer (AR2)	Amazon reviewer (top 100)	This reviewer in the United States started by reviewing books. Once she became well known, she started reviewing other products she received for free. She thinks many other reviewers are paid for their reviews, something she is adamantly against.
Amanda Gailey (real name)	Amazon reviewer (activist)	Gailey is a faculty member at the University of Nebraska. She wrote an Amazon review of a cell-phone case as a form of activism. Because it criticized a gun manufacturer and not the product, this review inadvertently went viral. She became the target of conservative news sites and blogs. I discuss her case in chapter 8.

they found readers would focus on one sentence or minor issue and subsequently ignore larger, complex issues. Generally, my participants told me that readers did not read carefully or recognize the intense labor required of digital writers.

While I am continuing to interview participants on a rolling basis, I interviewed enough participants to make broader claims on the basis of *data saturation*. In this study, data saturation is the point at which participants began to provide answers that repeated prior participants' responses. While I still learn new and interesting things from each participant, I found that after I interviewed about eight to twelve people in each category type, broader trends emerged that could be discussed across the categories.

CONCERNING FINDINGS AND CONCLUSIONS

A final word here about researcher bias, which is unescapable. Update culture invests me in the notion of change. I am invested in change for reasons that blur the line between professional and personal. As an individual, I was first attracted to the idea of writing because of its apparent permanence; well-known writers are remembered after their death, and I found this attractive when I was in high school and college. As a researcher, however, I have found writing to be anything but permanent, especially in terms of digital content. Writing this book has challenged my perceptions of what writing can be and what being a writer entails; it's been the exact opposite of confirmation bias. My research into the history of writing and the internet has reminded me of this ephemeral nature. In terms of digital writing, old writing can find new life and contexts. New writing can be completely forgotten or deleted with simply a keystroke—something I've observed (frustratingly at times) as I interviewed my participants who appear in this book. And all writing—but especially digital writing—seems to have an afterlife we must attend as scholars of writing, rhetoric, and social media.

2
TEMPLATE RHETORIC

The argument throughout this chapter, and this book more generally, is that we live in an *update culture*. Update culture, as I mentioned in the introduction, is an ongoing need to reread, edit, and update texts in digital environments mediated by interactive and participatory internet (IPI) templates. These templates provide the technological capability for audience participation and for writers to receive that participation. Central to update culture, then, is that people interact with each other through their digital activity.

We even have statistical evidence of an update culture. A Pew Research Survey found that adults of all ages revise and edit their texts as well as monitor their digital writing and discursive information (Madden 2014). With respect to "adults who have asked someone to remove or *correct* material about them online" (emphasis added), the report notes that

65% have asked that a *photo or video* be removed or corrected.

39% have asked that *written material like a comment or blog posting* be removed or corrected.

13% have asked that *something else, such as a court record or financial statement* be removed or corrected.

As these statistics bear out, everyday users are savvy about taking down material or correcting (updating) material that has been posted to the internet. Digital writing in this sense shifts and moves. Digital writing is updatable, and it seems to be widely accepted that updating occurs.

Update culture consequently yields an *expectation* that writers and readers communicate with one another through mediated means that are emergent and ongoing. These interactions prompt us to think about how people react to comments and develop strategies for negotiating digital audience participation. Since writing is changeable, we expect it to change, and we often accept that it will change, sometimes rapidly.

IPI templates enable these updates, changes, and moves, but they do so in structured ways. If we assume, as Barbara Warnick and David

DOI: 10.7330/9781607329749.c002

Heineman do in *Rhetoric Online: The Politics of New Media* (2012), that "the Web employs a logic of referentiality and intertextuality where discourse is often characterized by fragmentary and disjointed statements and questions" (41), then IPI templates *enable* communicative acts to reference each other by linking users to other users and discourses to seemingly unrelated discourses. While the internet employs referentiality and intertextuality, what's often overlooked is that interfaces shape these characteristics. Practically, interfaces must undergird any theory of the internet and social media, including everyday users who cannot create their own websites.[1] IPI templates are thus the everyday structures internet users employ without programming and designing their own websites.

Investigating IPI templates opens up avenues of inquiry for understanding why we so frequently update, read, and write in update culture by providing an analytical framework about the technological, interface-based reasons for some of our digital behaviors, including the structural reasons users may share their internal thoughts and everyday experiences in online forums. Interfaces are highly ideological (Selfe and Selfe 1994), structuring our interactions online. Templates facilitate the majority of internet communication because they allow technical experts and novitiates alike to join digital forums, conversations, and debates without requiring specialized training or skills. Instead of programming or using markup languages, users turn on their machines and devices, open a browser or web application, and manipulate a template built by designers. Because IPI templates facilitate participatory media and user-to-user communication, they structure how users persuade, produce consensus, and convince various groups to identify (or not) with one another. They form, to use an imperfect metaphor, the roads and channels by which user-to-user rhetoric and communication travel in digital environments.

Despite concerns from writing studies scholars Kristen Arola (2010) and Kathleen Blake Yancey (2004) about the deleterious effects templates have had on web-design practices, templates dominate most user-end aspects of digital communication, especially social media (Gallagher 2015b). Moreover, as technology becomes increasingly mobile and wearable, quick and easy-to-use templates will continue to gain a more prominent role in our lives as the twenty-first century progresses. For these reasons, we need to analyze *how* IPI templates provide coercive structures and procedures for users who rely on technological interfaces of other designers, programmers, and website hosts.

Not only do templates enable a rapid and frequent writer-audience relationship, but as I observed in my participants' interview responses,

templates have a subtle way of shaping the writer's means of communication. The participants featured in this book tended to draw upon
the language of templates when I interviewed them, which I realized
only after transcribing interviews and reviewing participants' writing in
retrospect. Many writers use templates to compose their texts, as was the
case with the reviewers, redditors, and bloggers I interviewed. (Journalists
tended to have more freedom, except on Twitter.) The writers who used a
content-management system deeply considered the display of their texts.
Consequently, the unit of writing I choose to focus on is the discourse that
can be entered into a template; in this sense, I use writing to mean discursive communication that includes alphabetic text, images, emojis, GIFs,
and other information that can placed into a template. Thus studying the
choices made in these interfaces can provide a theory about the way templates shape writer-audience relationships that explains subtle tendencies
of writerly experiences as being deeply structured by coercive interfaces.

The remainder of this chapter has two main parts. First, I define IPI
templates. Second, I argue that IPI templates give rise to template rhetoric, which is a type of procedural rhetoric that allows update culture to
form in a technological sense. I describe four characteristics of template
rhetoric: repetition, time-space compression, ambient affordances,
and standardization.

DEFINING IPI TEMPLATES

I define IPI templates as *interactive interfaces of ongoing prefabricated designs
and cultural forms.* These templates contain empty spaces designated for
writing or *filling in.* This empty space is surrounded by a variety of interactive fields. IPI templates include obvious sites like Facebook, Twitter,
Instagram, and Snapchat, as well as websites with standardized profiles,
qualitative affordances, and prescribed interactions, such as digital
reviews on Amazon or Yelp.

To elaborate on this definition, I initially need to explain the difference between IPI templates and WYSIWYG (what you see is what you
get) word-processing editors, such as Microsoft Word or Macintosh
Pages. IPI templates are inherently connected to the internet, whereas
WYSIWYGs are not. They can be, as with the case of Google documents,
but such connection is not automatically at given. WYSIWYGs are templates designed for document production, whereas IPI templates are
designed for user-to-user communication on the internet. For instance,
Word is not designed for user-to-user interactions. People can communicate within the documents of Word, through tracked changes for

example, but the foregrounded purpose of the program is to produce documents (which can then be used for communication).

Matthew Kirschenbaum's *Track Changes: A Literary History of Word Processing* (2016) gestures toward the differences between WYSIWYG applications and IPI templates. In examining word processing, Kirschenbaum compares and contrasts WYSIWYGs like Google Docs with Twitter. Kirschenbaum writes that "unlike Twitter . . . Google Docs is a fully featured word processor, freely available. . . . Users tend to gravitate toward it because it relieves them of having to worry about which files are stored on which individual machine" (239). Kirschenbaum's extensive discussion and conceptualization of word processing in *Track Changes* provide a clear comparative point: WYSIWYGs have files and documents, whereas IPI templates are for user-to-user communication. With WYSIWYG word-processing editors, messages are contained in documents, many of which are now only digital, but documents remain the purpose of messages. With IPI templates, messages are produced, received, and distributed within their frameworks for internet-based user-to-user communication. The purpose of text in IPI templates is to communicate messages without expectation of a document per se. There is no document within an IPI template; it is often perceived as an empty vessel for communicating messages—incorrectly, as Johndan Johnson-Eilola's *Nostalgic Angels* (1997) observed over two decades ago. Johnson-Eilola writes, "Hypertext (or any technology) is never neutral or transparent to our intentions" (14). Technologies such as templates are extraordinarily important to communication because they are ideological structures that connect users to other users.

Because there is no document undergirding the messages of IPI templates or their environments, rhetoric and discourse can flow rapidly and on a larger scale but nevertheless in structured ways. IPI templates thus extend an ongoing interest in what Chris Mays (2015) calls "thinking in terms of the movement—in the sense of the circulation, flow, interaction, and evolution" (para. 3). In terms of circulation, IPI templates are literally designed to move texts, images, videos, memes, emojis, and GIFs for the explicit purpose of user-to-user communication. While this interest in movement picks up the work of a long line of scholars who investigate how writing, rhetoric, and communication transform (Biesecker 1989; Coe 1975; Cooper 1986; Dingo 2012; Edbauer 2005; Edwards 2018; Gries 2013, 2015; Jung 2014; Rivers and Weber 2011; Syverson 1999), IPI templates orient this transformational and circulatory process to focus on the *structures* that enable such movement. Like Chun's perspective on habit in *Updating to Remain the Same*

(2016), IPI templates focus our analytical understanding of digital communication on the conditions that make viral spreading possible rather than simply seeing viral spreading as haphazard phenomena (15). Thus, focusing on IPI templates helps us see that the viral nonlinear spread of internet communication is not random. Interrogating templates and their rhetoric places an emphasis on the structures undergirding digital communication.

Through this highly structured mediation, IPI templates assist in the construction of wider public deliberation by connecting the social and technological aspects of digital rhetoric and communication. If "rhetoric emerges already infected by the viral intensities that are circulating in the social field" (Edbauer 2005, 14), then investigating IPI templates enables digital writing scholars, media theorists, and digital rhetoricians to see the intersection of social forces and design structures of digital rhetoric and communication. Making IPI templates an object of inquiry helps us understand *how* digital rhetorics emerge in digital environments. In terms of this book, templates provide us context for the language that writers and their commenters use as insight into how writers contend with the afterlife of their texts, such as making updates, managing commenters, and so forth. In fact, all the participants in my study used IPI templates to distribute their writing and interact with their audiences. They used templates as their primary mode of interface.

Defining Templates: Interactive Interfaces

IPI templates are a type of interactive interface. In its technical definition, *interface* means a moment of discontinuity wherein two systems meet. Media theorists such as Alexander Galloway (2012) adopt such a perspective: "The interface becomes the point of transition between different mediatic layers within any nested system" (31). Each time a user encounters an IPI template, a moment of discontinuity exists because the user must bring to bear their own purposes and intentions on the ways a template is designed. Communication designers and digital rhetoricians commonly adopt a related definition of interface: the means by which a user manipulates a computer program, through either hardware or software manipulations.

IPI templates are common for screen-based digital devices because everyday users without specialized coding knowledge can communicate quickly and easily online. Rebecca Tarsa (2015) states the importance of interfaces: "Since most of us cannot reach right in and work with the computer languages in which the programs we use are written, we need interfaces to bridge the gap" (13). While designers of IPI templates, such as Facebook's and Twitter's templates, attempt to make moments of discontinuity fade to make money, these aims simultaneously ensure faster moments of communication with fewer moments of miscommunication for user-to-user interactions. Without explicitly investigating templates as the primary ways users communicate in digital environments, we may miss the role of interfaces in the production and circulation of digital conversations, emotions, exchanges, and experiences.

I emphasize this point because IPI templates are aimed, to varying degrees of success, at producing an invisible interface and medium so that users can communicate faster and with greater ease. Because IPI templates cause users to write faster and more often, these templates encourage users to inculcate habits of updating, revision, and change without the user noticing the interface as a source of those habits. In *Interface*, Branden Hookway (2014) notes that interfaces tend to fade after initial user frustration.

> In the experience of the user, interface takes on a seeming transparency as it is worked through, and as its user is enabled through augmentation. Here the threshold is attenuated toward an apparent disappearance. . . . The immediate encounter of the interface as a form of separation, as a thing that challenges, that must be attended to, and is not yet but soon will be available for all users, blurs and fades into the experience of the interface. (123)

Hookway articulates an experience that internet designers desire: while an interface is an obstacle for users at first, over time it recedes into the background as a thing that has been worked through. Similarly, with their computer code hidden, IPI templates appear to users as objects that facilitate easy and fast communication. They are rhetorical of course, but it's easy to miss their profound influences since we often look *through* them rather than *at* them.[2] By categorizing IPI templates as interfaces, we can call critical attention to the way these templates influence communication and rhetorical discourse.

Defining Templates: Ongoing Prefabricated Designs

As interfaces, IPI templates supply users with ongoing standardized means of persuasion, providing expectation of decorum through updatable prefabricated designs (as I note in the introduction to this book). This means of persuasion produces an expectation for participation (user to user) and interaction (user to template). The *ongoing* nature of IPI templates is central to their role in update culture and the afterlife of digital writing because entering information into an empty field often results in an *incomplete* field from the perspective of a user. Unlike print templates, such as a résumé, IPI templates require continuous updating, posting, and digital inscription.

Because IPI templates habitually prod users to fill out empty fields, the situations that arise from them possess the potential to never end. Hence, the afterlife of digital writing is strikingly more intense in its scope and frequency than the afterlife of print writing. While a novelist may leave an email address at the end of a book, templates streamline the process of writer-audience interaction as a fundamental, and not external, part of reading an online text. From this perspective, any text, picture, or discursive construction does not change, accumulate, or move neutrally. For instance, Facebook status updates do not go viral randomly; they are sorted, quantified, distributed, and circulated through visual display that combines the intentions of designers, the input information of audiences, and the proprietary goals of website hosts, for example, via algorithms and content managers.

IPI templates, as ongoing prefabricated designs, produce somewhat of a paradox: emergent rhetoric that moves rapidly and at great scales is nevertheless highly structured. These flows do not move freely or outside economic, environmental, institutional, military, or social forces. In particular, as prefabricated designs, IPI templates reorient what Gries, in *Still Life with Rhetoric* (2015), articulates as the ongoing circulatory aspect of rhetorical ecologies and rhetoric within the contexts of digital environments. These templates shift Gries's key observation that we need creative and distributed methodologies to understand "rhetorical becomings" or "rhetorical transformations" (108). By tracking the transformative, mimetic, and viral nature of Shepard Fairey's famous *Obama Hope* poster, Gries is able to not only observe changes in objects and images but also account for "*how* things become rhetorical as they circulate and transform with time and space and contribute to collective life" through a new material account that examines the "consequentiality" that things "spark in the world" (3). The notion of rhetorical ecologies, for Gries, is important to visual rhetoric "because it challenges us to imagine how images emerge and flow within a network (or field) of forces, affects, and associations" (27). But contra Gries's work, some of these same flows are actually within the same website occurring between writer and commenters (audiences).

In the context of this book, the majority of digital circulatory spatio-temporal flows and forces are constrained by IPI templates. Discourse can move in an ongoing fashion, but that ongoingness has forms. Because templates compel everyday users to act in certain ways, the

rhetoric that emerges from them is structured and habitual, a devia-
tion from Gries's new materialist perspective. The characteristics of IPI
templates provide a level of predictability, which emerges when users
fill in and fill out IPI templates to communicate. The type and level of
interactivity are standardized, and IPI templates restrict users' ability to
format and provide a range of expressions. Users cannot add pictures to
their profiles, update a status, write in unstandardized ways, or produce
discourse in totally free ways. The afterlife of digital writing, like the
afterlife of print writing, is therefore influenced by political, cultural,
social, and design structures.

While the design of these templates provides a range of discursive
expression, users still choose, to varying degrees, what texts to write,
what posts to share, and what images to circulate. Users make use of
constraints creatively. Users' interactions with these templates become
imbricated with those templates. Prefabricated designs provide a prescribed way of communicating while allowing users freedom to produce
and craft rhetoric. In this sense, IPI templates are cultural forms.

Defining Templates: Cultural Forms

Because IPI templates, as interfaces, provide writers and audiences with
standardized expectations and decorum through a prescribed available
means of discourse, this discourse is integrated into and throughout
users' languages. IPI templates habituate us to act in certain ways,
persuading us through repetition (Chun 2016), thereby becoming
cultural forms. For instance, the words Friend, Status, and Like from
Facebook's template are obvious ways that IPI templates function as cultural forms. Despite having meaning outside Facebook's context, these
words have meaning inherently tied to the affordances (Norman, 1988)
of Facebook's template. Users Friend one another, post Status updates,
and Like those statuses. Alternatively, we Tweet and Favorite on Twitter.
It's not merely that these words have taken on new meaning. All words
evolve and change through use. Rather, these words are cultural forma-
tions derived from template affordances, which are themselves designed
by user-experience architects.

While writing scholars have good reason to take issue with his
hasty dismissal of rhetoric from new media (Eyman 2015, 52–55), Lev
Manovich's (2002) notion of cultural interface provides a useful way to
frame IPI templates as encouraging types of discursive culture to emerge.
Manovich uses "cultural interface" to "describe a human-computer-
culture interface—the ways in which computers present and allow us

to interact with cultural data. Cultural interfaces include the interfaces used by the designers of Web sites, CD-ROM and DVD titles . . . and other new media objects" (69–70). Manovich goes on to argue that cultures look the way they do because they stitch together "elements of other, already familiar cultural forms" (71). Included in his list of other cultural forms are cinema, the printed word, and the page, all of which are remediated on the internet.

IPI templates, like any cultural form, draw upon previous instantiations of prior media, social expectations, and technological affordances. For instance, Facebook's template emerged as a remediated mashup from the website Friendster and college facebooks, the latter of which are notable for the misogyny inherent in the fraternity world of collegiate life. When considered as cultural forms, IPI templates function ideologically. They formulate ontologies of digital writing, offering us guides about how to communicate with, and thereby specific types of knowing, one another. They infuse our ways of being with the discourse they supply to users while providing a procedural rhetoric between users.

TEMPLATE RHETORIC

As interactive interfaces of ongoing prefabricated designs and cultural forms, IPI templates form a peculiar type of standardized "procedural rhetoric" (Bogost 2007; Brown 2015; Holmes 2014, 2017; Matheson 2014) that I label *template rhetoric*. Template rhetoric, in the context of this book, is applicable to IPI templates and their environments. Procedural rhetoric connects rules of behavior with the authoring of rules: "Procedural rhetoric is a general name for the practice of authoring arguments through processes. . . . [Procedural rhetoric's] arguments are made not through the construction of words or images, but through the authorship of rules of behavior, the construction of dynamic models" (Bogost 2007, 29). Template rhetoric, like procedural rhetoric, is the idea that the possible range of interactions are authored for us by templates. While Ian Bogost locates procedural rhetoric in relation to programming videogames, the concept can be extended to IPI templates and their users because "procedural rhetoric is a technique for making arguments with computational systems and for unpacking computational arguments others have created" (3). IPI templates are part of computational systems that template designs create for users to employ. They are the aesthetically pleasing masks computational systems wear; everyday users without coding or markup knowledge need intermediaries to communicate online. Template rhetoric provides a basis for user-centric behavioral rules while allowing users to employ the rules flexibly and work creatively inside the rules. IPI templates author rules of behavior by providing users standardized methods of inscription, sometimes literally through blank forms and other times with specific rhetorical choices.

Yet, template rhetoric coerces users not through literal procedures, like videogames do, but through an ideology of procedure,[3] a reflection of the work other scholars have applied to procedural rhetoric. In *Ethical Programs* (2015), Brown works through the Levinasian Other and Derridean hospitality of software to broaden Bogost's procedural rhetoric by looking at the ideology of procedures. Brown writes, "We interact with procedures on a daily basis, and those procedures express particular worldviews" (48). Brown's version of procedural rhetoric involves worldviews, which, in synthesizing Galloway's theory of protocol, offers a way of seeing how users enter arranged networks where choices remain available even if they are coercively structured—as users are when they engage in template rhetoric.

Brown's revitalized version of procedural rhetoric helpfully lays out a way of understanding the textual and visual rhetoric of template rhetoric. Reworking procedural rhetoric with the example of Barack Obama's 2008 campaign mechanisms, Brown (2015) offers the following: "While digital rhetoricians have often attended to visual rhetorics and to the genres emerging in digital spaces, procedural rhetoric offers a way to deepen this work by thinking about the authorship of procedures that generate image and text and that invite or discourage interaction" (48). Brown goes on to examine how a phone-banking script for working on Obama's 2008 campaign is incomplete without volunteers (fig. 2.1).

The code in figure 2.1 is the procedure aimed at emphasizing the rhetorical work of both code and user simultaneously. Brown (2015) observes the following: "In many cases the procedures for attempting to persuade supporters of McCain or Clinton were authored not by the campaign but rather by the volunteers themselves" (64). For Brown, and I extend this sentiment to IPI templates, fulfilling the "script" of templates successfully requires users.

Template rhetoric, in keeping with Brown's perspective, encourages users to perform a series of structured tasks and processes that are never fully explicit until they are completed and extended by a user. This is a key distinction between users participating in template rhetoric and users being simply forced into an action by a prefabricated design. As Brown (2015) notes, "Procedural arguments in the form of phone-banking scripts were distributed by the campaign, but Obama volunteers were not rigid, unwavering machines. They did not always

```php
<?php
boolean $supportObama;
boolean $volunteer;
string $name;
string $phone;
string $email;

if ($supportObama==TRUE) {
  print ("Great! Would you be willing to Volunteer for the campaign?");
    if ($volunteer==true){
    $name = $_GET('name');
    $phone = $_GET('phoneNumber');
    $email = $_GET('email');
    }
        else
        {
        print ("Okay, no problem. Please remember to vote on November 2!");
        }
  }
else {
  print ("Thanks for your time. Have a great day.");
  }
?>
```

Figure 2.1. Brown's version of the Obama campaign's phone-banking script (63–64)

execute the campaign's code, or at least not in the way that we normally imagine the process of execution. *They interpreted it, changed it, and made it their own*" (66; emphasis added). In the context of my argument, while users can't redesign IPI templates, they can interpret the meaning of certain fields within these templates; for example, the meaning of a retweet on Twitter, a Reblog on Tumblr, or a Share on Facebook can have numerous implications and interpretations for users. Users can make certain functionalities their own, such as Checking In on the app Foursquare at a location where they wish to be as opposed to a location where they actually are. Template rhetoric depends on what and how users fill in these templates as much as the designs of the template. From this conceptual understanding, four characteristics of template rhetoric are useful to understanding the qualitative data in this book: repetition, time-space compression, ambient affordances, and standardization.

Repetition

The first of these characteristics is repetition. Because IPI templates can be filled out repeatedly, unlike a printed page, template rhetoric induces continuous filling in and filling out of templates, thereby providing

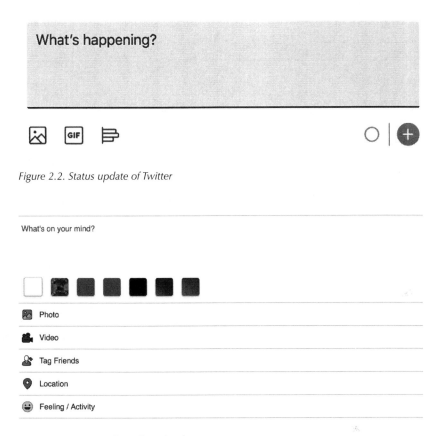

Figure 2.2. Status update of Twitter

Figure 2.3. Status update of Facebook

users with expectations of input information and behavior. Template rhetoric continuously prods users—but does not force them—to provide information and content using prestructured designs that occur through a visual array of interactive fields and qualitative affordances. Examples of repeatable templated fields are the status-update fields of Twitter (fig. 2.2) or Facebook (fig. 2.3). Other examples include review templates, such as Amazon and Yelp reviews. Content-management systems, such as WordPress, enable constant updating capabilities.

Empty template fields, as in figures 2.2 and 2.3, encourage users to fill in the template by posing a question—one that most likely becomes naturalized over time as users adjust to viewing the questions "What's happening?" or "What's on your mind?" repeatedly. These empty-state pages, as they are known in industry contexts, introduce users to instructions through habits (Gallagher and Holmes 2019). The act of filling in these templates thus never ceases and becomes a type of habit, disposition, or *hexis*—and is then forgotten. Template rhetoric prods users to write again through a naturalized interface, unlike previous methods of writing. Sending a paper note to a friend, coworker, or classmate, for instance, does not instantly yield another empty piece of paper to write *another* note. IPI templates have this effect.

Repetition intensifies the afterlife of digital writing, especially with respect to the construction of a habitual identity. Via repetition, template rhetoric hails, in an Althusserian way, users to form a particular kind of identity wherein they must monitor and manage their content. I will say more about monitoring and management in chapter 5, "Textual Management."

Time-Space Compression

IPI templates afford time-space compression, or the idea that technology increases the speed of production, distribution, and circulation, especially in regard to the flow of capital (Harvey 1989). Time-space compression usefully describes the way discursive information quickly moves around the internet; Brown (2012) has argued it is important for writers to know information moves quickly in the dromosphere, where rhetors must know speed is crucial (83). Similarly, Gries (2015) notes,

> From the perspective of [information and communication technology] time . . . our messages seem much more everywhere at once and nowhere in particular. This is especially the case in network culture in which information spills from network to network both on the Internet and outernet and messages do not flow from a sender to receiver, but spread, mix, mutate, converge, diverge, and interact in a complex of multiplicity of communication channels. (31)

I would extend this description to template rhetoric because, as a widely engaged user interface, IPI templates warp understandings of time *and* space, like "information and communication technology" does to our sense of "duration" (30). IPI templates compress temporal relations through visual display, often with a tendency to background temporal relations. (I say more about this idea in terms of interface and algorithmic timing in the next chapter, "Textual Timing.") As an illustrative example, Facebook's template timeline infamously defaults its layout to displaying "important" items, with the emphasis here being that "important" is guided by proprietary algorithms (formerly known as EdgeRank). Other examples include instances when digital comments on reddit or Tumblr aren't displayed linearly, leading to confusion about how to read digital texts. Comments on news articles or blogs can be displayed literally close together and may be read as an accumulated, singular text even when timestamps indicate lapsed time.

In the context of the afterlife of digital writing, time-space compression has a major implication for the habits of users: the *when* of reading is crucial to *what* and *how* users read. (I say more about this in the next chapter.) Texts, images, videos, and other discursive information are not static. Information moves and changes—and because it's expected to do so, users must account for this updating. Users end up writing in ways oriented toward recursive, iterative distribution and circulation. Readers and other audiences, such as algorithms and software programs, may process information that took significant amounts of time to accumulate, such as a large digital thread or set of comments, in the short space on a screen.

Ambient Affordances

IPI templates have literal affordances (Norman 1988) that are crucial to template rhetoric because they enable writers and audiences to move text and develop affective responses to content. These ambient affordances intensify what can happen after a text is delivered and discourse circulates in and around an initiating text. They literally create an afterlife to text that has no print analogue. I label these *ambient affordances* to describe the ways users and templates coalesce to form persuasive digital rhetoric beyond the bounds of technological determinism or social construction. This reflects Thomas Rickert's approach in *Ambient Rhetoric* (2013): "The individual is already a part of the invention in the wild environment, since to exist at all is already to suppose a world. Thus subjects exist not as separate from world but as a complex folding within other complex foldings of material and discursive force" (96–97). Within the context of template rhetoric, users' language and a template's language cannot be readily separated from one another. Via Martin Heidegger, Rickert usefully demonstrates that templates and technologies, including embodied forces, have an active and primary—not a passive and secondary—role in the rhetorical situation or event of digital writing. To extend Rickert here, to write is to be enfolded as part of a mood (*stimmung*) in the presymbolic realm of affects for any digital writer.

Terminologically, *ambient affordances* identifies this relationship between the affordances of IPI templates and users' own purposes, a topic that has been taken up by numerous scholars, notably through what Mel Stanfill (2015) calls "discursive interface analysis" and Tarsa's (2015) "qualitative affordances." For Stanfill (2015), discursive interface analysis engages users by undergirding users' ability to produce discourse; essentially, it is an approach to identify how users' discourses are informed by interfaces.

> Discursive interface analysis goes beyond function, examining affordances broadly—the features, but also what is foregrounded, how it is explained, and how technically possible uses become more or less normative through productive constraint. (1062)

Useful here is Stanfill's observation that affordances do not completely delineate user communication. Designers build them with intention, creating normative features of digital behavior and discursive exchange. But these normative communication features are the most accessible and intentional features available to users.

Noting that easy-to-use affordances entice users to employ them, Tarsa (2015) identifies qualitative affordances (QAs) as a way to articulate how users can interact and manipulate templates to communicate. Though her argument is couched in reddit and social media, I extend it to template rhetoric more broadly because her examples highlight the complexity of audience participation in IPI environments.

> A qualitative affordance, in its simplest form, provides a system through which readers' opinions of a text are tracked and displayed back to the community. These systems generally fall into one of three categories: share-based, "like"-based, or two-way. (22)

QAs are interactive affordances that allow users to register and accrue responses, such as feelings and shares. QAs record these registers, often counting them. Ambient affordances—though prescribed by designers—are slippery outside of user-to-user communication. Ambient affordances account for the surrounding context and possible interactions. Let me use a brief example to illustrate ambient affordances: Facebook's Like affordance. The Like button on Facebook, first rolled out to users in February 2009, had no counterpart (such as a Dislike button) or complement until February 2016, when reactions were introduced. Users had to obey the procedures of Facebook's template. Messages in statuses could not be Disliked, only Liked. Affectively, this means that the template rhetoric within a Facebook status was decidedly positive since users could not express dissatisfaction with a status via a qualitative affordance. In terms of template rhetoric, Facebook audiences could only express a positive sentiment unless they chose to write a comment. (They could ignore a post or comment, but ignoring was not a clear expression of negative sentiment.)

Ambient affordances are crucial to update culture and the afterlife of digital writing because they provide users with habituated ways to respond to one another and a common language, if not necessarily meaning, for understanding that response. By clicking or tapping a template, audiences can easily register a reaction of some sort, and other users have a general frame of understanding this discursive reaction. In conjunction with the two previous characteristics, repetition and time-space compression, ambient affordances create the possibility for closing the gap between writer (or discourse producer) and audience.

Standardization

Repetition, time-space compression, and ambient affordances of IPI templates are inextricably tied to the fact that these templates standardize user input. IPI templates are part of the forces behind the spreading, mixing, mutation, convergence, divergence, and interaction of digital messages. IPI templates inform users about what kind of information is supposed to be input. Input fields contain surrounding context without which the information collected couldn't be standardized. Through standardization, these templates—and their programmers and designers—impose hegemonic communication practices on users. This hegemony manufactures a sense of expectation and decorum for user-to-user relationships in IPI template environments—all of which accelerates the afterlife of digital writing.

CODA

In this chapter, I defined IPI templates and described template rhetoric to provide context to the writer-audience relationship in digital environments wherein neither writer nor audience programs the website. Due to the four characteristics of template rhetoric—repetition, time-space compression, ambient affordances, and standardization—writers and audiences share certain words, expectations, decorums, and habits. These templates enable the intensity of digital writing's afterlife by uniting writer and audience. For instance, on reddit, the word *karma* is used and discussed prominently. Likewise, the idea of helpfulness, which comes from the Amazon review template, was often brought up during my interviews as part of participants' writing goals. Reviewers frequently discussed the need to be helpful with a review and not just funny or entertaining. Reddit's karma and Amazon's helpfulness are examples of the way template rhetoric is infused into a particular digital environment. Template rhetoric produces environments that provide writers with expected types of responses and provide audiences with a means of response.

Now that I have set the stage and provided a bird's-eye view of the context and technical reasons for update culture, I turn to the strategies that I found writers demonstrating when they were contending with their audiences in update culture. Each of the next three chapters addresses a particular concrete strategy that is important to the afterlife of digital writing: textual timing, textual attention, and textual management. Each strategy addresses a question with which writers contend with update culture. In the next chapter, "Textual Timing," I take up the question of *when*.

3

TEXTUAL TIMING

In the fall of 2016, Russia ran a disinformation and propaganda campaign to interfere with US elections. Buried in the story was the sophisticated *timing* strategy the Russians employed. As Donie O'Sullivan (2018) of CNN writes, "Once the operation was up and running, staff in St. Petersburg worked day and night and were instructed to post in accordance with U.S. time zones." Russian workers considered not only the content of their writing, memes, and images but also *when* the content was posted, circulated, and moved. Good timing for them meant careful, consistent, and precise coordination. As a 2018 report on Russian interference states, "The [Russian] specialists were divided into day-shift and night-shift hours and instructed to make posts in accordance with the appropriate US time zone. The ORGANIZATION [Internet Russian Agency] also circulated lists of US holidays so that specialists could develop and post appropriate account activity" (R. Mueller 2018, 14). The operatives *timed* their writing and discourse production. *When* they wrote and circulated texts was a crucial and explicit strategy. They understood rhetorically savvy timing meant attending to the time of day and time zone when delivering and circulating texts, as well as coordinating series of texts with each other.

This example shows that *when* is a crucial and relevant writing strategy in our digital lives. *When* to write, revise, share, and update, as well as *when* to respond to audiences, are significant questions to consider. Do digital writers adopt a *kairotic* approach, aiming to find the right sliver of time? In light of Debra Hawhee's (2004) view of *kairos* as an "immanent, embodied time," are these writers aiming to find the right place and time for the "due measure" of their remarks (11)? Alternatively, do these writers turn to a *chronos*-based approach to time, deciding to respond at specific moments of clock time? What other timing strategies and conceptions are useful for digital writing and rhetoric? These are radical questions, ones that may have been naturalized by our media-saturated and screen-infused world. In face-to-face communication, deciding when to respond is not at all a new quandary. But responding to readers *in, around, on,* and

DOI: 10.7330/9781607329749.c003

through text radically changes writer-audience relationships. Because a text can change, or because of the mere *possibility* of change, investigating and developing answers to these questions can assist with understanding the role of temporality for the afterlife of digital writing.

Broadly, this chapter argues that digital writers pair *chronos* and *kairos* together as they wrestle with when to deliver and circulate their writing as well as when to respond, redeliver, and recirculate. If IPI environments overload users with discursive information and create the possibility for every discursive act to be a *kairotic* moment, then writers develop concrete internal strategies for producing rhetorical discourse that seizes upon the right, decorous moment, or "attunement to a situation" (Rickert 2013, 98) in terms of quantitative approaches. From my interviews and textual analysis, I have found that *chronos*, understood as "time as measure, the quantity of duration, the length of periodicity, the age of object or artifact" (Smith 1969, 1), can be usefully paired with *kairos* to describe the timing strategies digital writers employ in update culture. While David Sheridan, Jim Ridolfo, and Anthony Michel's (2012) *The Available Means of Persuasion* argues that honoring *kairos* has a destabilizing effect on this issue of *when* (27), I argue that pairing *chronos* with *kairos* can help restabilize writers as they navigate the chaotic nature of digital writing and rhetoric. To be direct, the writers I studied learned qualitatively *when* appropriate moments to write and respond were and then translated those experiences into a quantitative perspective. As a concrete example, journalists learned that pushing and recirculating content were often best done at lunchtime and after work, which translated to noon (EST) and between five and seven in the evening. They learned kairotically and then paired—fused—their *kairotic* knowledge with chronic knowledge.

Drawing upon qualitative and quantitative approaches to timing and temporality can be expanded to more complex notions of timing that I label *template timing* and *algorithmic timing*. Template timing argues that temporal concerns related to delivery and circulation of texts are related to the interface of a platform, namely, the way a template displays the various discourses. Template timing therefore extends the notion of timing to account for spatiality on digital screens. Algorithmic timing is related to template timing in that discourse is displayed within a platform's variety of fields, such as the way an update status is displayed in a Facebook newsfeed. However, algorithmic timing is more about the inner, black-boxed workings of a platform rather than its template. These three models of timing—*kairos-chronos* fusion, template timing, and algorithmic timing—serve to demonstrate the complexity of timing writing when writers attend to the afterlife of their digital texts. My broader goal in this chapter, then, is to describe the variety of timing activities my participants reported to me, including the strategies that exceed typical understandings of rhetorical temporality.

The rest of this chapter has six sections. First, I discuss how the internet inverts rhetorical understandings of *kairos*. Second, because the internet provides an inordinate number of *kairotic* moments, I argue that *chronos* can be paired with *kairos* in order to better understand digital timing. Following this theoretical discussion, I provide three accounts of textual timing helpful for understanding *when* writers respond. These accounts are (1) *kairos-chronos* fusion, (2) template timing, and (3) algorithmic timing. Fifth, I discuss how participants were unable to stop responding and writing. I argue that accrual and persistency buttress digital notions of timing. Because it might seem as if my participants were simply pandering to human and nonhuman crowds, I conclude by discussing *ad populum* and pandering in digital contexts.

THE INVERSION OF *KAIROS* ON THE INTERNET

Since James Kinneavy revived *kairos* in "*Kairos*: A Neglected Concept in Classical Rhetoric" (1986), numerous scholars have picked up the term *kairos* to describe the way speakers, rhetoricians, and communicators intervene in a timely manner that results in identification, persuasion, and change. Kinneavy, in discussing Plato's *Phaedrus*, notes that *kairos* describes a "propriety of time" in order to show the term's full range of connotations and rich dimensions (86–87), including ethical, epistemological, rhetorical, aesthetic, and civic (87–93). Elliott Jaques, in *The Form of Time* (1982), reminds readers that "*kairos* is the time not of measurement but of human activity, of opportunity" (15). *Kairos* is "the family of terms . . . concerned with the time of movement, with change, with emergence of the new and with active innovation" (15). In *Bodily Arts*, Hawhee (2004) posits that "*kairos* marks the quality of time rather than its quantity, which is captured by the other, more familiar Greek word for time—*chronos*. *Kairos* is thus rhetoric's timing, for the quality, direction, and movement of discursive encounters depend more on the forces at work on and in a particular moment than on their quantifiable length" (67). *Kairos*, despite subtleties in its definitions, retains its rhetorical core around a timely moment of intervention, persuasion, or language use.

In his attempt to extend Hawhee's *Bodily Arts* (2004) and John Muckelbauer's *The Future of Invention* (2008), Rickert, in *Ambient Rhetoric* (2013), adds a spatial, contextual component to *kairos*.

> The art of *kairos*, as most commonly understood, is the ability of a rhetor to invent appropriately in a given situation. . . . The situation presents itself in such fashion that the appropriate action will be understood, after effective results are achieved (i.e., retroactively), to have been *kairotic*. Thus, a context or situation is crucial to the appearance of *kairos*. . . . (75)

Rickert points us to a version of *kairos* that is in some ways uncontrollable and unteachable because it can only be activated and harnessed within a given temporal and spatial moment. Seizing the *kairotic* moment is at least partly beyond the control of individual rhetors and, likely, dependent on a host of factors beyond the control of individual agents in a given situation.

Understood in this way, *kairos* functions paradoxically in that it can be identified when it has passed. The act of analysis to identify what was and what was not the right or opportune moment must be retroactive. *Kairos* requires not only contextual factors, similar to the constraints in Bitzer's "The Rhetorical Situation" (1968), but also a temporal point of view that *looks back* upon rhetorical events and discourse. While we can teach rhetors to look for the right time or location, achieving *kairos* is a much more difficult and inexact task. We simply don't know whether a moment is *kairotic* (or not) until the moment has passed and we can see the outcome of the intervention. And this is the rub with the concept: it requires seeing the outcome(s) to determine whether *kairos* was enacted.

While *kairos* presupposes a retroactive perspective for many of its definitions, I am going to retheorize it differently, based on my case studies of digital writers, because IPI environments seem to invert the latent expectations of the concept. Canonically, *kairos* has been largely assumed to be scarce; *kairotic* moments are uncommon in traditional conceptions. Traditionally, speakers and writers must find the delicate opportune moment.

In my conversations with participants, however, digital writers self-reported that there are a vast number of *kairotic* moments and reported that they could be "always on"—a phrase that, incredibly, all but five (and these five were redditors) of my participants used at least once during interviews to describe their writing. This phrase, *always on*, helps describe a counterintuitive aspect of *kairos* for digital writers. *Kairos* is a possible feature, due in part to template rhetoric's characteristics, of *all* interactions and discursive exchanges in update culture. Every interaction on the internet might be *kairotic* but might also be forgotten.

This perspective of endless possible *kairotic* moments in update culture can be described in contemporary terms as *going viral*. On the internet, discursive information can attract attention, organically or inorganically (meaning either unpaid or paid, respectively). Any discourse can thus go viral, however likely or unlikely that is. Virality itself might be seen as a contemporary instantiation or permutation of *kairos* because viral content is a somewhat imprecise art, science, or algorithm, depending on one's perspective.

Recent scholarship has theorized the importance of virality. In *Going Viral* (2013), for instance, Karine Nahon and Jeff Hemsley argue that viral content needs to be socially shared with sharp acceleration and dramatic rate of decay. Such content needs to reach a large number of people and a large number of networks, both informal and corporate (19–34). Central to virality, for Nahon and Hemsley, is that "a viral information event creates a temporally bound, self-organized, interest network in which membership is based on an interest in the information content or in belonging to the interest network of others" (34). If we use Nahon and Hemsley's perspective, then viral discursive information on the internet includes *the right kind of timing*. Hawhee's (2014) remarks about *kairos* are significant here because they can be applied to digital templated environments as much as to ancient rhetorical arts in an Athens gymnasium: "*Kairos* is thus rhetoric's timing, for the quality, direction, and movement of discursive encounters depend more on the forces at work on and in a particular moment than on their quantifiable length" (66). Discursive encounters and interactions on the internet involve the quality, direction, and movement Hawhee invokes. Whether a tweet goes viral involves not only its clock time, that is, when it's initially sent out, but also on who sends a tweet out, what followers that person has, and a host of other factors, including the corporate structures, such as algorithms.

With respect to the prevalence of IPIs and the expectation of audience interaction during a digital text's afterlife, any discursive moment or exchange may go viral or intervene in a *kairotic* moment. Every act of rhetorical discourse may become *kairotic*, perhaps inadvertently. Even if most discursive exchanges don't go viral or intervene in the opportune moment, they possess the possibility to do so. Digital users observe and manipulate their templates when they decide which moments are the ideal contextual moments of interaction.

KAIROS AND CHRONOS ON THE INTERNET

Because any discursive act on the internet may go viral and become *kairotic*, however unlikely it is, I have found that writers develop *repetitive, consistent practices* accrued over the course of chronological time—*chronos*. Knowing when to deliver and circulate writing, and when to respond to and intervene with audiences, requires a day-by-day or hour-by-hour approach to temporality. With an intense degree of audience interaction available at all times, *kairotic* moments become an unceasing wave of never-ending qualitative time. Writers reported learning to cull quantitative moments out of their qualitative experiences. I thus found that my participants approached their writing with a fused understanding of *kairos* and *chronos*, or what I call *kairos-chronos fusion*.

Examples from my reddit case studies illustrate my point. When writing on the forum-based website reddit, posts accrue *upvotes* in terms of karma, which (as I note earlier) is the website's form of currency in terms of audience approval. In the subforum, or subreddit, AskReddit, users can accrue karma rapidly if they know when audiences will give them the most karma, that is, audience approval. As the redditors Kijafa and DiegoJones4 told me independently of one another, karma is a "metric of visibility." Kijafa told me, "Karma is not necessarily a measure of quality but of visibility." He later said that being successful in terms of karma is about "pattern recognition." What appears to be savvy *kairotic* intervention, however, can also be described as a pattern based upon when most users are active.

Several redditors remarked about when to write to accrue upvotes, as well as receive voluminous participation in terms of both *kairos* and *chronos*. AndrewSmith1986 told me that writing when "America is awake" is the key to timing on reddit. When I asked him what he meant, he said, "When people are awake, from about eight to four eastern time." Another participant, RamsesThePigeon (Max Patrick Schlienger) told me that a good time to write on reddit was "whenever people are going to work." RamsesThePigeon reminisced that he became well known, which he meant as having accrued karma, by recognizing that whenever he logged onto and read reddit, he was on his way to or from work. He started commenting on this basis and successfully accrued karma. (People who aim to accrue karma on reddit are referred to as, even by themselves, as *karma-whores*.)

Timing writing on reddit thus involves matching patterns between what people are doing in their lives with the time of day they do them. For instance, the well-known redditor StickleyMan advised me to write on rising threads—that is, posts gathering karma at a high rate of acceleration—between seven and ten in the morning EST because this strategy yields a dramatic amount of karma in AskReddit. StickleyMan told me this accrual was likely because people are arriving at work and are "a little bored." Using this advice from StickleyMan, I experimented for two weeks in the summer of 2017 and accumulated over 15,000 karma during my two-week experiment—quite a bit of karma for a novitiate! During the summer of 2018, I did this in May, June, and July and reached 100,000 karma.

Accruing karma on AskReddit, then, entails seizing the opportune, qualitative moment *and* carefully monitoring and observing patterns of chronological time. The appearance of *kairos* for the uninitiated to reddit is actually a quantitative strategy for those who are intimately familiar with the website. Opportune timing combines systematically and methodically deciding when to write at particular times of the day and week with a bit of luck and, sometimes, previous reputation. In contexts such as these, textual timing—the *when* of writing—involves a systematic approach to delivering and circulating discourse at specific clock times in real time.

In terms of *when*, then, I believe we should treat *chronos* and *kairos* as equally useful and valuable in digital writing and rhetoric, an approach that complicates rhetoric's stance toward *chronos*. Most studies of time have assumed *chronos* is either fairly straightforward (chronological or quantitative time) or less useful than a *kairos*-based approach to time. Even John Smith, whose pivotal articles "Time, Times and the 'Right Time': *Chronos* and *Kairos*" (1969) and "Time and Qualitative Time" (1986) explicitly discuss *chronos* as an avenue of inquiry, tends to emphasize the importance of *kairos* over the role of *chronos*. *Chronos* is lexically more familiar to English speakers; from chronology to anachronism to chronometry, derivatives of *chronos* abound in English, whereas the only common use of *kairos* is the phrase *kairotic moment*. For an emblematic example of the prioritization of *kairos* over *chronos*, see Brooke's treatment of *chronos* in *Lingua Fracta* (2009), in which Brooke briefly mentions *chronos* and then proceeds to discuss *kairos* in depth. Alternatively, Liz Losh's *Virtualpolitik* (2009) mentions *kairos* in her discussion of digital rhetoric without ever mentioning *chronos* (49–50). Likewise, Peter Simonson's "Reinventing Invention Again" (2014) provides a succinct and valuable account of *kairos*—but neglects any mention of *chronos*, as if *kairos* exists as the only rhetorical concept of time.

Because *chronos* has been traditionally conceived as chronological and quantitative time, I argue that *chronos*, as clock time and quantitative time, helps digital writers negotiate a paradox of information overload on the web. That is, if all moments could become *kairotic*, then how do writers choose when to write, rewrite, edit, and respond? Rhetorically, if writers and users are inundated with "amalgamations and transformations—the spread—of a given rhetoric within its wider ecology," then writers need a framework that allows them to approach rhetorical situations and ecologies in a coherent and organized fashion (Edbauer 2005, 20). Infusing *chronos* into a *kairos* approach helps to do so.

An important caveat to the perspective I am taking is the acknowledgment that individuals are not autonomous agents in IPI environments and cannot reach all audiences or be monolithically successful. What might be a moment of failure one day may be a success story a few weeks later—and vice versa. Because of the continuous, repetitive, and recursive nature of writing on the web, participatory audiences are part of the expected background decorum, creating a general sense of what might be called *kairotic noise*.

Temporally, to write in IPI environments means to write not only for a general audience or publics but also for possible audiences who have yet to announce themselves. Sometimes the timely moment never arrives, but other times it appears quickly and overwhelmingly. Yet other times the opportune moment emerges days, months, or years later—without regard to the initial writer's intentions or audience members' responses. In other words, while writers have intentions, audiences can pick up a writer's discourse at various times. The question of when, then, is often a question of producing discourse at consistent, repetitive, and organized intervals to ensure some audiences will read or process the text. (I offer more details about interacting with these audiences in the next chapter, "Textual Attention.") Because of this expectation of a participatory audience, digital writers likely have less agency than writers who do not have such audiences.

Such a view pushes against early depictions of web users, notably Barbara Warnick and David Heineman's first edition of *Rhetoric Online* (2007). Douglas Eyman's *Digital Rhetoric* (2015) offers a sharp synopsis of Warnick and Heineman's manuscript (30–34), noting that digital rhetoric must do more than simply "adjust" (34) theories of rhetoric to the web. Written when websites were not nearly as interactive, lacking RSS feeds and complicated JavaScript, Warnick and Heineman (2007) write, "Web users do not constitute a mass audience since each of them consumes Web content at his or her own pace and within the constraints of the user's environment" (37). Elaborating on this assertion, Warnick and Heineman posit, "Web users . . . initiate digital experience in their own time and as individuals, although they may form communities of common interest related to mass media content" (38). Warnick and Heineman's description positions users primarily in control of their web experiences. In IPI environments, however, the website's designers and structure control a user's experience, especially with respect to social media corporations and proprietary algorithms. While Warnick and Heineman recognize the role of the "user's environments" in the former passage, the subsequent quotation prioritizes the intention and autonomy of the user over uncontrollable aspects like website navigation. Users must contend with the priority of recent time in IPI environments and encounter time through structures and designs outside their power.

DEFINING TEXTUAL TIMING

This background theory helps frame digital timing as a qualitative-quantitative process important to the afterlife of writing. In the terms I lay out, digital writers may publish, post, and circulate at strategic times of day or on strategic days of the week to contend with being "always on" or guard against an insatiable need to "go viral." Textual timing is a process writers employ to cope and strategize because messages and other digital discourse are in a state of flux. Textual timing, broadly defined, is a process for describing a quantitative approach—*chronos*—to find the opportune moment—*kairos. Kairos* alone is not enough because while it may help writers respond to readers on a situational basis, considering innumerable factors can be time consuming, overwhelming, and simply not possible. *Chronos* alone is not enough because while "grid time" and quantitative time may help writers manage the massive number of opportunities, every moment is *not* the same in IPI environments. Practically and empirically, textual timing combines these approaches. From my interviews and textual evidence, participants in my study developed three types of these approaches: (1) *kairos-chronos* fusion, (2) template timing, and (3) algorithmic timing. I present these three types of timing in order of increasing complexity while recognizing these approaches are related to each other.

KAIROS-CHRONOS FUSION

Participants wrote, circulated, and pushed content from qualitative and quantitative perspectives. They accounted for the context of what people are doing (for example, responding when people are coming home from work and on their lunch break, not writing when people are going to bed) and the *quantitative* time of the day or week (for example, responding between seven and nine in the morning, between five and seven in the evening, and at noon, and avoiding pushing content after nine at night, all in EST). Participants considered when to write, when their audiences were most likely to respond, and when they ought to respond to audiences. They did so for any number of reasons, including to accrue attention (via reddit's karma system or Amazon's helpful-vote system), avoid overload (a reason noted by Amazon reviewers), and maintain work/life balance (a reason noted by many participants). Bloggers and Amazon reviewers often want to keep their audiences guessing as to when they will respond. Redditors typically want to instigate large discussions and, therefore, need to find effective times to initiate such engagement. The distinguishing feature between how digital writers consider time and more traditional, rote understandings of *chronos* is that digital writers pay attention to the context of clock time. I label this type of timing *kairos-chronos fusion*.

The journalists I studied were keenly aware that certain days were a poor time to share content and respond to audiences, notably, Friday night and Saturday, which are known as "news dumps" in the media. While all journalists I interviewed paid attention to the time of day and day of the week when they shared their content, two spoke directly to the issue of time. The first was Tracy Monroe, a science journalist and educator, and the second was Matt Grimes, a nutrition doctor, writer, and blogger.

Monroe's provaccine advocacy work placed her in the position to fight against the ignorance of antivaccine trolls at the opportune time on a continual basis. From this perspective, Monroe searched for a *kairotic* moment that was simultaneously repeatable and sustainable. To be direct, Monroe wanted to reach a large audience of readers who could be convinced to vaccinate—and she needed to find a time to do that. In highlighting this effort, Monroe told me, "You have to be strategic about [when you share]. It's not just about writing. You have to share it at the right time of the day and on the right day. Saturday mornings are the worst. Don't share anything after 9 p.m. eastern time. Share at lunchtime and after work. You know, noon and after five o'clock." In this statement, Monroe illustrates a *chronos*-infused *kairotic* approach to timing her content. As part of the production and distribution process of savvy circulation, timing digital writing means paying attention to *patterns* of effective quantitative time and considering why those times are useful. For example, noon is a time when people are on their lunch break from work and therefore more likely to consume (read, watch, listen to) digital content.

The second case involves Matt Grimes, a nutrition doctor who wrote for a variety of digital venues. Of importance, simply because *any* moment can be opportune does not mean *every* moment is such. Grimes did not believe that *every* moment is timely or *kairotic*; context of time mattered to him. "Consistent delivery" combined with context of that delivery is a key approach to timing. That is, if one is consistent *and* strategic enough with circulating content on the internet, an audience can be reached. An effective time to post content, for Grimes, entails monitoring social media platforms for a relevant news story and then sharing one's own writing at savvy times of day, such as "lunch breaks" or "news breaks." Consequently, Grimes's *kairos-chronos* fusion approach was similar to Monroe's: not every moment may be a good time to create and share content, but having a contextualized quantitative sense of timing is a way to conceive of the opportune moment.

Redditors also expressed a related understanding of the way *kairos* and *chronos* are fused. Redditors frequently talked about specific times of day as being inextricably linked and related to what "reddit is doing." (This phrase came up independently during interviews with redditors, including AndrewSmith1986, RamsesThePigeon, Way_Fairer, StickleyMan, Just1MoreFix, Roboticide, toxicbox, and Kijafa.) "Good timing" on reddit is surprisingly specific: somewhere between seven and ten in the morning EST. *Chronos* in this sense provides inventional *topoi*. Seven to ten in the morning EST is a good time, as toxicbox told me, because most of the "drones are getting to work and need a distraction." AndrewSmith1986 told me that reddit is "American-centric" and is most active when people are coming from and going to work. Kijafa, Omnipotent_Goose, Portarossa, RamsesThePigeon, Roboticide, Just1MoreFix, and Way_Fairer specifically mentioned times that correspond to seven to ten in the morning EST, noting this time is when people are commuting to or arriving at work in the United States. RamsesThePigeon, Just1MoreFix, DiegoJones4, and DevasoHouse explicitly discussed people arriving at work, although not all affirmed a particular time. Mattreyu wrote in an email, "Best times would probably be kind of early in the morning if you're posting links. Comments are more forgiving, but both don't usually do well when you post in the evenings and especially on weekends." Bound up in redditors' sense of good timing is the idea of karma, reading layout, and algorithms, which I address in the next two sections.

Kairos-chronos fusions on reddit account for specific times along with the context of that time. When writing on reddit, participants considered the time of day and what other redditors were doing behind the screen, a key gap that seems to be missing from research about the website (Brooker et al. 2017; Gallagher 2015a; Massanari 2015, 2017; Pflugfelder 2016; Sparby 2017; Thompson 2014). Moreover, this audience behavior, at least in terms of time, is abstracted. Participants did not just imagine a set of users or individual redditors but rather imagined their audience in broad demographics. With the exception of Portarossa (notably, the only redditor who self-identified as a woman), redditors described their imagined audiences as men between twenty-three and thirty-six years of age. Some said older ("mid-to-late thirties or forties"), but most actually articulated late twenties to thirties. This imagined demographic illustrates their perceptions of timing because they imagined their audiences as on the way to work or arriving at work. In this sense, the way redditors conceive of their audience influences when they decide to write and the frequency with which they decide to write.

If journalists and redditors consider when to create, share, and circulate content in accordance with *kairos-chronos* fusion, then Amazon reviewers consider when to write, as well as when to respond to audiences, in a similar fashion but with the purpose of those fusions turned inward. The reviewers I studied developed strategies for timing their writing by considering their quality of life, consistency of response, and quality of response. Since none reviewed products professionally, some woke up early to write reviews and respond to comments, while others reviewed when they got home from work. Others were retired and could respond to questions and comments at any time; as a result, many had notifications pushed to them on their digital devices. The key distinction between reviewers' sense of timing and that of journalists and redditors was the goal of guarding their time and developing a consistent practice. Many of them, like journalists, took a business-like approach to reviewing.

While the reviewers' timing strategies cannot be described monolithically, general trends can describe their approach to when to respond to comments. The following four reviewers articulated emblematic *kairos-chronos* fusions that protected the reviewers from information overload and being "always on."

- I check my comments in the morning at 8 a.m. and only once. Otherwise, it's overwhelming. (AR1)
- The helpfulness vote is all that really matters. You can't sit around and watch it. I check it <u>once an hour</u> and that's it. When I do, I'll respond to comments too. <u>On the hour.</u> (Bill Elijah)
- I don't read comments together. I get them sent to my phone and <u>read and respond immediately</u> and then forget about them. (Seymour O'Reilly)
- I'm embarrassed to say this, but I sometimes spend 8 hours a day. I have to limit it somehow. I have to pick when to respond to questions, I write for <u>two hours</u> before work. (AR2)

The underlined words in these passages reference specific times of day, showing how reviewers deployed *kairos-chronos* fusions in order to protect their own time. Although this *chronos*-based feature was also commonly mentioned by journalists, the reviewers more often articulated specific times and days as a way to protect their own time because they reviewed as a hobby or an aspirational vocation.

The qualitative (*kairos*) timing feature of reviewers' viewpoints is that they have developed strategies for avoiding being "always on." They defined how to be a productive writer in an environment, such as the review culture of Amazon, where they could always be writing and responding to comments. They carved out time for writing and responding, which means they simultaneously defined time for *not* writing—I return to the idea of *stopping* later in this chapter.

Kairos-chronos fusion for Amazon reviewers could easily be seen as a helpful writing strategy for any writer, offline or online, especially in light of the reviewers' sense of being "always on"—a pressure inculcated by Amazon's review system and culture. Several reviewers, including the reviewers Mike W, Liza Margulies (the Amazon reviewer who goes by longwayfromhome), and Jason Rob (pseudonym), told me writing reviews had to happen "as soon as possible" or "quickly as possible" (all three used these phrases). While these three reviewers have reduced their reviewing dramatically since I first began talking with them, in part due to changes in Amazon's reviewing guidelines and process for "purging" older reviews, they explained that savvy timing involved writing immediately: "sooner the better" (Rob). Mike W told me of the intense pressure to respond rapidly:

> I probably had 150 to 200 emails waiting for me each day upon waking with offers to review something. I would probably pare that down to five to ten a day. There were days when I had ten to fifteen packages on my doorstep. Almost everyday, minimum at three [packages]. I would bump into the UPS guy around town and he would say, "Who the hell are you?" They all knew my house. [laughter from both Mike W and myself]

Likewise, Rob told me,

> Because once more reviews start piling in, there's less likelihood that your review is going to float to the top where it's going to be more noticed by people who are going to view it as helpful, hopefully. If your review is buried under 300 other reviews, a lot of people may never even see it. For the same reason that if you're searching for something in Google, you rarely go past page one of the results because you've already seen a page full of results, and you can usually get what you need to get from that first page. But you don't ever go to page 14 of the results.

Liza told me,

> The only time timing is important to me is if I . . . if there's a product that I really want my review to be noticed on, I'll post it . . . I'll try and post something that is a relatively new item as quickly as possible after I've gotten a sense of it. Just to see if I can, you know, make it a more prominent review.

During their peak years (2014–17), Mike W reported writing seven to ten reviews a day, and Rob reported the same number. Liza reviewed fewer during her peak years, most likely because her reviews were longer than those of the other two (she told me she was known for quality reviews). Nevertheless, all three were contending, during this time, with update culture taken to its highest intensity, when shrewd timing meant as fast as possible.

In general terms of *kairos-chronos* fusion, digital writers' timing behaviors might be described as *pacing* and *patterning* their writing. Pacing echoes recent scholarship about consistent digital content production, including the production of YouTube videos (Ledbetter 2014, 126–27). Likewise, patterning echoes Brooke's (2009) theoretical reworking of the canon of arrangement into sequencing and then pattern (92–97). Digital writers learned to pace their reviews, articles, posts, and other content while developing strategic patterns for distributing, delivering, and circulating content. Together, pacing and patterning provide insight into rhetorical timing. Rather than persuasion occurring with one text, speech, or moment of discourse, digital rhetoric in IPI environments unfolds across a given set of exchanges, accruing and accreting. Digital rhetors learn to cull these series of texts and their exchanges, searching for opportune moments within the grid of all times while developing ways to anticipate when best to intervene.

TEMPLATE TIMING

Yet *kairos-chronos* fusion is but one aspect of textual timing for the writers I studied. They considered more than just qualitative and quantitative times. They also considered when their audiences would encounter their writing and content on a *screen*. These writers had a spatial awareness of when audiences would encounter their writing, a spatial awareness that accounted for interfaces, specifically the layout of a website's template.

All participants paid attention to the layout and design in which their writing would be received and read. They not only considered the best times of day, day of week, or qualitative activity but also when audiences encountered their writing on the screen via its interface. *When* thus becomes as much about spatiality as temporality. In terms of broader audience theory, *template timing* moves our understanding of participatory audiences into the realm of interfaces and templates, along with their display of discursive information. Because IPI templates move that information, this understanding necessitates timing.

The notions of *default display*, *first*, or *recent* demonstrate template timing across all case studies. Digital writers covet getting their content displayed first or by default (Powers 2015). This aim in turn shapes how participants understand timing because, for them, *when* becomes a way to achieve this coveted or "pole" position (StickleyMan). When writing reviews on Amazon, for instance, posting a review first is generally considered the best *when* (this also holds true for reddit and, generally, on twitter for journalists). As AR1 told me, "There's a recency bias to reviewing. The first review usually gets all the attention and so it becomes the most helpful [because] it preexists at the top of the reviews because that's what Amazon organized." Good timing on reddit also means which posts and comments receive large amounts of karma or get "good responses" (this phrase came up with seven reddit participants, all independently of one another). Journalists wanted their articles shared on Facebook and Twitter with enough ambient affordances to boost their content into the newsfeeds of potential audiences.

To determine when is the best time to write effective reviews (reviewers), posts (redditors), or online content (journalists), writers consider the optimal time in which that writing can be *received* well. This is due to the autotelic algorithmic nature of default displays and first posts, which use ambient affordances to organize the display of content. Accruing ambient affordances on a particular platform leads writers to garner helpful votes (reviewing), karma (reddit), and Likes, Shares, or Retweets (journalists and bloggers) because more readers will see that content due to the interactive display of IPI templates.

Template timing, more generally, shows that digital timing requires a spatial consideration that novitiate writers might not instinctively possess. While novices might want ambient affordances, such as helpful votes or upvotes, seasoned writers understand such affordances control the display of texts, thereby enabling writers to be read more widely. While those in game studies might label one element of this phenomenon as *gamification* (adding game elements to nongame activities), the crucial element of separation from gamification is that writing needs to be timed. Because that timing occurs on screens and devices, digital timing thus necessitates a spatial awareness of digital temporality, including the way that participatory audiences have a role in shaping a writer's encounter with those very same audiences. I now detail template timing for reddit and Amazon reviewing, two venues in which spatiality is crucial to timing.

Template Timing on Reddit

On reddit, template timing is particularly noticeable due to the website's intricate threaded conversations. Posts (initial writing) and comments are displayed according to karma upvotes and downvotes; users are more likely to read comments that have upvotes because of the threaded default display. Unlike online conversations on Facebook, which limits respondents to one level of exchange, reddit enables replying to comments infinitely (creating threaded exchanges difficult to read for novices). Comments on a post can be displayed in several categories: best (the default), new, top, controversial, rising, old, and Q&A. Savvy redditors, including my participants, get read if they consider these elements.

Redditors' complex sense of template timing is informed by the way these posts and comments are displayed—redditors ensure their writing is at the top of a post, where they know the writing will be read (and garner even more upvotes). In this sense, the *kairos-chronos* fusions I mention earlier (for example, knowing to write between seven and ten in the morning EST) also involve finding "rising" threads. Nearly every redditor also mentioned, unprompted, the need to find a rising thread, which is a thread that has a high rate of acceleration in terms of upvotes and number of comments. Finding a rising thread requires changing the default display of reddit. On the surface, this may simply be a way to game the system of reddit to accrue karma (karma-whoring).

However, there is more to this approach than simply gathering karma. The role of karma means that redditors understand how audiences encounter their texts from a spatial-temporal perspective. To have good timing on reddit means embedding a comment in a conversation that will hopefully be read widely, perhaps even making the "front page" of reddit, where many casual users and digital passersby will read the comment. Doing so requires finding posts in their infancy (rising threads) and then determining which threads will get the most attention (upvotes). To do this, redditors told me that they need to come to a rising post early in its life cycle (similar to the recency bias mentioned by reviewers). Roboticide, for instance, told me, "You need to get there within two hours of the post to embed yourself." Toxicbox remarked that commenting on the post early "really embeds you in that post so people can see your comment." Several other redditors mentioned the word *embed* when discussing timing, including DevasoHouse, Way_Fairer, and StickleyMan. By "embed," they mean that while a post may not be successful immediately, it becomes successful as a post or a comment continues to evolve and mutate as it receives attention.

In terms of templates and website layout, redditors perceive and predict the way general users encounter and read a text. Redditors know how most other users read threads through interface-display defaults; redditors recognize that elements of an interface's template shape users' reading processes. These redditors understand that to be read widely means they can't write a post or comment on another *popular* post. Instead, a comment needs to be embedded in a conversation and "ride the karma wave" (StickleyMan) up to the top.

Template Timing for Amazon Reviewers

The templates and rules of writing Amazon reviews articulate a complex version of template timing. While reviews can be sorted by a number of different metrics (such as most critical and most positive), their default display is arranged by the metric of "helpful votes," which is a pair of electronic buttons for voting Yes or No. Accruing helpful votes is a type of spatial timing for IPI environments. Those writers who produce reviews quickly on new products, while still writing useful reviews, can accrue helpful votes. This recency plays a role in reviewers' writing processes, for as Sandy Winston told me, "When I sit down to purposely review something, I don't read other people's reviews first, I just want to get my reviews out first." Because reviews with the most helpful votes are displayed first, they thus receive more helpful votes. Indeed, this cycle of accruing ambient affordances is a phenomenon that exists for redditors and journalists, as well as in my own experiences.

In light of these metrics, reviewers implicitly consider template timing through what I have come to label *helpfulness template timing*. As reviewers frequently stated in our interviews, they consider the questions "When can I be most helpful?" and "When is this review going to be read?" when they prepare to write. These two questions invoke the spatial layout of their reviews, via the Amazon review template. They paid careful attention to the number of helpful votes they received because these votes determined how a review was displayed (similar to reddit, Twitter, and other platforms). They looked at the threaded display of comments, as redditors and journalists also do, deliberating carefully about when to respond. (*How* they responded is an issue I discuss in the next chapter.) In doing so, reviewers paid attention to timestamps of comments—and often disregarded disingenuous comments or older comments. Reviewers looked at the way their review was displayed in the context of other reviews (something redditors frequently engaged with savvy precision). Put simply, their questions of *when* involved the spatial display on a screen—a display overtly influenced by interfaces and, specifically, templates.

To provide more context to helpfulness template timing, I need to describe the intense environment of Amazon reviewing, which takes shape for two reasons. The first is Amazon's Vine program. The second is the layout of Amazon's review template. These factors are the origin of the helpfulness language that my participants so frequently used. As I note above, Amazon reviewers have developed this concept of helpfulness as a way of considering when they should write. In essence, being helpful as a reviewer is about accruing more votes so that one's reviews are displayed sooner to review readers. Yet helpfulness is a concept filtered through Amazon's review template and reviewing guidelines, which assist reviewers with considering the timing of their writing.

In the competitive world of writing Amazon reviews, highly ranked reviewers take great pride in their writing despite—or perhaps because of—getting many items for free from the Vine program, a program that emphasizes helpfulness as a concept. As Kennedy has argued in *Textual Curation* (2016), "Policy dictates content and it does so in ways that shape not only the text but also the contributing collective" (71). In light of Kennedy's argument, it's clear the reviewers' texts and behaviors were driven by the Vine program's policies. The Vine program prioritizes helpfulness as a concept when inviting

> the most trusted reviewers on Amazon to post opinions about new and pre-release items to help their fellow customers make informed purchase decisions. Amazon invites customers to become Vine Voices based on their reviewer rank, which is a reflection of the quality and *helpfulness* of their reviews as judged by other Amazon customers. Amazon provides Vine members with free products that have been submitted to the program by participating vendors. Vine reviews are the independent opinions of the Vine Voices. The vendor cannot influence, modify or edit the reviews. ("What Is Amazon Vine?"; emphasis added)

Of the Amazon reviewers I interviewed, only two weren't participating in this program. Members of the program are denoted as such on their account, a marking that, according to reviewers, provides some degree of prestige because it indicates the reviewer has "made it."

The program is a source of both reward and consternation. It sends reviewers, based on their ranking, free items to review without the pressure of a positive review from the manufacturer. It asks for items to be reviewed within "30 days of receipt." In this respect, the Vine program inculcates a truly intense version of update culture. The number of items sent to reviewers continuously supplies them with new materials to write about. Importantly, once items from the Vine program became taxable income in 2017, the intensity of reviewing was significantly reduced because many reviewers did not want to pay taxes on commodities they did not want.

The Vine program sets a general decorum around reviewing, one reflected in the reviewing template. The guidelines of the Vine program ask writers to review, as noted previously, for the express purpose of being helpful, thereby creating a culture of competitiveness because reviewers who do not abide by the program can be removed from the program. Being removed from the program likely has a deleterious effect on reviewers' rankings because receiving free merchandise enables them to review products easily, quickly, and authoritatively (the last being true because the program marks them as having genuinely received items they review).

The second part of helpfulness template timing is the review template, which emphasizes helpfulness. This IPI template has a five-star system that sets out a limited range of evaluation. Reviewers may choose a star to rate an item by hovering their cursors over the desired star. Underneath this rating system is an opportunity for users to write a review. In the early review system, writers were required to use at least twenty words. Amazon removed this word minimum in 2013, much to the consternation of my participants. While there is currently no word or character minimum, several of the reviewers I interviewed expressed a desire for a word minimum to "ensure quality reviews" and produce "helpful reviews."

The reviewers I interviewed used the language of helpfulness during our interviews—a crucial reflection of the review template, the Vine program, and the ideology of Amazon's review system. Each review can be rated by other readers, presumably potential customers, as helpful or not. In fact, all reviewers used the phrase "quality reviews" or "helpful review" when describing their writing goals. Reviewers also discussed a need to be "engaging" and "authentic," which I took to mean an effort to be as helpful as possible.

The language reviewers employ does not emerge ex nihilo from the templates. It is written into Amazon's official guidelines. In these guidelines, Amazon specifies frequent and high-level reviewers as "enthusiasts." The following selection from the guidelines demonstrates how Amazon reviewers come to define their values and priorities:

Be active. Post reviews and answer questions on products related to your interests and hobbies often. Posting more frequently encourages other customers to follow you and keeps them interested in what you have to say.

Be engaging. Make sure your reviews or answers are compelling or helpful to customers. It's a good sign that customers are engaged when your posts earn helpful votes or you earn more followers. You can view more on how to write a great review in the Customer Review Creation Guidelines.

Be authentic. Your reviews and answers should be based on your personal experience with products you've actually used or consumed. Being authentic earns trust and helps you build an audience that shares your interests. ("About Top Contributors")

As I learned over the course of my interviews, the emphasis on engagement, authenticity, and helpfulness in these guidelines has a clear effect on the way highly ranked reviewers conceptualize their writing processes. It is clear this language of helpfulness from the reviewers derives from the review template and Amazon's guidelines. I've established this extensive background because reviewers understand when to write their reviews, when to respond to comments, and when to delete their writings in the context of helpfulness template timing, an idea that informs the textual timing of Amazon reviewers.

Every reviewer I talked with prioritized being helpful. As AR2 said, "The main reason I write reviews has been for self-gratification, although I do get a lot of pleasure out of people upvoting, and I get pleasure out of people commenting and saying, 'You helped me.' It's not like all for other people [reviewing], I do get something out it." This reviewer pointed out to me that "helpfulness" is a murky term that other reviewers contend with. AR2 said,

Sometimes people misunderstand "Helpful" and "Not Helpful" for "I agree" or "I don't agree." . . . A review can be incredibly helpful, but it's of my experience, this is what happened. Or this is my experience with the book, and . . . There are certain authors, and this is one of the reasons I stay out of fiction, from famous authors like Anne Rice to self-published authors that you've never heard of, they will absolutely come in and get all their friends and families to downvote your review of them. They have nothing to do with the review at all. I don't know if it's harsh, but this is one of the reasons I stopped reviewing, mostly stopped reviewing fiction. Every once in a while I'll break down and get a book from Vine, and then I'm pretty much always sorry I did. I don't need a bunch of fan boys and girls all over my butt because I didn't like their favorite author's books, because vampires don't sparkle or whatever.

This amusing passage provides an emblematic perspective on the qualitative feature of the helpfulness. Reviewers train themselves to target helpfulness, read Amazon's guidelines carefully, and pay close attention to the review template's features.

Helpfulness and the helpfulness template determine the way reviews are displayed and *when* readers encounter a review on their screen—the more votes, the sooner readers encounter a review. Helpfulness thus becomes an approach to timing, learning how to predict and prefigure audience demands, including updating or deleting reviews that were ignored. (I discuss this in chapter 5, "Textual Management.")

ALGORITHMIC TIMING

While the concept of template timing explicitly connects the spatiality of interfaces to temporality, algorithms are at play behind interfaces and their templates. If template timing describes the explicit features of a spatial-temporal display, then algorithmic timing describes the implicit features behind the screen. Algorithmic timing describes how participants time their writing according to various elements that are distilled implicitly into a platform's display and interface.

Every group of participants mentioned algorithms, albeit with different perspectives. Amazon reviewers talked about the "review algorithm" and generally had a vexed relationship with it because it controlled their ranking. Journalists had a pragmatic take on algorithms, understanding that the algorithms of Twitter, Facebook, and other sites circulated their content (for better or worse). Bloggers explicitly talked about Google's search-engine algorithms and frequently mentioned using keywords as a way to "boost" their writing into the results of their audiences. Redditors extensively talked about "reddit's algorithms" and considered the algorithms as a way to be read widely. In terms of algorithmic timing, the writers I studied considered when to write in terms of the templated spatial display of a screen when that mutable display is determined by an algorithm. Part of timing for them, then, was to consider the various factors of an algorithm, including the ways that algorithms prioritize certain types of writing and other discursive information. Part of writing for participatory audiences, then, is to consider how algorithms *aggregate* audience response.

These findings complement and reorient other studies of online writers. Unlike the ebook authors in Laquintano's *Mass Authorship* (2016), who believe they can overcome the power of algorithms (94), the writers I studied did *not* believe they could overcome the power of algorithms. Rather, they tried to take advantage of algorithms in various contexts. I attribute this difference to the type of writing they engaged: my participants did not produce novels or books, whereas in Laquintano's study, writers are framed as authors, with all the prestige a term like *author* entails. And, of course, they were producing traditional books (in ebook format).

In my interviews, not every participant mentioned algorithms directly, although all the redditors mentioned the term at least once, and half of the journalists discussed algorithms explicitly. The Amazon reviewers and journalists discussed algorithms implicitly; they mentioned algorithms, but they also mentioned terms such as "automated sorting" (AR1) and other terms that implied automation. More generally, algorithmic timing fell into two categories: direct manipulation of algorithmic timing and experiential algorithmic timing. The former category was significantly less common than the latter. Direct manipulation of algorithmic timing describes the way writers conceive of their timing when they explicitly have an awareness of an algorithm's elements. Experiential algorithmic timing describes the way participants develop timing strategies based on their direct experiences with an algorithm but without explicit access to an algorithm's elements.

Direct manipulation of algorithmic timing frequently occurred with journalists, bloggers, and redditors more often than with reviewers. For instance, the journalists and bloggers I interviewed mentioned considering the "weight of content" and "time decay" as being important when they shared their content on Facebook. These phrases are derived from the older model of Facebook's algorithm, called EdgeRank. Estee Beck (2016) describes the algorithm effectively:

> Facebook's EdgeRank algorithm [$\Sigma = U_e \times W_e \times D_e$ (Σ = rank; U = affinity; W = weight; D = decay; e = edge)] calculated data based on: (1) affinity—how close or many times users came into contact (the edge) with each other through viewing pages, commenting on posts, etc.; (2) weight—the rank of the type and frequency of contact from the edge; and (3) decay—the time from last contact on the edge.

For instance, Heather Armstrong and Penelope Trunk understood that in order for their content to reach a large number of users, they needed a number of comments and Likes on a publicly accessible post on Facebook or Twitter. Trunk also told me that if she wanted to push an older piece of content (such as a photo) into the timelines of others, she'll comment on that photo to reset the "time-decay" factor. Direct manipulation of algorithmic timing in IPI environments therefore considers the factors that go into a spatial display, even those that are not easy to distill or discern from the visual cues of an interface.

Savvy redditors discussed, anonymously because it's against reddit's policies, direct manipulation of algorithmic timing when they told me about creating "bot" accounts written with computer scripts. These bots posted on certain comment threads, targeting threads that were "rising." These bots thus had "good timing" because they could comment on threads that had high rates of acceleration. In this sense, what appears to be good timing is manipulation of algorithms. In fact, I found out by contacting several redditor accounts that some of the top-level accounts are actually bots or groups of people who have written a script. The well-known account Trapped_in_reddit is actually a bot run by several users. This bot was written with a computer script to find the popular threads on reddit and repost them.

Experiential algorithmic timing occurred with all but three of my participants (only StickleyMan, Kelly Salasin, and Seymour O'Reilly did *not* discuss the experiences of an algorithm). Participants consistently imagined how an algorithm was processing ("reading") their texts and redistributing those texts based on the defined parameters of an algorithm's equations. Digital writers time their texts by attempting to unbox the black box of proprietary systems.

Writing for Amazon's review algorithm is, for example, experiential algorithmic timing. The review algorithm ranks reviewers through a balance of four elements: number of reviews written, number of helpful votes, number of unhelpful votes, and recent reviews. Although the precise algorithm remains black boxed by Amazon for proprietary reasons, this lack of access does not stop reviewers from *conceptualizing* their writing processes around this procedure and reconsidering the temporal nature of their writing.

The review algorithm is a crucial part of when reviewers produce discourse spatially. It encourages them to track their helpful votes as well as delete and subsequently rewrite reviews that don't accumulate positive votes. The way reviewers respond to questions and queries also shapes the number of helpful votes, including reader comments that can come at any time of day or on any day of the week. Reviewers must therefore be prepared for reader response at all times. Reviewers may predict patterns of response based on *chronos* approaches, notably on Black Friday and Cyber Monday around Thanksgiving, but the precise response is unpredictable, requiring careful intervention so that reviews maximize (or "game") the *helpfulness* of their reviews. The complexity of algorithmic timing demonstrates the intimate relationship of algorithmic timing with *kairos-chronos* fusion and template timing.

In addition to Amazon reviewers, professional journalists and blog-gers rely on experiential algorithmic timing when they decide to write for a platform's algorithm as their audience. They know their audi-ences read across various platforms, understanding that each piece of content is displayed according to a particular system's proprietary algorithms. These writers consequently negotiate several algorithms as they circulate writing around the web, including Facebook's EdgeRank, Google's search engine, and Twitter's algorithm, among others. Like Amazon reviewers, these writers understand algorithms as part of their timing processes because the algorithms control the display of texts. Participants attempt to manipulate algorithms, understanding that algorithms display when users encounter content, regardless of whether participants understand the elements that control the display.

Here I focus on one particular blogger, Heather Armstrong, who crystallized the habits of many well-known writers who time their texts, including Monroe, Grimes, Trunk, and others. Armstrong, who was once considered the "world's number one mommy blogger," pro-vided me with an emblematic example of what I call *algorithmic display*. Considered one of the thirty most influential women in the media by *Forbes* magazine, Armstrong was a well-known blogger and "influencer" who maintained her social media sites on a frequent basis. She posted her writing directly to Facebook, Twitter, and other social media sites; she circulated her articles and other content around the internet by posting links to various social media sites and forums. On these sites, she received numerous comments and ambient affordances, such as Likes and Retweets. And these were important to her because, she told me, comments and Likes are "addictive" and "[comments] are gratifying. When I get them, I get a jolt of happiness."

Due to the importance of surrounding context, Armstrong keenly attended to the inner functioning of Facebook's algorithm, EdgeRank. While an exact understanding of EdgeRank's equation is not possible for proprietary reasons, Armstrong understood that certain strategies pushed her content back into the newsfeeds of her readers. The EdgeRank algorithm favors recent content; thus, as Armstrong told me, "I give my content a bump by commenting on it." The term *bump* here means that Armstrong commented on her own posts and texts in order to push content back into the newsfeeds of her readers. "You need to push content back into people's feeds," she told me. "Any good blogger should do it. You should tell that to your students." She later told me that the weight of content, the language of EdgeRank, requires monitor-ing content and keeping content recent, preventing time decay. These factors also play a role when thanking the commenters, an idea I examine in the next chapter.

For Armstrong, and this is true for other writers who navigate multiple social media sites, deciding when to respond on the internet involved thinking about how content is displayed in users' RSS feeds. Her understanding of when to post content and when to reply to comments was geared toward the display of that content in order to get her writing to rise in her audience's timelines. This approach of algorithmic timing thus fuses a human and nonhuman approach, via temporal and spatial relations, that neither *chronos* nor *kairos* fully captures.

Algorithmic timing expands the query of when to respond to include the spatial display of text. IPI templates allow writers to alter text rapidly and at scale, often with complex algorithms undergirding the movement of discourse displayed in those templates. As Hawhee (2004), Rickert (2013), and Muckelbauer (2008) have also shown, rhetorical timing has a spatial component; important to note, building on their work, this discussion foregrounds the spatial component to *chronos*-based time in addition to *kairos*-based time. When writers consider digital algorithms, they consider the various input features that become homogenized into a display on people's computers and mobile devices. To make the decision about *when* to write, these writers think about the calculations and procedures of an algorithm in addition to context-appropriate texts.

NOT STOPPING IN UPDATE CULTURE

But when is it a bad time to write and respond in update culture? This last section responds to this question by addressing the need to be "always on," including the pressure of responding to audiences. As the redditor Roboticide and reviewer Margulies both said, "I stop when people stop responding." Whether or not they'd written a good text, from a self-evaluative stance, they were always gearing up to write more. Within hours or days of conducting my interviews and reading their texts, more writing appeared—reviews, new articles, or pushed posts. While I say more about this continuous production in chapters 6, 7, and 8, discussing *when to stop* helps make better sense of their textual timing strategies, provides a depiction of the effort and labor these writers expend, and guards against an overly positive view of update culture.

The writers I interviewed discussed the experience of their writing as being "always on," an aspect related to participants' deployment of clock time. Amazon reviewers reported writing for up to eight hours a day, while many wrote for at least two hours. (The ones who regularly wrote for more than two hours considered it part of their hobbies during retirement.) Regardless of whether these estimates accurately reflect the average amount of time spent writing, these reviewers at least had the perception of spending many hours per day writing. The journalists I talked with recalled writing all hours of the day, from early morning (Grimes) to staying up until three or four in the morning (Monroe). Bloggers told me they wrote at any time they could (Armstrong). Redditors told me they wrote around the clock and during work hours, keeping reddit open on their computers. To be blunt, timing the afterlife of digital writing is exhausting and affectively draining. One reviewer told me he was "depressed" when he fell out of the high-level rankings, despite his efforts to review on a daily basis. More distressing, he stopped responding to my queries, and his email account is no longer active.

When I asked participants "How do you cope?" and "When do you stop responding," many of them had no clear-cut strategies or answers. Some of them told me that was part of the "gig." The reviewers frequently talked about how they were addicted to the rush of writing and receiving helpful votes. Redditors often told me about the dopamine rush they received when a post was upvoted. (Interestingly, many redditors and reviewers explicitly talked about the dopamine rush.) While bloggers told me they'd learned to avoid posting too many times per week (no more than three times per week was the consensus for "right number of posts"), their specific answers were diverse and lacked any discernable pattern.

I have found, thus, that the question of when to stop has no stable or unifying answer. This finding could be due to my methodology because I studied writers who actively considered their audiences and comments; in doing so, I may have found people who were "always on." Nevertheless, this finding has implications. If writing is part of digital content production and writers are branching out into positions such as social media manager, then becoming successful at digital writing involves producing content on a continuous basis. To be a writer in update culture means to write at any time, as well as monitoring one's writing on a frequent basis.

I would be remiss not to articulate an outlier in how one participant coped with being "always on." Trunk, a blogger who has evolved into a controversial writer since I first interviewed her in the summer of 2013, writes what is called "evergreen" content. This approach is sustainable because it's supposed to be timely or accurate at all times. A nonevergreen piece of writing might be a basketball game recap; the writing is out of date rather quickly. Evergreen content, such as Trunk's blogging advice about how to interview on the job market or ask for a raise at work, is designed to be useful and timely at all times. Trunk is the only participant to discuss this type of content.

OVER THE COURSE OF TIME

These perspectives of textual timing show the diversity of rhetorical timing for digital rhetoric and how *chronos* and *kairos* are connected. By turning to *kairos-chronos* fusion, template timing, and algorithmic timing, rhetorical theory can account for rhetorical aspects of *chronos*, as well as expand the ways rhetoricians can investigate and discuss timing, more generally, in digital environments. To persuade others in digital environments involves timing discourse in complex ways that involve qualitative (*kairos*) and quantitative (*chronos*) approaches *over the course of time*. That is, when contending with participatory audiences, digital writers consider rhetorical timing in ways that accrue. Rhetorical timing is learned by negotiating templates and other interfaces, as well as through the collective emergent behavior of audiences.

Framing rhetorical timing as accruing is important to theories of persuasion because it highlights the ongoing nature of digital rhetoric and, consequently, rhetoric writ large. Audiences are not persuaded in single-serving speeches, texts, or situations, nor are rhetors single-serving producers of rhetoric. The question of when to write and respond appears to be best answered with continuously—and in ways that are informed qualitatively and quantitatively by what audiences are doing empirically. Agency requires an *ongoing* sense of one's purpose and awareness of what others, including algorithms and procedures that drive nonhuman sorting mechanisms, are doing at a particular time *and* over the course of time.

This emergent and ongoing nature is crucial for participants. At the end of my first interview with each participant, I asked them if they had advice for students interested in writing online or producing digital content or advice specific to different platforms. Invariably, they answered with some permutation of *consistency* and *persistence*. While I return to these habits in chapter 6, for now I emphasize that my participants encouraged interested writers or content producers to create content consistently. According to several participants, even if a blog or website has no readers, it still needs to have relevant and updated content. It is better to have no blog or website than inconsistent or out-of-date content. Persistent and consistent content, then, is a mark of successful digital timing.

CODA: *AD POPULUM* AND PANDERING

At this juncture in *Update Culture*, I want to step in as a researcher and offer some perspective. Template timing and algorithmic timing became somewhat of a game to my participants. Picking the best time or "gaming the system" were frequent refrains used throughout my interviews. It struck me, as a researcher, that writers were perhaps *pandering* to their audiences, algorithms, or both. I was also struck by the connection between textual timing and being dictated by systems, institutions, and structures.

I have wrestled with the issue of pandering throughout the project. Are writers simply trying to gin up readership, even if it means pandering to the crowds, *ad populum*? With respect to participatory audiences, is timing a digital text a matter of pushing content frequently and responding often? Part of me, as a researcher, believes this is the case.

Another part of me knows that writers, or at least the ones I studied, don't simply appeal to the crowds. (This view might be a function of who agreed to participate in this study.) They search through—cull from, really—an ocean of audience response. When they do so, writers look for genuinely engaged comments, reading carefully and deciding which comments to give attention. In this sense, when examined in isolation, textual timing might lead us to the conclusion that writers are pandering to quantitative systems, institutions, and structures. But textual timing is part of a broader panoply of strategies. Writers do not just consider *when* to write and respond. They also consider *how* to write and respond, an issue to which I now turn.

4

TEXTUAL ATTENTION

While the previous chapter describes and analyzes the timing strategies digital writers deploy, this chapter examines how writers respond
to their participatory audiences. Echoing previous work on rhetorical
velocity (Ridolfo and DeVoss 2009) and digital delivery (Morey 2015;
Porter 2009), the afterlife of digital writing requires writers to do
more than time their texts. Template functions are quite unique in
this regard because their empty-state pages are procedurally built for
interactivity (Gallagher and Holmes 2019). The afterlife of texts thus
asks writers to respond to their readers, both as actual readers and as
imagined constructs. Writers do so by giving their audiences *attention*,
an idea previous digital writing and rhetoric researchers have examined, notably in the early blogosphere (Pfister 2014), the information
economy (Lanham 2006), and social media ecologies (Citton 2017;
Rivers 2016).

While my participants did not respond to all their comments or
readers, most still gave attention to comments by "reading" them in
some form or another. I put "reading" in quotation marks because my
participants didn't read comments in the way someone might read
print texts—or even blog posts. Instead, digital writers skim comments
strategically, ignoring the vitriolic ones while answering questions they
deem sincere. They rhetorically *filter out* certain comments, give attention to audiences that demonstrate sincerity, and then respond to those
audiences. Digital writers develop means of filtering which comments
are worth interacting with and which ones are not. They "rhetorically
eavesdrop" (Ratcliffe 2006) on their audience's responses in order to
gauge the types of participation their writing garners. They give *textual
attention* to the writing of their audiences and the ambient affordances
of their respective IPI templates.

This chapter thus uses attention as a trope for the way writers read,
deliberate, and respond to the variety of response, feedback, and
participation they receive from audiences in IPI environments. Using
textual attention describes the discursive actions digital writers employ

DOI: 10.7330/9781607329749.c004

when giving attention to their audiences. While rhetoricians and compositionists have discussed attention for public, political, cultural, and pedagogical purposes (Citton 2017; Lanham 2006; Rivers 2016), I reorient the trope for responding to participatory audiences in digital, templated environments.

The trope attention captures the conversational nature of reading audience response from a concatenation of public voices. Many of these voices compete with one another, leading digital writers to contend with audience response by developing particular discursive strategies that substitute for the loss of an affective encounter, body, or gesture in these environments. With respect to in-person settings, we need gestures and oral methods for acknowledging that others are present and communication occurs. However, listening and haptic metaphors privilege a particular sensory system that simply is not present in digital exchanges with participatory audiences (my previous work was guilty of this privileging when I labeled it *textual listening*). Attention is proprioceptive; that is, it includes the entire embodied range of functionalities rather than being limited to a specific sensory system.

In using the phrase *textual attention*, I aim to describe more fully the self-reported activities of my participants who actively (and passively) contended with the rapid respond of their IPI environments. Textual attention accounts for the way text literally moves and circulates via updates, revisions, and ambient affordances. As I make explicit in the examples later in this chapter, textual attention attempts to account for ways writers attend to the circulation and afterlife of their texts in IPI environments. Textual attention integrates producing and delivering discourse in digital environments, an issue I address in this chapter's conclusion. With this integration comes the expectation that initial texts—texts that prompt audience participation and response—may be responded to and equipped with the possibility for audience participation to be spatially close to the initiating text (often below or next to an initial text). I am thus using textual attention to describe a way of reading multiple audience members' reactions within a written digital environment with the express aim of responding to some—but not all—comments. It's also important to note that participants already had reader attention and needed to determine the value of various types of participation. In other words, textual attention cultivates the means to determine what to pay attention to rather than merely driving up pageviews.

This rest of this chapter has five parts. First, I examine listening scholarship that highlights the connection between attention and the presence of others. I note that attention involves others, an obvious but necessary observation. I then discuss attention in a way that moves the concept away from its economic import and toward its rhetorical implications in digital rhetoric. Third, I define textual attention as a holistic strategy participants use in order to contend with this negativity. Writers use textual attention and *attending* as a strategy to identify genuine or sincere comments that deserve response, thereby helping writers determine exigence. Fourth, I offer examples of textual attention and attending, along with my participants' rationales for writing in such a manner, in order to document and theorize various forms of textual attention. Last, I discuss the pragmatic and theoretical significance of textual attention.

BEYOND READING: ATTENTION AS NEEDING OTHERS

While digital writers read their comments and other responses by their participatory audiences, to use the word *read* here does not adequately describe the act of textual attention. While participants were certainly reading their texts, they were also responding to their commenters and deciding which comments or exchanges to ignore. In this sense, reading is inadequate to describe how digital writers respond to their audiences because reading does not capture the rapid activity of responding to audience participation or the changing nature of digital writing exchanges. Reading print texts and even some "Web 1.0" texts does not engender the *expectation* of returning to a changing, mutable text. Reading, without the need to respond, lacks the dialogic import of textual attention. Those involved in the production of discourse also don't necessarily expect to reread their response on that text (once those texts are published). And those who read a text are not necessarily *responding* to that text on or near that text.

The language of attention foregrounds the existence of exchange not readily present in the language of reading. With a few notable exceptions, such as children learning to read, the process of reading tends to be individual, especially when it is conceived in print texts. Even when people read for the purpose of discussion, reading mostly occurs silently, and then discussion takes place *after* reading. In this project, participants read the literal texts of their readers and attended to the writing of their readers.

Attention, rather than reading, better describes the peculiar manner in which my participants reported reading and *filtering* through their comments and then deciding which comments *deserved a response*.

Interestingly, when participants talked about a particular comment, they used the word *read* to describe their activity. However, as they generalized or described their experiences more abstractly, they used the word *listening*. Attention, in my view, better captures this oscillation; attention is a thicker description for a variety of activities involved in contending with participatory audiences.

The importance of attention and the role of "others" can be found in scholarship associated with listening. While listening invokes a relationship to sound, it is etymologically distinct from hearing because it conceptually involves attention rather than a body organ (ears). In terms of language origin, listening implies *multiple people* and the presence of others, whereas hearing invokes "self-experience" (Lipari 2010, 349). Lisbeth Lipari, in "Listening, Thinking, Being," finds a profound distinction between listening and hearing.

> Listen and hear are not simply synonyms, but are inflected with different meanings that suggest different ways of being in the world. Etymologically listening comes from a root that emphasizes *attention* and giving to another, while hearing comes from a root that emphasizes perception and sensation of sound. Indeed, the ideas of "gaining" and "possessing" found in hearing foreground a focus on the self's experience, while the ideas of *attention* and obedience found in listening focus on the other. (349; emphasis added)

I focus here on the role of attention as needing other bodies and beings, a characteristic that scholars such as Kate Lacey (2013) have addressed through a *variety of voices in a community* (14). Drawing on public sphere theorist Susan Bickford, Lacey writes, "Listening . . . constitutes a kind of *attention* to others (and otherness) and, importantly, *being attended to* that is the prerequisite of both citizenship . . . and of communicative action" (165). With its roots in others and attention, listening invites a relationship between communicator (a writer in the scope of this book) and audiences, one that is collaborative in terms of discourse production.

While some might not share the optimism for democratic action that Lipari and Lacey invoke, *listening* has a pragmatic grounding when the term is used for attention and *attending to*. The writers I interviewed, for instance, attended to their audiences who wrote *back* to them. The relationship between writer and audience becomes less a binary when *attention* is used as a descriptor. Attention helps describe the efforts of my participants to exchange communicative acts with readers while not responding (or even reading) every audience response.

Using attention in conjunction with writing helps disrupt the relationship between writer and reader in IPI contexts, where the categories of "author" and "audience" are murky. My participants frequently described responding to comments and rereading their own texts, often with a new perspective. Likewise, their readers wrote back to them; in fact, the methodology of this project assumes writers have audience response, albeit in a variety of discursive forms, including text, visuals, emoji, GIF, and ambient affordance. Attention, in the way I use it, illustrates the multidirectional, temporal roles of digital writing, especially the oscillating role of being both writer and reader in IPI environments.

ATTENTION BEYOND THE ECONOMY

The way I use attention decouples it from its economic connotation, a connotation that has gained traction in an information economy in which digital commodities are no longer scarce, thereby requiring attention in order to function economically. Like Nathaniel Rivers in "Paying Attention with Cache" (2016), I need, due to the attention exchanges between digital writers and their participatory audiences, to move past attention as a special object to be accrued and accumulated. As I am using it, attention pushes against how Richard Lanham (2006) positions it in *The Economics of Attention*, in which "attention is the commodity in short supply" (xi). But to extend Rivers's view, attention in my case studies emerges as more than a synecdoche. When Rivers writes that "attention is not what's brought to bear on, given, distracted or captured, but rather what is always at stake in any interaction—it is an assembly, and it is one that emerges *kairotically*," he disperses attention into any (and perhaps every) interaction. While I tend to agree with Rivers's assertion theoretically, the way I use *attention* in this book keeps the term empirically grounded in giving attention to audiences and adds a type of filtering meant for responding to those audiences. In this sense, I use attention to describe how concrete exchanges happen in digital, interactive environments. I use attention to include responding to audiences.

In pushing attention beyond its economic connotations, I join Yves Citton in *The Ecology of Attention* (2017), which orients attention toward ecology, endeavoring to examine different types of attention and the way attention affects us culturally and societally. Pointing out that attention is not a new concern (10–15), Citton argues that attention "should be thought of as an *interface*: it is what links a subject to an object it has selected in something external to it" (175). While offering a diverse taxonomy of attention, Citton's "reflexive attention" is most relevant here, for it is defined as follows: "The individual may pay attention to the dynamics, constraints, apparatuses, and above all to the evaluations, conditioning their attention" (139). Citton goes on to mention autore-ferential circles of attention: "I give my attention to what I value and I value what I give my attention to" (139). Reflexive attention also, accord-ing to Citton, contains "co-attention" (84) and "bidirectionality" (85), which again highlights the interactive nature of attention and presence of others I mention earlier in this chapter. Citton's approach helps me push attention away from an economic force and toward a writerly type of strategy that includes responding to readers.

I turn to reflexive attention because it describes the type of attention I found occurring between participants and their audiences. Digital writers give attention to the comments they deem relevant and on topic. The implication here is that, at least in terms of the participants I studied, writers give attention to the attention they already receive and choose to give more attention to the sincere or genuine comments that are, for the most part, giving the right *kind* of attention.

Textual attention, I believe, has utility for writers overwhelmed and overloaded when writing online and receiving a multiplicity of audience responses. On the internet and on social media, writers are surrounded by notifications, comments, and ambient affordances. Textual attention is not about getting attention but about what to do once a writer has audience participation. It is a useful strategy for inculcating the type of communication a writer wishes to have. While textual attention does not guarantee control, it does provide readers some orientation for digital conversations, exchanges, and guidelines. I say more about control and guidelines in the next chapter.

DEFINING TEXTUAL ATTENTION

Textual attention is both a reading and writing strategy writers use to conceptualize and respond to a participatory audience. This strategy shares similarities with attentive listening in conversation but happens with and around alphabetic text, images, videos, and other digital dis-course. The mechanics of textual attention differ from those of read-ing a single-authored monograph, most noticeably in that audience response is continuing and emergent. Ultimately, textual attention accounts for the need to be open to the composite audiences (Perelman and Olbrechts-Tyteca 1969) of a text's afterlife *and* the way that the after-life of digital writing encourages writers to respond textually to audi-ence responses. Textual attention captures the paradox of reading and responding textually to multiple audience members' reactions within IPI environments.

From my observations, textual attention is a multidirectional strategy writers use to identify sincere audiences and to show audiences they understand them. I believe there are multiple ways to implement textual attention. Anecdotally, a simple version of textual attention is when someone makes a comment on one's Twitter account or Facebook post and one uses an ambient affordance, such as Like or Favorite, on that comment to indicate acknowledgment that one has perceived the commenter's contribution. (It resembles a phatic expression.)

Lexically, textual attention draws a relationship among reading, listening, filtering, and responding to discourse in IPI environments. When my participants produced a text or initiated discourse, they didn't ignore comments they had received. Many in fact reported feeling addicted to comments, and several remarked, "If I have haters I have an audience" (a remarkable phrase independently used by Armstrong, Trunk, and Grimes).

Textual attention thus better captures the dialogue of an ongoing series of emergent texts. Participants recognized not all comments are relevant. Not all texts need to be read. But these texts must still be skimmed (that is, quickly processed) to determine whether to respond or not. This strategy includes indicating that a response or comment, such as Liking a comment, has been received because in IPI environments, these contexts lack physical cues.

Beyond physical cues, however, the act of attention involves multidirectionality (Carnegie 2009) not present in the stance of reading. I use this level of interactivity and temporality in my deployment of the term *textual attention*. The interactive writer's stance establishes the point from which activity is initiated. To clarify one facet of stance, textual attention necessarily includes the position of the *initial writer*; it is not a strategy of commenters or "secondary writers"—those writers who might be considered audience members (readers by all means could adopt such a stance, but this kind of study is outside the scope of this book). These latter individuals occupy a position typical of readers, and by acknowledging their stance, I concretize the difference in stance occupied by the initial writer. The purpose of textual attention is different from what we typically associate with reading text: writers use textual attention in part to acknowledge commenters.

Given my participants' position as initial writer of the comment-initiating text, textual attention is influenced by the decorum and expectations of their templated digital environments. Textual attention is thus *specifically* used to meet the challenge of interacting with the frequent responses prevalent in digital communication, which a writer must choose to do. Why they do this differs in the details among writers, but in the examples to follow, I lay out how writers search for a certain type of comment, that is, one that deserves a response from the writer's point of view. With textual attention, I aim to capture the presence of the multiple responses writers must sort through to both build themselves a mental image of their audience and also determine which responses are genuine or sincere.

My participants, for instance, did not just agree with comments or challenge information they viewed as incorrect. They encountered a public concatenation of texts, all written with a variety of styles and tones—two words that describe talking as well as writing. Without describing too idealistic a picture, I can say my participants actively contended with audience participation in order to account for the presence of others. While digital writers, my participants included, certainly ignore vitriolic participation (something I revisit in the next chapter), they still ponder negative comments and the act of response in relation to their previous and future texts. Participants considered their own position in the ecosystem of a particular IPI environment. They read, filtered, and gave certain comments ("the good ones") attention.

My participants attended to comments in a way that made them reconsider older writing in new ways. Consider a reviewer who developed new ideas by revisiting not only older writing but also the products themselves. As AR1 told me,

> Listening to comments doesn't just make me consider my review. Well it does but it also makes me consider my other reviews and sometimes to consider older products. I'll sometimes go back and try out the item again, even if it was just a crappy salad spinner. Or I'll go back and read other comments with that comment in mind.

This reviewer went on to tell me, "Not all comments are valuable. But some really hit home and make you think. Those comments are the best, the ones that make you think." AR1 revealed to me that while some comments simply get ignored, others can have a profound impact, especially if comments are particularly helpful. This reviewer engaged comments in a way that demonstrates a sense of responsibility for attending to one's comments and, more broadly, audience participation.

THE FOCUS OF ATTENTION

Before I continue to my examples of textual attention, I need to clarify what my participants are *paying attention* to. Writers in these environments contend with three features: metrics via ambient affordances, lengthy responses, and a large number of questions. Writers reported they contend with ambient affordances such as Facebook Likes, Twitter Retweets, and reddit's karma system. Writers need to cull through a large number of comments, and they can receive lengthy comments. In light of these factors, they need to search through negative responses in order to find positive ones. Writers must contend with a variety of comments, and if they choose to respond—as my participants did—they must likely craft a process for how to respond. As the redditor Roboticide told me,

> You can't respond to all of them [the comments]. I try to respond to everyone early on that is contributing something. If you have a post with 500 comments, after five hours or something, that's just way too many to respond to. So at that point, you try to find somebody that is contributing something constructive. It sort of depends on what kind of engagement you're getting. . . . I'll definitely respond to someone asking about rule enforcement versus someone saying "That's neat."

Comments need to be waded through because they can be lengthy and, despite some positivity, generally skew negative in their sentiment.

Textual attention is such a process for navigating a large number of negative comments, as well as a small but significant percent of positive comments. In this sense, participants cultivated and attuned themselves to certain types of attention. In rhetorical terms, textual attention could be considered a *techne* or *hexis* for contending with digital *doxa*. Due to the possible immense scale of circulation on social media, writers need crafts and habits for contending with, and sorting through, the common beliefs of participatory audiences. In less rhetorical terms, textual attention is a craft or habit for dealing with the hate and vitriol of comments while filtering the treasure out of the digital trash.

TEXTUAL ATTENTION IN ACTION

I observed textual attention to have three parts. First, writers read through, and made sense of, a concatenation of public voices. They gave textual attention often to their most successful texts. By successful, I mean texts that had accrued numerous pageviews, comments, or ambient affordances. If a review, article, or post was well received, participants gave it textual attention. My participants discussed not only reading comments but also piecing those comments together because they are disparate texts with diverse styles and voices. Second, participants searched for sincere or genuine comments and audience participation. An important caveat here is that sincerity or genuineness was wrapped up in participants' writing goals and purposes. Notably, most participants discussed ignoring vitriolic insults, sea-lioning (men barging in on women having a digital discussion), or concern trolling (feigning concern), features crucial to defining sincerity. Third, participants expressed recognition of sincere audience response, via text, image, GIF, and so forth. They thanked commenters and deployed strategic uses of ambient affordances while attempting to express sincerity and genuineness themselves.

Reading through, and Trying to Make Sense of, a Concatenation of Public Voices

The first step participants reported was attention to a concatenation of comments. I use the word *concatenation* here to echo Jenny Edbauer's (2005) language. By way of Michael Warner, Edbauer writes of Bitzer's rhetorical situation, "Situation bleeds into the concatenation of public interaction. Public interactions bleed into wider social processes. The elements of rhetorical situation simply bleed" (9). Concatenation better captures the wider range of people and texts writers contend with. Participants read through comments, their readers, their own texts. But they were not solely reading for comprehension. Additionally, I use the phrase *making sense of* to imply that participants read to determine which comments needed responses and which ones did not.

Numerous participants alluded to the language of attention to describe reading through a concatenation of comments. Three quotations from my participants help illustrate my point. In each, participants slide between reading and listening to their comments. Each of these quotations occurred after I asked the question, "How do you respond to commenters?" I did not use the word *listen* or its derivative in any of my questions.

As AR1 explained to me, "After I *read* the comments, I feel like, 'People are *listening* to me? Really? Me?' You know what I mean? I feel like a million dollars after I read them" (emphasis added). Tracy Monroe, the savvy medical and provaccine journalist, said commenters needed to be contended with: "You really need to *listen* to their [commenters'] arguments so you can read and respond or deconstruct it" (emphasis added). A well-known and somewhat controversial reviewer of dietary supplements (that do not, most likely, work), Seymour O'Reilly told me, "I'm not saying this to brag but my reviews get a lot of attention and a lot of respect. How do I know this? Read the comment section of my reviews. *Listen* to them, not me. If you take a look at any one of my reviews and read the comments section of almost anyone of them, you can see what people have to say. Most people are very appreciative of the information that I provide. That's an incentive" (emphasis added).

I note three aspects from each of these interview interactions. First, participants' language not only slid between reading and writing but also between comments and commenters. Comments and the people making those comments are mixed up. I believe this mixture reiterates the combination of oral and written modes. Writing and speaking, as well as people and comments, are not easily discernable. People become texts, and texts become people, at least in terms of conventionalization. Second, the responses have value, albeit to varying degrees and extents. O'Reilly believes the comments provide his writing validity. Monroe finds the comments valuable as sources of insight into avenues of persuasive arguments and discourse. Third, as far as they are distinct concepts, *reading* references the comments themselves and *listening* refers to the individual writing those comments. But in IPI environments, these comments are layered onto one another, which again recaps the need to textually attend.

Searching for Sincere or Genuine Comments

Participants reported that after reading through, and trying to make sense of, a concatenation of public voices, they searched for certain types of responses. The second aspect of textual attention, as a strategy then, was to search for sincere or genuine comments. Sincerity is important because it allows writers to "continue the conversation," "have a conversation," "get a lot of responses," or "start some big shit" (in the case of the redditors) about a text they produced. I use these phrases because they were exceptionally common across all participants, regardless of purpose, writerly occupation, and platform.

As a researcher, I am not entirely sure why these phrases were used so frequently, but I believe it is due to writers' desire to have an audience, something IPI environments may inculcate. Writers want to see (literally) reader discussion of their writing. Thus, to "keep the conversation going," another phrase participants frequently used, writers responded to the genuine responses. Matt Grimes stated this aim succinctly when he said, "It's hard to create *genuine* engagement. It's either effusive praise or trolling. You have to look for the truly engaged. And you have to find the right audience, the *sincere* readers" (emphasis added).

While no participant defined sincere or genuine in precisely the same way, there was general agreement about what was *not* sincere or genuine. These types of responses fell into three broad overlapping categories.

First, participants avoided, ignored, or even deleted responses that were vitriolic, including racist, misogynistic, sexist, and homophobic insults. Second, writers, especially those who identify as women, avoided sea lions—male commenters who feign interest with the intent to disrupt a comment-driven exchange between women. Third, writers sought to eliminate concern trolls, which is an act of faking concern about an issue, often political, in order to destabilize a sincere exchange. A concern troll then is a commenter who feigns interest, typically by asking a question, only to attack a digital exchange or derail an ongoing debate.

While these three reasons are distinguishable from each other, they are clearly related. The most obvious connection among them is the act of ignoring. While it seems obvious that writers ignore these types of comments or commenters, every single participant mentioned ignoring specific comments and categories of comments. The notable feature here is that to ignore comments, participants must have read the comment and accrued enough experience to develop categories to ignore. I write more about ignoring comments as a management strategy in chapter 5, "Textual Management."

In the following examples, I explore the ways participants dealt with nonsincere comments, and then I turn to genuine comments. In terms of vitriolic responses, participants reported ignoring or deleting comments (the latter if their template allowed them to do so). Bloggers, who controlled their own content-management systems, frequently reported deleting. For instance, Heather Armstrong said, "I heavily moderate my comments section to keep out the abusive language. You don't get to poop in my living room. But real comments, the *genuine* ones, are addictive." Kelly Salasin, the Vermont blogger I mentioned in the opening of this book, told me she simply ignores insulting comments. Penelope Trunk, who makes a full-time living by offering "advice at the intersection of work and life," articulated a similar perspective.

> GALLAGHER: How important is audience feedback for what you write in the future?
>
> PENELOPE TRUNK: Oh, really, really important. I think of it as a conversation. Also, I don't . . . if a topic doesn't get a lot of *genuine* comments, I don't write about it again (emphasis added).
>
> GALLAGHER: Do you ever have commenters who interfere with your writing?
>
> PENELOPE TRUNK: No, I can just delete them. I just ban them. If I don't like a commenter, I just ban them.

In addition to using the keyword *conversation* I mention earlier, Trunk mentioned deleting and banning commenters who interfere with her writing. What's notable here is that Armstrong, Salasin, and Trunk—all bloggers—mentioned the sincere/genuine construct as an inverse. They noted insulting, trolling comments as comments they would not respond to. Thus, despite clearly reading through a slew of nasty or off-topic comments (often both), participants did not respond to them. In this sense, textual attention as a broad strategy involves not responding to types of response and feedback.

Now I turn to the most explicit form of textual attention, which is attending to sincere questions. While questions from concern trolls and sea lions are for the most part easy to identify, genuine questions are intimately tied to participant purposes. Consequently, Amazon reviewers responded to questions about product specifications; bloggers about a point of clarification in their sentences; journalists about a potential error in reporting or grammar, spelling, or syntax; and redditors about comments that seemed friendly. Jason Rob, a savvy reviewer who had been a top-ranked reviewer for several years and described himself as a "digital influencer," emblematically said, "I respond to commenters, and usually to the commenters [that] are just asking a *genuine* question on maybe something that I haven't covered in the review. They might want to ask, 'Well, how long is the cord?' In response to people's questions, I have modified my review process. . . . Because of people's questions, I now include information in my reviews that I might not have included" (emphasis added). Rob, who has been profiled by a number of digital magazines, described the key feature of this aspect of textual attention: there is an opening for an honest exchange, however minor.

In my view as a researcher, the culling of sincerity from digital exchanges and question posing is a search for an *opening*—a chance to "continue the conversation" or have some sort of exchange in which those having the exchange view it as productive. Although an opening may look different in tone, word choice, and length across the diverse array of IPI digital environments, participants searched for these openings because their position as writer inculcated a responsibility to respond. Attending to writing has historically been true for writers: among a variety of other activities, they give talks about their books and articles, as well as go on book tours—all while answering some questions from audience members.

But in update culture, the writing *itself* must be attended, not simply activity instigated by the writing. Responses are literally close to the text—under, next to, or over—and need to be monitored for the "good stuff." I say more about monitoring the "bad stuff" in the next chapter, but for now I turn to what participants did after they determined a comment or question to be sincere or genuine.

Recognition of Sincere Response

As I've alluded to already, textual attention is not simply reading comments; it is doing so with the aim of responding to those comments. I identify three levels of response, each with increasing complexity. First, writers can simply acknowledge response, either through a mention of thanks ("thank you!") or using an ambient affordance (Liking). I found multiple examples of this from every writer I studied. Second, writers can respond with a comment, often accompanied by a mention of thanks. On this level, writers can pose questions back to commenters. These two levels are generally similar to the discourse of customer service, albeit the writers attend to their own writing. On the third and most complex level, writers can alter their general approach to writing or initiating discourse.

The Amazon reviewer Liza Margulies told me about the first- and second-level responses. She said, "I write back and forth with these people [commenters], all the time. Somebody will say, 'thanks to you, I'm buying this. It's arriving on Friday. I can't wait.' And I'll wait until Saturday, and I'll write them back and say, 'Did it arrive? Do you love it? Let me know what you think.'" Margulies engages in a call-and-response chat. All my participants reported doing this at least once, although for journalists this strategy was less common than it was for reviewers, bloggers, and redditors. It was most common for the redditors due to their conversational purposes and the layout of reddit's template.

Let me return momentarily to the reviewer, Jason Rob, to briefly illustrate the third type of response. In the previous section, I include Rob's quote about searching for genuine questions and how these responses changed his habits: "Because of people's questions, I now include information in my reviews that I might not have included." In a media interview (redacted for privacy), Rob said he revisits and updates reviews after he receives comments (and after enough time has passed). Embedded in these perspectives is what I identify as the response aspect of textual attention. Rob reads the various responses he receives, *and* those responses play a role in his future writing process.

With all three types of responses, my participants generally strove for a positive, upbeat tone when responding, which seems understandable considering these were comments they decided were sincere or genuine. As Maggie Skinner, a digital environmental journalist, told me, "Answer them [the commenters] right away and get super excited. You have to put effort into it and respond in a way that isn't alienating. It's really hard and requires a lot of energy and time. And never start anything with 'actually.'" Skinner's advice here about *actually* is meaningful, as it was *the most frequent recommendation from all my participants.* As StickleyMan told me, "'Actually' is terrible. Never use 'actually.' You sound like a jerk." Heather Armstrong told me the word "serves to sever the conversation."

The word *actually* serves as a correlative to the issue of sincere or genuine tone. If writers search for such comments, then it follows that they should respond in kind. Participants frequently mentioned responding to comments in ways that reflected the tone and style of the comment, all of which echo the idea of attention I've described. Way_Fairer, once the most upvoted redditor of all time, told me to match the punctuation of any comment when responding to audiences because it better matches the tone of the commenter. One significant exchange with an Amazon reviewer, the reviewer Ciaran, focused on responding affably.

> GALLAGHER: Do you ever respond to comments about your reviews?
>
> CIARAN: I do. It's probably one of the most rewarding things. You can get helpful votes all day long, but when someone actually takes the time to comment, whether it's positive, or constructive criticism, that's always great to know that your reviews aren't just floating in the state of Amazon, but are actually really helping people make their decisions. If it's a positive response, I always try to thank the person for writing that. It's oftentimes I find that a product's comments, on your reviews, turn into a discussion forum of their own. If you go to some of the more popular products, you can see that these sheets have exceeded 100 pages of comments that people commented. That's a lot [of] support. Obviously, with any, I'm like "It's either going to be some flare ups every now and then." You do get comments that are—that would've been rude. With this, like with anything, you're putting yourself out in the public, and it's almost putting your reputation out there. Your comments back to people are almost a reflection of who you are, so you always try to be gracious or appropriate. Ignore anything that could be incriminatory. Just try and make wise decisions.

Ciaran describes all three levels of response while simultaneously articulating the importance of tone. Ciaran implicitly notes the search for positivity or at least "constructive criticism." Then he thanks the commenters while also noting the possibility of a discussion forum popping up unexpectedly. The importance of replying with an appropriate tone ("gracious") emerges to finish the process for Ciaran. I present this long

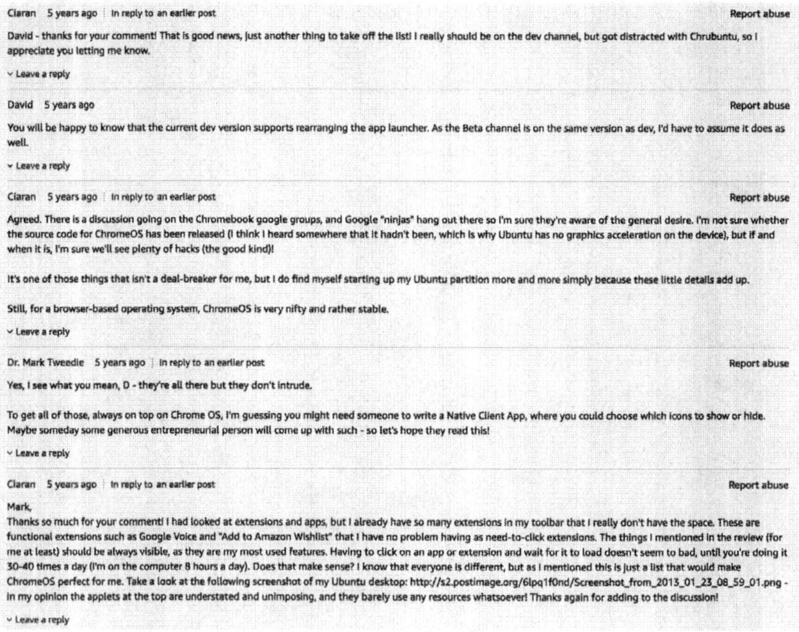

Ciaran 5 years ago | In reply to an earlier post Report abuse

David - thanks for your comment! That is good news, just another thing to take off the list! I really should be on the dev channel, but got distracted with Chrubuntu, so I appreciate you letting me know.

Leave a reply

David 5 years ago Report abuse

You will be happy to know that the current dev version supports rearranging the app launcher. As the Beta channel is on the same version as dev, I'd have to assume it does as well.

Leave a reply

Ciaran 5 years ago | In reply to an earlier post Report abuse

Agreed. There is a discussion going on the Chromebook google groups, and Google "ninjas" hang out there so I'm sure they're aware of the general desire. I'm not sure whether the source code for ChromeOS has been released (I think I heard somewhere that it hadn't been, which is why Ubuntu has no graphics acceleration on the device), but if and when it is, I'm sure we'll see plenty of hacks (the good kind)!

It's one of those things that isn't a deal-breaker for me, but I do find myself starting up my Ubuntu partition more and more simply because these little details add up.

Still, for a browser-based operating system, ChromeOS is very nifty and rather stable.

Leave a reply

Dr. Mark Tweedie 5 years ago | In reply to an earlier post Report abuse

Yes, I see what you mean, D - they're all there but they don't intrude.

To get all of those, always on top on Chrome OS, I'm guessing you might need someone to write a Native Client App, where you could choose which icons to show or hide. Maybe someday some generous entrepreneurial person will come up with such - so let's hope they read this!

Leave a reply

Ciaran 5 years ago | In reply to an earlier post Report abuse

Mark,
Thanks so much for your comment! I had looked at extensions and apps, but I already have so many extensions in my toolbar that I really don't have the space. These are functional extensions such as Google Voice and "Add to Amazon Wishlist" that I have no problem having as need-to-click extensions. The things I mentioned in the review (for me at least) should be always visible, as they are my most used features. Having to click on an app or extension and wait for it to load doesn't seem to bad, until you're doing it 30-40 times a day (I'm on the computer 8 hours a day). Does that make sense? I know that everyone is different, but as I mentioned this is just a list that would make ChromeOS perfect for me. Take a look at the following screenshot of my Ubuntu desktop: http://s2.postimage.org/6lpq1f0nd/Screenshot_from_2013_01_23_08_59_01.png - in my opinion the applets at the top are understated and unimposing, and they barely use any resources whatsoever! Thanks again for adding to the discussion!

Leave a reply

Figure 4.1. Textual attention in Amazon reviewing

passage (Fig 4.1) because it exemplifies textual attention as described in detail by one of my participants. While numerous other participants demonstrated textual attention in their writing, Ciaran articulated it most clearly in our interviews.

Following this self-reported description, I found an example of Ciaran's strategy deployed through an exchange that occurred on a Chromebook review (Fig. 4.1). In reply to Dr. Mark Tweedie, Ciaran thanks the commenter, recognizes he read the comment by using the same language as the commenter ("extensions and apps"), and proceeds to provide details that seem to echo Tweedie's sentiment. Ciaran not only "continues the conversation," a phrase numerous participants used in my interviews, but also extends the conversation. Accordingly, with respect to the phrase "need to click extensions," he explains his point of view by detailing the repetitive nature of his task. Then he poses a question to the commenter—who did not reply to this comment—about what the commenter thinks. Ciaran concludes his comment with a *second* mention of thanks. Combining this textual evidence with Ciaran's perspective better describes textual attention broadly and captures the third arc of the strategy, that is, the response.

My participants frequently responded to commenters with an array of discourse. They posed questions, answered questions, extended their commenters' statements, and added relevant details. Ultimately, participants' responses function as evidence to commenters, and to their audience more generally, that they exist and that they will respond if the comment adds to the substance of the content—"the conversation."

StickleyMan: A Case of Textual Attention

I now want to offer a thick description of textual attention through a paradigmatic case study of StickleyMan. StickleyMan was the screen-name of the fourth most popular redditor, at the time of our interviews. StickleyMan aimed to orient members of reddit toward taking an atti-tude of learning while looking for a random but constructive experi-ence for himself within his texts. It is important to note two facets of his persona: (1) StickleyMan was an extensive producer of GIFs and aimed to be humorous in his non-alphabetic-based texts; and (2) he had garnered a reputation as an insightful commenter. In fact, several well-known GIFs that repeatedly circulate online are his creation. These two features, I believe, are what gave him the digital authority to occasion-ally have "meaningful" and "productive" conversations on reddit. The purpose of his conversations or texts was fundamentally dialogic: other redditors helped him learn and gain insight, and he hoped that other redditors learned from him and each other.

StickleyMan oriented other redditors to engage in an "organic," con-tinuous conversation using textual attention. StickleyMan took a stance of openness in regard to the cultures, persons, and texts of reddit. Textual attention enabled him to achieve his goals because it prodded the audience to respond in an unstructured way that allowed a public to form. It was a two-pronged approach. His well-established position on reddit actually came from his GIF production, in which his aim was to be humorous. I believe StickleyMan's well-known position as a humor-ous redditor enabled him to have these more serious conversations. StickleyMan, independent of my questioning, brought the following example (Figs. 4.2, 4.3, and 4.4) to my attention because he considered the exchange to be a representation of the ideal kind of organic discus-sion he aimed for outside his GIF posts.

For StickleyMan, this technique emerged in the subreddit known as AskReddit. AskReddit is essentially an opportunity to ask the com-munity of reddit a question and let it respond. Nowhere is textual

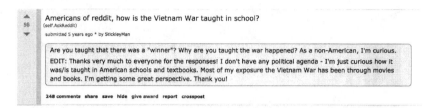

Figure 4.2. StickleyMan posing a question on AskReddit

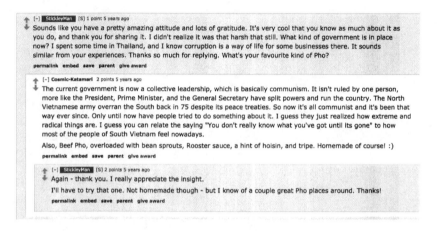

Figure 4.3. Screenshot of exchange in Vietnam thread between StickleyMan and Cosmic-Katamari. Mentions of thanks are circled.

attention more salient and paradigmatic than in the AskReddit thread on which StickleyMan posed the question, "Americans of reddit, how is the Vietnam War taught in school?" (fig. 4.2). In this Vietnam thread, StickleyMan comments eleven times. In ten of the eleven instances, he thanks readers and asks them questions in his role as the initial writer. In the remaining instance, he makes a lengthier comment about his context and life. In addition to the "thanks" StickleyMan offers in the comments, this initial text is later edited to include two mentions of "thank you" (fig. 4.3).

Originally, the text read as "Are you taught that there was a 'winner'? Why are you taught the war happened? As a non-American, I'm curious." With this phrasing, StickleyMan denies any vested political interest, instead constructing his position as one of personal interest. He positions himself as a non-American, wanting to be informed by the strangers of AskReddit. Throughout the thread, he continues to emphasize his openness to others' perspectives by recognizing participating

[-] **Insidia** 2 points 5 years ago
I can tell you how I teach it...

1. I frame it within the context of the Cold War. I want my students to understand why US leaders took the actions they did, and why leaders of other nations responded/acted as they did. We spend a lot of time on the climate of fear that was created, and how we perceived Communism at the time. We also look at which perceptions were grounded in reality (Communist governments tended to kill off a HUGE number of dissidents), and which were not.

2. When we start the actual war, I teach it through the lens of how difficult it is to know the truth of historical narratives when we are faced with conflicting sources. So, we do some big overviews of the historical context (colonialism, basic timeline, involved parties), then I have the students analyze a bunch of primary sources about the Gulf of Tonkin using historical thinking skills like sourcing, corroboration, contextualization, close reading, and reading the silences. Then they have to write a narrative that answers the question, "What really happened in the Gulf of Tonkin?" They also have to talk about their degree of confidence in their analysis.

3. Finally, we look at the war from the perspective of the individual soldier. For this, we read The Things They Carried, then videotape an interview with a Vietnam veteran for the Library of Congress Veteran's History Project. It's pretty awesome.

This takes about 5-6 weeks of 2 hours a day, in a combined history/English class. Our school explicitly values depth over breadth, so we cover fewer historical topics in much more depth.

permalink embed save give award

> [-] StickleyMan [S] 1 point 5 years ago
> Very cool to get a teacher's perspective. Thank you!
>
> Those all sound like really effective and engaging methods of teaching what happened. The third one especially must make things very personal and real for the students. How do they usually react? Are there any restrictions placed on what you teach through the curriculum or the board?
>
> You sound like an awesome teacher and your students are lucky to have you. Thanks again!
>
> permalink embed save parent give award
>
> > [-] **Insidia** 2 points 5 years ago
> > Thanks! I love my job. :)
> >
> > As far as restrictions, we do, of course, have to teach to state standards. I'm lucky in that CO's standards for history are written to be much more skill based- they're far less prescriptive than the history standards of states like CA. I'm at a charter school that allows enormous freedom for teachers to design their own curriculum, so no pressure there. Our school was designed with this type of teaching in mind.
> >
> > My students love this project, particularly the veteran interviews. We've gotten some amazing footage of veterans telling stories that even their wives have never heard. It's a really powerful experience for my 15 year olds to have.
> >
> > permalink embed save parent give award

Figure 4.4. Repeated questioning from Vietnam War thread

members with thanks and an overtly excited tone indicated by exclamation points. He told me that exclamation points help "to create a positive, sincere thread." Figure 4.3 illustrates the important and consistent use of thanks. In using "Thanks" or "thank you" and the words "cool" and "appreciate," StickleyMan expressly recognizes Cosmic-Katamari, the commenter. Sincerity accompanies StickleyMan's words of thanks; he gives textual attention by recognizing the audience member's input in his reply, picking up the language of the reply, and appearing to genuinely desire a type of educational experience with this thread. He neither identifies with the audience nor persuades them toward a particular view, but rather he attempts to entice the audience to participate on their terms.

Additionally, StickleyMan prods his audience with repeated questioning to keep the thread moving forward. Engaging the audience in this way requires not one initial question but recurring questioning (fig. 4.4). Note that he thanks twice. This exchange shows StickleyMan inciting participation in a knowledgeable manner that then dovetails into repeated questioning, thereby forming textual attention. The redditor insidia provides an organized and coherent response, most likely because insidia claims to be a teacher.

StickleyMan's response in this case is indicative of textual attention in three ways. First, he opens his response with the phrase "Very cool to get a teacher's perspective." I asked him what the word *cool* means to him here: "It's just a way of acknowledging and recognizing somebody and their opinion, being like, 'Yeah okay I digest what you're saying. That's cool. Here's my response to it.'" Because reddit assumes a level of informal tone and word choice, StickleyMan must use a tone that can stand in for a formal level of positivity while also encouraging a commenter who offers a cogent and engaged response. The phrase "Very cool to get a teacher's perspective" shows insidia that StickleyMan has read the comment and reflected upon it while understanding the appropriate word choice and tone to use in this community. Second, the two instances of thanking insidia demonstrate StickleyMan's encouragement of a positive tone in the thread, reiterating his goals through example. Lastly, he affirms insidia's teaching methods by asking questions that display concrete details from insidia's comment; he actually references insidia's text and then prods insidia with more questions. Because StickleyMan's purpose is to encourage an organic, continuous conversation, he had to respond to other redditors regularly. He also had to choose which redditors to respond to and which to ignore. In this way, textual attention is a multilayered technique aimed at a specific reader *and* readers of the thread at large. Textual attention encourages continuing already-present *and* future conversations by establishing the initial writer's willingness to interact.

TEXTUAL ATTENTION AS A PRAGMATIC SOLUTION

Textual attention is ultimately a writing strategy used by writers who are interested in reading comments on their texts but are faced with numerous comments. It is a description of how writers in templated digital environments respond to the comments of their participatory audiences. The importance of textual attention is threefold. First, the goals of textual attention extend beyond those of reading, which is often associated with the purpose of understanding a text. In addition to seeking an understanding of a text or texts, writers employing textual attention seek out a genuine audience. In this sense, textual attention implies evaluating multiple, even competing, responses from audience members.

Second, textual attention differs from listening. That is, while it is a strategy that shares some purpose with active listening, it is meant to account for IPI environments that lack the benefit of vocal intonation or body language. My use of the word *attention* to describe this strategy arises from the near oral speeds at which text can be exchanged in IPI environments, speeds that for the writer are multiplied under the pressure of a quantitatively large response. In speech, we accommodate this rapid, multidirectional transmittal of information through attentive listening, employing body language such as eye contact and posture, and questioning and showing affirmation in appropriate verbal tones. In doing so, we aim to engage the speaker by showing our genuine and sincere interest in their words. Within digital templates, we currently lack the ability to provide these kinds of human feedback. Depending on the template interface, we can be limited to text exclusively, or we have access to digital approximations of human feedback, including ambient affordances, emoticons, emojis, GIFs, or memes. The digital-feedback component of textual attention describes how writers deal with missing human feedback when the writer's aims parallel those of oral listeners.

Third, textual attention provides us with a way to understand digital writing *after* delivery. After a text is delivered, writers still have rhetorical activity, often in the form of labor. In rhetorical terms, invention continues after initial delivery; delivery occurs again and again, as does production.

Textual attention, then, is a strategy that forms in update culture wherein writers recognize they must attend to the afterlife of their writing. For writers that employ it, textual attention becomes part of their writing process(es). Textual attention attempts to identify one process digital writers use *after* the initial production of a text, in other words, during the circulation of a text. Historically, the writing process after circulation was limited to versions of the original text. While one after-effect of textual attention can be an updated initial text, it is more important to recognize that for some digital writers, textual attention, as a production process, *accompanies* the circulation of their writing. For example, writers might choose textual attention as a means to extend the lifespan of a text, or in choosing textual attention, writers might be forced to contend with an extended lifespan of the text. An example of the latter is responding to comments on zombie posts, or posts that are very old. If digital writing and rhetoric are committed to tracing the contours and spread of digital discourse, then part of that commitment is describing how writers react and develop writing strategies subsequent to those contours. Textual attention is one such description for postproduction production.

ATTENTION AS EXIGENCE IN DIGITAL RHETORIC

In light of these postproduction strategies, textual attention complicates our understanding of exigence or the issue or problem that demands a response. In Bitzer's now canonical "The Rhetorical Situation" (1968), exigence is defined as the "organizing principle" that "specifies an audience to be addressed and change to be effected" (7). While Richard Vatz, in "The Myth of the Rhetorical Situation" (1973), famously sees exigencies as created, and Bitzer sees them as objective aspects of situations,[1] textual attention complicates what it means to "demand" a response. Because audiences in IPI environments are emergent, textual attention shows that multiple exigencies exist at the same time, and digital writers on the internet must choose which are most important. In this regard, I echo Scott Smith and Craig Lybarger's (1996) contention that exigencies are fluid and "everywhere shot through with perceptions and . . . institutional forces" (197). That exigencies are multiple in update culture is inherent to the nature of participatory audiences.

Across my case studies, participants appeared to be filtering exigencies and choosing which ones to attend to and which ones to ignore. To echo the previous chapter, textual attention inverts our understanding of exigencies: there are so many exigencies that digital writers need some sort of mechanism to filter, sort, and determine which acts of discourse need or deserve attention. The act of filtering, sorting, and giving attention is a highly rhetorical act. Textual attention is the primary strategy I observed as a way of giving active attention to audience participation, via comments. Textual attention helps writers sort through exigencies and choose which ones are deserving of a response.

My point here is that exigencies are rife in digital-media environments. Exigencies come and go, emerging and vanishing at rapid rates and on massive or tiny scales. In the context of this study, they aren't spectacular, special, or unique. Audiences can provide and create them; writers can also create them. Likewise, due to the thin distinction between writers and participatory audiences, both writers and audiences encounter exigencies, even if they are simultaneously created. Exigencies might be said to be commonplace and demanding, with a stress on the ongoing, multiple nature of exigencies. Textual attention is the constellation of practices meant to account for the multiple, emergent exigencies in update culture and, more generally, digital cultures.

CODA: NONLINEARITY IN UPDATE CULTURE

At this point in *Update Culture and the Afterlife of Digital Writing*, I want to stress that the linear nature of this book might make it seem like textual timing precedes textual attention. I need to make clear that textual timing and textual attention occur repeatedly, in a nonlinear recursive fashion. They intersect as strategies that writers use in order to cope with the afterlife of their texts. In a similar vein, the next chapter, "Textual Management," documents several strategies that occur before, during, and after textual timing and textual attention. These are smaller but significant ways in which writers develop brands and enact impression management in IPI contexts. In other words, even though timing, attention, and management are useful tropes, they become even more useful and effective as ways to manage the circulation of digital texts when viewed in an interlocking manner. It is to this chapter that I now turn.

5
TEXTUAL MANAGEMENT

While the previous two chapters took up the questions of *when* and *how* writers negotiate their participatory audiences and the afterlife of their writing, this chapter answers the question of *what* writers do while they contend with these audiences during the afterlife of their writing. In broad strokes, writers manage their audience response. However, under the auspice of the term *management* falls a remarkable and heterogeneous constellation of textual practices. Because texts themselves can change in digital and social media environments, writers revisit their writing, rereading their texts after delivery, during circulation, and postpublication, all with a fresh editorial eye due to comments, ambient affordances, and other types of participatory response. Textual management consequently refers to series of actions writers deploy to enact control over their writing.

Textual management expands and reorients theories of impression management, originated by Ervin Goffman in *The Presentation of Self in Everyday Life* (1959), for IPI environments. Like Carolyn Cunningham's edited collection *Social Networking and Impression Management: Self Presentation in the Digital Age* (2012), this chapter seeks to add to and expand upon various theories of impression management by applying them to social media. Simultaneously, I am aware of the striking differences between a general theory of impression management for digital contexts and what the individual writers I have studied do. Thus, as I note in the introduction of this book, the scope of this chapter only applies to individual writers in IPI environments.

I dwell briefly here on my writers' purposes, something often lost in digital contexts, because purpose clarifies two questions. First, to what end are these writers managing their writing? Second, after initially publishing or delivering a text, what are digital writers doing that audiences might directly see or experience? The most common purpose my participants reported, with respect to their comments and participatory media writ large, was to "continue the conversation," "keep the conversation going," or initiate large comment "exchanges." While these phrases are not monolithic in their meaning among various writers, they do share

DOI: 10.7330/9781607329749.c005

resonances. As I mention in the previous chapter, writers aimed to continue conversations because these conversations centered on *their* writing.

Thus, if conversations continued, writers knew they were *being read*. Even if those conversations were critical, without being vitriolic, readers inherently signaled they had engaged the text in some way. In fact, nearly all writers mentioned being interested in sincere critical engagement. Self-reported mentions of continuing conversations attested to a desire to grow audience engagement and to be read. Digital writers, in this sense, valued increased metrics and flow of electronic traffic to their websites because it signaled being read. They were not simply trying to win "imaginary internet points" (redditors) or get "helpful votes" (reviewers) or "get as many retweets as possible" (journalists). They wanted these things because they represented *being read*.

Managing texts in various ways assisted participants in achieving these ends. The concept of textual management thus suggests that writers take on administrator-like positions and deploy time and energy to exert control over texts. These writers often marshaled readers to act in certain ways by embodying certain writerly roles and explicitly policing the writing of others in the venue. My participants did not force commenters or readers to respond in terms of content; they typically requested a particular manner of response (tone, style, etc.) or tried to model the kind of response they desired.

To put it less formally, writers who consider their comments are concerned with how audiences respond and whether audiences are genuinely engaged. It is for this reason I use the term *manage* because it emphasizes that my participants did not control their audiences but instead created parameters for behaviors and initiated certain roles in the group. Writers try to influence the *doxa* surrounding their writing, but participatory audiences retain a sense of autonomy. Like a manager in the workplace, textual management makes certain behaviors both possible and more rewarded than others. Yet commenters and readers still make choices on their own. Textual management, then, describes the way digital writers may direct communities or groups of readers so that the writers can (1) achieve their goals of having a particular kind of successful debate and (2) retain a productive relationship with audiences in order to be read.

Participants active on similar platforms reported similar purposes. Amazon reviewers reported a strong desire to be helpful, which I mention in chapter 3, "Textual Timing." The articulation of this desire as "helpfulness" is drawn directly from Amazon's reviewing template and from reviewing guidelines provided by the corporation. Digital journalists expressed a desire to report news and studies as clearly as they could while serving a public interest. Bloggers, like Heather Armstrong, valued circulation on social media sites: Shares on Facebook, Retweets on Twitter, and embedded hyperlinks on fellow bloggers' posts. Redditors wanted to initiate large comment exchanges and get read widely. When discussing their writing purposes, participants' language also reflected the labels and language of their respective templates.

The writers I studied did not aim to produce ebooks, as Laquintano details in *Mass Authorship and the Rise of Self-Publishing* (2016). Unlike Laquintano's participants, who wrote electronic novels and poker guidebooks, the writers I studied wrote shorter pieces, more akin to everyday writing. In addition to length of text, another crucial difference is that the writers Laquintano studied wanted, in addition to being paid, the cultural capital associated with authorship. That said, Laquintano's book details many digital-management practices related to *Update Culture and the Afterlife of Digital Writing*. I draw points of comparison with his work in this chapter to identify larger patterns of writerly habits on the internet.

The rest of this chapter has four main parts. First, I provide a thick description of textual management, drawing on theories of impression management and curation. Second, I identify the writerly move to generalize audience response so that writers grasp the response better—and in turn, write back. Here, I use the term *hivemind* (and other terms) to develop the concept of *identifying digital groupthink* as it relates to initial writers who respond to participatory audiences. Third, I lay out the concrete strategies writers reported and demonstrated. These include macromanagement (framing the conversation and establishing forums), indirect management (monitoring, curating, and controlling the conversation), direct management (fighting or battling trolls), and responsive management (ignoring, deleting, correcting, and updating texts). Last, I discuss reasons textual management is useful to twenty-first-century writing practices: digital writers often engage in *aspirational branding*. *Aspirational branding* is the term I use to describe the largest, most generalizable aim I could identify throughout this project and across the writers I studied. While I write more about this at the end of this chapter, for now, I simply describe the concept as the writerly purpose of being read and being aware that one is read.

DEFINING TEXTUAL MANAGEMENT

Textual management describes the work of writers who "successfully stag[e] a character" (Goffman 1959, 208). The most useful part of

Goffman's approach, for my purposes here, is his *dramaturgical* lens of analysis. Namely, both backstages and frontstages of performance exist in digital environments. Frontstage means that readers may view some of the management strategies writers employ. Backstage choices and processes are often not presented explicitly on social media sites. These include managing aspects that may disappear (such as edits that are not indicated from an initial piece of content) or are never accessible in the first place (such as approving or deleting comments).

Researchers often can't identify backstage activities from simply reading texts, a methodological issue I discuss in the final chapter of this book. Yet, even when they are documented in content-management systems, such as WordPress, backstage activities can be difficult to follow and design choices may be lost. Having interviewed numerous digital writers, I found that these writers consciously engaged in frontstage and backstage activities, although participants did not use these terms explicitly. Most notably, participants frequently used the message function to communicate with other writers with similar positions to share ideas, circulate writing, and get Upvotes, Helpful Votes, Retweets, and Likes.

However, textual management exceeds the boundaries of impression management because textual management encompasses *editorial activities* once reserved for professional editors in print and cohesive organizations, as well as *curatorial practices* reserved for preservation specialists. Such activities and practices emerge from constellations of social, economic, and historical factors, including the collapse of writerly occupations and the rise of ecommerce with seemingly zero-cost distribution of texts. Rising up alongside these factors—or perhaps due to these factors—writers are frequently open to a wide range of public audiences, including but not limited to welcome readers, invasive algorithms, trolls, surveillance software, and unexpected readers. As Brown (2015) observes in *Ethical Programs*, "Politics in the hospitable network means that the rhetor has already welcomed multiple audiences to the rhetorical situation, audiences that exceed the intended audience and that arrive with conflicting and competing interests" (168). While Brown's observations are couched in software studies about the ethics of code and software swarms that exceed their programmed intention, his perspective sheds a light on the reasons digital writers engage in management practices. To extend Brown's perspective, digital writers frequently encounter audiences with "conflicting and competing interests" and, in my view, need strategies after encountering such audiences. Writers in these contexts need to corral, control, and influence their audiences to extend the effectiveness of their texts. I now go into detail about *editorial activities* and *curatorial practices* as defining components of textual management.

With editorial activities, I aim to emphasize the variety of activities that may be overlooked with respect to labeling my participants as *writers*. They are editors, copyeditors, promoters, managers, publishers, content moderators, and even agents. The historical capitalist apparatus associated with professional writing, one that isolated the act of writing from the act of distributing and delivering writing, has nearly vanished with respect to my participants. Only a few of the journalists I spoke with had editors, and these editors had a limited role and even less liability; the writers I studied effectively became moderators of their own work. Only Heather Armstrong explicitly mentioned an editor as having influence on her work. The redditors and reviewers clearly did not have any editors. In other words, these contingent writers are trying to get read in a world on their own—a general sentiment that Laquintano's *Mass Authorship and the Rise of Self-Publishing* (2016) confirms.

Writers and writing are part of a larger trend in digital labor becoming contingent. As Clay Spinuzzi has observed in *All Edge* (2015), information and communication technologies (ICTs) have led organizations to hire or rely upon nonemployer firms with rotating casts of contract labor. These groups of laborers, called all-edge adhocracies by Spinuzzi, are inordinately flexible, giving organizations the frontstage appearance of unity when in reality they mainly consist of individuals unfamiliar with one another (1–6). All-edge adhocracies are contract workers putting on a theatrical performance.

All-edge adhocracy is a two-part concept. First, adhocracies are "rotating teams of specialists who come together to swarm a project, disperse at the end of it, and reform in a different configuration for the next project" (Spinuzzi 2015, 1). Second, all-edge means "able to rapidly link across organizational boundaries" (2) that "temporarily connect specialists across organizations rather than just within an organization" (3). In all-edge adhocracies on the web, writers are hired on a freelance basis. They may categorize themselves as journalists for a digital newspaper or magazine, such as *Wired* or *Forbes*, but they are not full-time employees. These organizations largely maintain their brand through the social media presence of their part-time writers. Individual writers maintain their social media presences, which in turn extend an organization's "front-stage" appearance of "unity, stability, and competence" (53). While Spinuzzi covers a wide array of individuals, including search-engine optimization specialists who write numerous twenty-page reports per month, my observation here is that my participants partake in all-edge adhocracies taken to an even higher intensity than depicted in *All Edge*.

The writers I studied are part of organizations despite not being considered official members. Amazon reviewers and bloggers have no formal association with platforms or websites, even if they occasionally write a "guest post" for a corporation such as Medium (a self-publishing website). With the collapse of newspapers, journalists are almost entirely adjunct workers. The journalists I studied discussed writing articles at odd hours of the day (without ever mentioning editors or other assistance) while needing to fulfill their day jobs that pay bills. My participant journalists also reported being *required* to monitor comments, which is emotional labor, intense temporal labor, and physical labor (staring at a screen for hours). Redditors are part of the reddit platform and are keenly aware that they make money for the paid administrators and corporation. (It's important to note reddit has moderators, who are self-selected users and *not* administrators). From this perspective, the writers I studied took on numerous roles that professional publication separated from writing. Whereas writers once dealt mainly with production, they are now producers, distributors, circulators, managers, editors, and marketers.

With respect to curatorial practices, I mean the act of editing comments, actively managing reader response (synchronously and asynchronously), and providing contexts and opportunities for discussion of texts. The act of curation here is meant as a thick version of the concept that exceeds simple preservation and maintenance techniques. My use of curation thus echoes Kennedy's *Textual Curation* (2016), which seeks to attend to the in-depth work and labor the term *curation* seems to have lost in our digital age.

> Describing and assigning meaning to curation as mere filtration, aggregation, or collection strips this compositional work of the essential skill and craft performed through the curator's labor. Those of us who work in fields that have adopted "curation" to describe filtered and recomposed compositions may forget that curation is a specialized craft and field of study in multiple curation-focused disciplines that award advanced degrees, train specialists, launch distinguished careers, and create robust scholarship. (5)

Kennedy's description highlights two aspects relevant to my argument in this book. First, curation for Kennedy is filtration, aggregation, and collection as well as significantly more than just these acts. The writers I studied had to filter, aggregate, and collect audience response on a constant basis. Second, curation is a professional, laborious endeavor. While Kennedy is clear about the disciplinary aspect of curation that is not applicable in this book, I do use the term to imply that responsibility for some of the laborious practices, once reserved for those in specialized careers, has fallen on writers. That is, in using the term *curatorial practices*, I am echoing again that digital writers do more than simply write on the internet.

Curatorial practices in the context of update culture implies writers attend to their writing without discrete end points. As many public critics have noted, including Carr (2010) and Turkle (2011), social media demands constant attention of users. Throughout my study, I've found that this line of reasoning can be extended to writers. Texts never end, and the need to keep writing never disappears. Kennedy notes this with the rethinking of curation for our digital age.

> This understanding of the labor processes associated with composing in current digital environments leads us to a different conceptualization of collaboratively produced digital information structures, whatever their genre: open, interconnected, and not necessarily finished in the ways that we previously deemed projects to be complete once they were published and distributed as print artifacts. We typically consider print compositions to have reached a terminal point in development when they are published and made available to an audience. (7)

Here, Kennedy anticipates a crucial finding of this book: in many ways, terminal points for writing have ceased. Texts, of course, are discrete, but they can be rewritten, updated, and edited repeatedly in update culture. The production of text occurs frequently, nonlinearly, and recursively, much like the revision and drafting process, while simultaneously being accessible on the internet. The process of distributing, delivering, and circulating texts occurs repeatedly. Circulation can be potentially endless. And, as I mention in the previous chapter, production, distribution, and circulation occur during the distribution and circulation processes, alongside and interconnected with each other to the point that writers need to manage those texts.

Ultimately, the concept of textual management assists writers in navigating the interaction and participation inherent in IPI contexts. In such environments, textual management describes ways in which writers influence and shape a participatory audience while retaining autonomy over that audience. By retaining this autonomy, textual management highlights the production of an ongoing dialogue and conversation undergirded by a writer's purposes.

IDENTIFYING DIGITAL GROUPTHINK

Before I identify and analyze specific textual-management strategies, I first identify participants' key ability to generalize holistic trends in audience behavior in order to make management decisions. I call this ability *identifying digital groupthink*. The term *groupthink*, which originated in the field of psychology, describes the way individuals avoid disagreements and controversial issues to the detriment of themselves or their groups or communities. I use the term to describe the way emergent groups of users in IPI environments tend to respond in similar fashion. *Identifying digital groupthink* is my term that describes the way digital writers learn, and subsequently manage, patterns and trends in audience response.

The concept takes shape under the guise of many names: the *hive-mind* and *thought police* are just two labels for this phenomenon I found during my research. Many readers of this book are likely familiar with these terms, perhaps from their personal use of social media when they or friends "ask the hivemind" for advice or crowdsource advice. The act of identifying digital groupthink allows writers to coalesce concatenations of audiences, such as ad hoc emergent groups of readers, demographics, corporate interests, and algorithms, into something manageable *they can write for, to, and with*. Identifying digital groupthink reflects the need of writers to think about the ways their readers respond based on aggregation, an issue Jeff Rice theorizes (2016, 2017). The purpose of identifying digital groupthink is to manage audiences as effectively as possible for an emergent purpose or situation.

Identifying digital groupthink thus enables writers to characterize the collective nature of their audience and then make choices about what they should do with that groupthink, or hivemind, echo chamber, thought police. In *Participatory Culture, Community, and Play* (2015), Adrienne L. Massanari describes groupthink, via the hivemind, as ritualized performances with respect to the website reddit (21). She writes that the rituals and repeated performances on reddit involve a "series of stock answers, phrases, and memetic retellings" (21). While Massanari has noted that the hivemind is certainly a problem within reddit—itself part of a larger problem, that of the cultural retreat into filter bubbles and confirmation bias—I extend this perspective beyond reddit. In IPI contexts, understanding larger patterns of response better helps writers control and manage their audiences. As StickleyMan told me, "The hivemind is shitty and awful and problematic except when it's totally right."

Participants learned the groupthink of their respective platforms to accrue experiences about how their audiences would respond to their texts. In terms of impression management, this accrual enables writers to develop contextual awareness of the ways their texts will be received. As danah boyd (2014) notes, "Impression management online and off is not just an individual act; it's a social process" (49). While this social experience does not guarantee predictive abilities on the part of writers, it enables them to gauge a general level of response and trends. Writers create a composite idea of groupthink to then react and write in response to this composite.

A few contextualized examples describe identifying digital groupthink. First, I return to StickleyMan, the high-level redditor I discuss in chapter 4. StickleyMan discussed groupthink directly through the concept of the hivemind. As a mental construct, the hivemind allowed StickleyMan to characterize the collective negativity of reddit so he could more readily encourage an organic, ongoing public to form when he wrote. StickleyMan imagined a negative redditor, the hivemind, who embodied the ideas he believed are problems with reddit. By doing so, he could write to achieve his purpose of positivity and being read more effectively while prompting discussions to entice a negative redditor to join. StickleyMan spoke of reddit in an abstracted and generalized manner by explicitly using the term *composite* in the following exchange.

> STICKLEYMAN: I kind of commit to being positive. I don't put people down when I comment. And I don't engage in negativity at all. So, it is difficult being, you know, I guess a prolific commenter with a lot of karma. The hate comes in all the time. And that's the difference I think. One of the differences between something like, reddit and Facebook. Facebook, if you want to talk shit to the guy writing, you're accountable to it, right? Your face is right there.
>
> GALLAGHER: I can see that . . .
>
> STICKLEYMAN: Especially in the summer. And I'm not one of these "I hate teenager kids" [types], but there's a marked difference in the audience and the replies on reddit over the summer. You know, I get called a faggot at least three times a day. You know, at this point, what else can I do? And we talk about it. You know, there's this century club subreddit, that's for only people with over 100,000 [karma]. . . . it's interesting to get their insights. And kind of the, the prevailing approach [in the century club] is just never feed the trolls, right? No matter what I say in a thread, especially if it's one that I comment, people are just going to jump on it. So, you know, it depends. And now that being said, let's say I'm just retelling a story or, or recounting something, and it's an AskReddit thread. I'm not just recounting in a silly way, how I would to my brother. I'll put some flair to it that I know the average redditor doesn't. You know, *in my mind I have this composite of what the average redditor is.* And, you know, if I'm making

something there, I want them to enjoy it and get a laugh on it, and I want to get karma out of this one, right? (emphasis added)

StickleyMan refers to redditors but does not seem to include himself in the larger category of "hiveminded" redditors. Compositing in this way allowed StickleyMan to determine what he believed was an average, negative redditor.

By constructing this composite redditor as the hivemind, StickleyMan could characterize, and thereby identify, the variety of conversations on reddit. In other words, he used the composite to explain the larger body of reddit conversations to himself. StickleyMan seemed to have an intimate knowledge of hiveminded redditors. For instance, he spoke of reddit with deft acumen in the following exchange:

STICKLEYMAN: reddit loves to reference itself.

GALLAGHER: reddit loves to talk about reddit?

STICKLEYMAN: Loves it. Loves to talk about how much it hates reddit. Loves to talk about how much reddit does this and that. There is a lot of self-loathing in that. But it's all what they love. Reddit likes to talk about reddit. Reddit also hates Facebook. I'll tell you that.

GALLAGHER: Why do you think it is?

STICKLEYMAN: Because they look at [Facebook] as unintellectual. Because there is this massive ego and this elitism to reddit that is, I think, manifested by the anonymity. Right? No one is accountable for anything. Everyone loves science, everyone reads 100 books here. Right? On Facebook, there is room for duck faces, and "Like this if you want to fight cerebral palsy." "Check out this meme that was on reddit six months ago." Here [on reddit] there is no tolerance for it. There's no gray. It's all black and white.

GALLAGHER: So do you think that reddit is ahead of Facebook?

STICKLEYMAN: Absolutely, reddit sees itself as more important, smarter. It's amazing how many people talk about how much they hate Facebook. Like it's the vogue thing to do. You delete your Facebook account and your life has never been better. And the fucking turn signal! [lighthearted outrage] You want to talk about hivemind. In the reddit, it comes up once a week: If you could put anything into law, what would it be? Put people in jail who don't use their turn signal. You would think [not using a turn signal] was an epidemic. That it was the biggest problem in North America. *It's a hivemind, it's the same thing.* (Second Interview, my emphasis added)

StickleyMan again illustrates an ability to identify the digital groupthink of an average redditor. His general views were reflected by the other redditors with some variation, although many of them were annoyed by reddit's strange obsession with people who do not use turn signals (toxicbox playfully referred to this as a "dark time" in reddit's memetic discourse). This abstraction enabled StickleyMan to perceive general patterns and trends. He slipped here, unbeknownst, I believe, to him, calling reddit "the reddit," which shows in this instance that he perceives reddit as a mass or single entity. Reddit becomes anthropomorphized, delineated from individuals or groups in the sense that StickleyMan referred to the site itself. He saw the entire community as a single being, one that sees itself as intelligent, righteous, and elitist. The outraged and annoyed tone with which he delivered these lines during our interview told me he was intimately familiar with the hivemind and believed it is a feature of reddit *at large*. And this perception allowed him to anticipate responses, which he will account for when he "posts in the future."

Participants expressed a vexed relationship with groupthink, including nearly every redditor. Each redditor understood the hivemind to be an intrinsic part of reddit, albeit to varying degrees. Most redditors understood hivemind as a *shifting* type of groupthink, one that moves with the changing of seasons as well as time of day. They could discuss patterns at length, as well as understand that those same patterns were not monolithic. Three examples help articulate this approach to the hivemind. Mattreyu told me, "I hear people refer to the hivemind, but I think really it's just popular opinion. The design of reddit really enforces the idea, since things people like get upvoted and more visible, which creates a feedback loop that pushes things like that up while others sink and disappear." Landlubber eloquently articulated an emblematic relationship to reddit's hivemind.

> Reddit itself has acknowledged the influence of the hivemind by implementing an initial temporary shrouding of a comment's karma score, as to better encourage voting based on merit rather than Pavlovian adherence to upvoting what is already popular so you're always at the cool kid's table. There's no real way to combat the hivemind, and in a way I suppose it suppresses individual thought, but not to some dangerous degree.

Portarossa, the only female redditor I interviewed, said the following of the hivemind over email:

> I'm a bit torn on the whole idea of the "reddit hivemind." On one hand, I'm not entirely sure it exists—at least, not in the way that most people seem to think, where reddit is some homogeneous bloc that only has one view on a given topic (leftist, pro-marijuana, pro-life, atheistic, that sort of thing). I think there are a few exceptions to this, usually in heavily-moderated communities that actively try to be an echo chamber—most notably places like /r/T_D and /r/MGTOW, where *any* dissent from the norm is considered a cardinal sin—but in wider reddit I think you

can comfortably have most opinions, *if* you present them in the right way. That's the big sticking point that people who complain about the hivemind usually miss. Yes, if you come into a place that's generally pretty liberal and you're throwing around Benghazi conspiracy theories and talking about how "Shillary" would have been the worst thing ever, you're going to get downvotes; it's like showing up to a wedding and vocally arguing that love is a sham and anyone who believes in it is a sucker. On the other hand, if you say, "Yes, I know you feel that way, but I disagree. Here's a well-sourced reason why," I think you'll probably have a better time of it—you won't necessarily set the front page on fire, but you're also not necessarily going to be downvoted to oblivion just because you disagree. You only need to look as far as /r/AskReddit threads where people ask things like "People who are against abortion, why?" to see this in action. Most people disagree with the main thrust of the argument, but if it's presented in a way that's palatable, they're not going to downvote.

Portarossa's perspective was similar to those of numerous other redditors in that the hivemind, while seeming to be present and sometimes hurtful, could be pushed through.

These perspectives provide a nuanced perspective of groupthink that provides three insights. First, the hivemind could be talked about concretely even if claims about the hivemind were not universals. Second, redditors understood that appealing to the hivemind yielded a certain amount of influence. Third, the hivemind could be challenged if a certain type of tone and style is chosen. In other words, writers at the individual level could discuss the hivemind, as well as achieve agency to challenge that same hivemind. While writers could pander to the hivemind, they believed such pandering was not entirely necessary if one is careful and persistent about the tone used. For redditors, the hivemind was a problematic feature of their discourse that nevertheless allowed them insight into pattern identification that usefully complements the previous timing and attention strategies.

Matt Grimes, the digital journalist I've mentioned previously, also understood the problems of dealing with hiveminds and echo chambers but believed it is a useful, if unpleasant, experience. As he advised, "Predictability is useful for new writers. Follow a news cycle, either daily or weekly." Grimes understood that the accrual of experience *through time* (see chapter 2, "Textual Timing") is important when deciding when, how, and why to respond to audiences across various social media platforms. He told me that "predictability through experience" is the "best way to figure out what to respond to." The accrual of groupthink experience—experiencing the hivemind—may be vitriolic, off topic, and time consuming, but it helps with developing specific techniques for textual management, techniques to which I now turn.

TEXTUAL-MANAGEMENT STRATEGIES

I now turn to the concrete management strategies of the various writers I've studied. As I mention earlier, these techniques are heterogeneous in nature, and I learned about several strategies that did not reflect larger trends. Some of the strategies *not* reflective of larger trends include sending private messages (mostly the journalists and redditors), "doxing," or an effort to reveal a troll's real-life identity (reviewers), and emailing commenters (bloggers and journalists). These strategies came up in my interviews and field observations in multiple instances; they are uncommon, though certainly not rare. These three strategies were often part of a larger effort on the part of my participants to prevent disruptive readers from having a presence in their texts. I don't go into detail with these strategies because (1) they were reported less often and (2) I didn't have direct access to these exchanges.

Textual management has four categories: macromanagement, indirect management, direct management, and responsive management. The categories start out with the most general and broad activities and funnel down to more specific activities. While research in other disciplines, including journalism, marketing, and business, encourage many of these activities, I emphasize them from a writerly perspective. In my analysis, I discuss how participants' respective templates, as well as the larger corporate power dynamics at play in an IPI environment, seemed to influence their strategies. These strategies ultimately show that writers take on the role of managers and moderators of multiple digital forums, a role that echoes speakers trying to manage noisy crowds in an auditorium—even multiple auditoriums at the same time.

Macromanagement: Framing the Conversation and Establishing Forums

Participants often had the ability to shape the norms, conventions, and expectations of their participatory audiences, a feature I label *macromanagement.* Macromanagement was the direct result of the ways my participants perceived how their audiences generally behaved, identifying digital groupthink and deciding upon the roles they wanted their audiences to take on. Macromanagement had two distinct parts, the latter of which occurred almost algorithmically in response to vitriolic comments: framing the conversation and establishing forums. Participants framed the conversation around their writing through rule setting, guideline adherence, and modeling appropriate behavior that coincided with those rules or guidelines. If they could not inculcate an appropriate conversation based on their individual goals and desires, then participants often established a forum away from their writing.

Framing the conversation, as a type of discursive regulation, is the production of explicit or implicit rules and guidelines, often via comment policies but also through modeling discursive behavior for participatory audiences. These policies and this act of "officiating" enable digital writers to communicate in ways that allow them to take up rhetorical positions of their choosing within a specific IPI environment. The control participants exerted is thus not totalizing but strategic: they aimed for readers to follow rules, guidelines, and discursive norms on their own rather than by force.

Producing rules and guidelines is a rhetorically complex task, one dependent on several factors, including but not limited to one's writing goal(s), platform or website, current readers, targeted readers, imagined demographic, intended algorithm, and previous reader comments. Like textual management itself, producing rules and guidelines is a heterogeneous process. Bloggers and journalists in my study often set rules and guidelines for themselves for responding to audiences (when they could do so). On the other hand, Amazon reviewers and redditors adhered to the guidelines of their specific platforms or subreddit. Redditors, including AndrewSmith1986 and others, also became rule setters by becoming moderators of certain subreddits. This of course does not mean reviewers and redditors did not have their own personal systems or journalists never had to contend with the official comment-management systems of *Forbes*, *Wired*, *Science*, and a host of other magazines. Nevertheless, three trends emerged with respect to framing conversations: internal frames, external frames, and establishing forums.

Internal Frames

Internal framing means creating an implicit way of engaging digital commenters. The journalists and redditors I studied most often employed internal frames, namely, their own systems for managing commenters. However, participants from all groups discussed internal frames. Six brief examples are illustrative.

First, Tracy Monroe, the vaccine journalist I discuss in prior chapters, established her own system of flagging commenters who "simply spread falsehoods about vaccines." She deleted "out and out lies," such as comments that linked autism to vaccines. Monroe, however, didn't delete comments that might be perceived as rhetorical questions or sarcasm. If there was a small chance (a "shred" she told me) of a comment being genuine, Monroe responded. In this sense, she had a three-tier system for how she responded: thanking commenters for positive or supportive comments, responding rhetorically to questions that might be genuine, and deleting false or vitriolic comments.

Second, Maggie Skinner, who started as an independent blogger in 2004 and eventually wrote for multiple professional science societies, had a two-tiered system that involved a yellow card and a red card, although she admitted there is a third category of comment she labels "completely batshit crazy with no connection to reality." This third type of comment, which was generally incoherent or off topic, she ignored and deleted if she could. This two-tiered system acted as a warning system and was her way of "making a public statement about comments" that were "over the line." The system "really seem[ed] to help," although she warned that writers must be "really clear about consequences," meaning reader response, when choosing to delete comments.

Third, the redditor HitchhikersPie had a two-part internal system for responding to commenters. He told me there were "two categories" for responding, which depended on his purpose. The first tier was about wittiness and karma farming; here HitchhikersPie wrote "as fast as possible." He responded quickly to commenters and gave every comment that wasn't from a troll a "courtesy upvote." The purpose of a courtesy upvote is to upvote commenters simply for responding and to acknowledge that he read their comment (it's part of his textual attention). It's also useful because "it drives up the thread by adding upvotes." The second category was slower and more methodical, centering around debate and discussion. Here, HitchhikersPie read comments carefully, perhaps a few hours later to see who was genuinely engaging his writing. He looked for "longer comments because longer comments are either something serious or a good joke . . . [longer comments] are something a troll doesn't do."

Fourth, Mike W, the Amazon reviewer, responded to all comments that asked a question (textual attention) and ignored the rest. He told me,

> So, when I was first getting famous . . . air quotes . . . I felt this huge responsibility to answer every question and I would actually spend way too much time trying to go and help people, especially if it was a product and they had specific questions. I would take the time . . . I had to read a lot of drones and electronics and I would take the time to talk about all their little questions.

While Mike W has mostly stopped writing reviews as of 2018 (due to exhaustion and feeling, rightfully in my view, as if he is performing free labor for Amazon), his experiences were similar to other reviewers with whom I spoke. His internal frame was customer-service oriented: answer the questions while ignoring the compliments and insults.

Two brief internal frames demonstrate the diversity of such frames. Way_Fairer, formerly the top-ranked redditor for comment karma, responded to comments by matching the punctuation of his responses and those of other commenters. DiegoJones4 upvoted all comments that responded to him, even if the commenters were "jerks" or trolls. Both redditors talked about these strategies as effective ways to promote creative and sustained engagement.

On the whole, internal systems cropped up frequently in my interviews with writers but did not appear explicitly in writers' spaces. That is, I've named them *internal frames* because these are not formalized rules for banning or deleting comments; they are backstage in the Goffmanesque, dramaturgical sense. These internal frames were reported to me as experiences for ways of negotiating and responding to participatory audience response—that is, response to response.

While my participant journalists reported these types most often, likely because their jobs and social media brands pivotally clung to digital interaction, the other groups of writers in my study also frequently reported developing an internal system. Amazon reviewers, for instance, may have the explicit rules of the reviewing community, but many developed individualized rules based on the responses typical of that product category. When reviewing nutrient supplements, for instance, reviewers tended to ignore comments more than when reviewing appliance gadgets. While I could not discern any particular pattern from context to context with respect to specifiable internal framing, reviewers reported *having* them. In my view as a researcher, these internal frames are endemic to social media but are also highly individualized due to the individuation of social media platforms and the creation of specific participatory audiences based on both strong ties and weak ties. As such, internal frames are helpful for writers to develop and possibly unavoidable, but they generally accrete over time and experience, while changing and evolving.

Before I move on to external frames, I need to address the issue of gender with respect to internal frames because gender played a role in terms of *attention*. Women (or those who identified as such) reported what I have called *internal frames* at a higher rate than men did. Men also disproportionately reported ignoring comments and, importantly, being *able* to ignore comments. This privilege may or may not be generalizable to other writers or studies; I cannot attest to the veracity due to my sample size, although numerous other scholars have noted the gendered aspect of digital rhetoric and discourse. In my specific study, for instance, women journalists and women reviewers reported significantly more threats than did their male counterparts. I make no assertions here about the nature of the platform, because I was unable to find any correlations with respect to gender.

I do, however, make claims across the case studies I conducted: internal frames were more highly developed and rhetorically sophisticated for women than for men. While men certainly engaged in internal framing, they did so less often and spoke to the crafting of it with fewer details, for two reasons. First, participants who identified as women reported threats of violence from commenters more often and more serious threats. They were more often the target of rape threats and threats of sexual violence, some toward their children (even if they didn't have children). Second, as described to me, female participants took commenters' claims more seriously than male participants did, and female participants did not easily dismiss those they viewed as trolls. As I mention earlier, men reported ignoring or dismissing threats more often than women did. In terms of digital rhetoric and discourse, then, responding to comments has a higher emotional component and labor component for women than for men. To create an internal frame thus enables women to develop digital rhetorical agency and control over their writing despite the role and influence that participatory audiences may have on their writing. Men are simply less likely to do so because the claims of their participatory audiences do not, it seems, make as much of an impact on them.

The gendered aspect of internal framing should not be surprising since women are more likely to receive vitriolic responses than are men. Internal framing is predicated upon the notion that writers need to wrangle, moderate, and control their writing. As a writer, receiving and contending with threats, frequently violent in nature, is certainly an impetus for control over text. If women receive these comments, then they are more likely to turn to methods of control, precisely what internal framing seems to be about from my observations and interviews. Both women and men, though, adhere and pay attention to explicit frames, an issue to which I now turn.

External Frames

Writers in this study universally drew upon external frames. External framing means adhering to an explicit way of negotiating commenters.

I found two ways in which this occurred. First, writers obeyed and enforced the *official* rules of a platform, such as through the comment guidelines on Facebook, Twitter, reddit, and so forth. Writers enforced guidelines on websites, such as *Forbes, Nature,* and *Science* (back when these websites had comments). Redditors, alternatively, obeyed the rules of subreddits. Second, the writers developed *unofficial* but nevertheless explicit rules for blogs or individual accounts. Many participants adhered to official channels and created their own, such as reviewers who obeyed—vehemently, according to our interviews—the rules Amazon set forth while also establishing rules on their accounts about what they would or would not review. Bloggers wrote their own comment policies. With respect to personalized rules, writers gave themselves permission to control comments in numerous ways. External frames appeared with respect to *every* writer I researched. All participants talked about official rules and twenty-two (out of forty) made some mention of unofficial rules, such as in their personal profiles, community norms, or template conventions.

External framing enabled writers to manage their participatory audiences from a broad, macro point of view. External frames were reported as useful and helpful for four overlapping reasons. First, external framing gave writers control over their text, which I detail shortly. Second, it told commenters that they were being read. This gave writers the personal satisfaction of paying attention to their audiences without needing to respond to every comment. Third, as a consequence of the second, external framing provided writers with a way to save time. Writers set rules about which comments would be deleted, what kinds of comments were encouraged, and which comments deserved response. Once rules were set and established, writers did not need to worry as much about monitoring conversations. Fourth, external framing provided writers with an outside authority to fall back on in cases of conflict. Even if the rules were unofficial, writers could refer to violation of rules rather than risk being accused of relying on their own personal whims, an anxious sentiment that frequently cropped up during our interviews.

And, as with internal framing, gender disparities were noticeable, especially with respect to unofficial external frames. No distinction could be drawn with respect to official external framing, because participants obeyed and enforced the rules of their respective platform or website. With unofficial external framing, however, women were far more likely than men to report having developed personalized rules and to describe the writing process for these rules. Of the eighteen women I interviewed, seventeen discussed writing out rules, while just seven men discussed writing rules. (Portarossa, a redditor, was the only female participant who did not discuss writing rules; I attribute this to the platform.) Women could recall the process of writing rules in far more detail than men could. While their individual processes of writing rules were heterogeneous and without any clear identifiable patterns, the recall of such processes is, I believe, significant even if that recall is conventionalized. The act of writing out rules functioned as a coping mechanism for the vitriol they often received via their comments. Several of them told me that writing out rules was "liberating," a word used across my interviews without my prompting. Others told me that rules gave them an excuse to not read comments and to simply ignore their audiences "when it got bad" or "when it gets bad," two phrases used across interviews with women without my prompting. Men did not use these phrases.

The most common theme for external frames, both official and unofficial, included *policing* user behavior and comment content. That is, both official channels and writers themselves produced rules and guidelines that told users what *not* to write or post. With official external frames, identified patterns of rules and guidelines included a series of "do nots," such as do not offend users, do not violate copyright, and do not post obscenities, pornography, or illegal content. Other rules included creating a shared space of exchange and avoiding ad hominem attacks. Examples from Amazon's guidelines include

- Don't impersonate other people or organizations or pretend to be someone or something you're not.
- Don't repeatedly send messages or requests to other people.
- Don't attempt to drown out other people's opinions, including by posting from multiple accounts or coordinating with others.
- Don't engage in name-calling or attack people based on whether you agree with them. ("Community Guidelines")

While Amazon's guidelines are more casually written and designed to be read by actual users, many other official external frames are written as legal agreements and contracts—not aimed for actual users. The terms of service for *Forbes,* an official external frame for two of my participants, contains commenting policies and governing rules of behavior. For instance, *Forbes*'s "Posting Rules" contains sixteen rules, all of which are framed as what not to write or how not to behave. These rules include avoiding material that

- contains vulgar, profane, abusive or hateful language, epithets or slurs, text or illustrations in poor taste, inflammatory attacks of a personal, racial or religious nature, or expressions of bigotry, racism, discrimination or hate.

- is defamatory, threatening, disparaging, grossly inflammatory, false, misleading, deceptive, fraudulent, inaccurate, unfair, contains gross exaggeration or unsubstantiated claims, violates the privacy rights of any third party, is unreasonably harmful or offensive to any individual or community, contains any actionable statement, or tends to mislead or reflect unfairly on any other person, business or entity.

- violates any right of *Forbes* or any third party.

- discriminates on the grounds of race, religion, national origin, gender, age, marital status, sexual orientation or disability, or refers to such matters in any manner prohibited by law.

- violates any municipal, state or federal law, rule, regulation or ordinance, or attempts to encourage such an evasion or violation.

- unfairly interferes with any third party's uninterrupted use and enjoyment of the Website or Other Channels.

- advertises, promotes or offers to trade any goods or services, except in areas specifically designated for such purpose.

- uploads copyrighted or other proprietary material of any kind on the Website without the express permission of the owner of that material. (truncated list of rules from Forbes's "Terms of Service")

While these rules are prefaced by the phrase "we encourage freedom of speech and a marketplace of ideas," they clearly establish and guide behavior through negative framing.

My participants' external frames generally did not ascribe an ideal positive behavior but provided restriction. Managing writing in digital environments remains difficult because writers need to provide freedom of expression and motivation for participatory audiences while still maintaining their own *ethos* and credibility as writers. A tension exists here: the writer and the audience in these contexts exist closer temporally and spatially than with print texts. External frames thus primarily functioned to prohibit behaviors, rather than guide them, due to this tension. In terms of macromanagement, writers did manage to *resolve* this tension by moving their audience away from the writer's digital space. This is the final strategy of textual macromanagement: establishing forums.

ESTABLISHING FORUMS

Participants established forums if they could not take up a rhetorical position of their choosing due to the omnipresence of comments and qualitative affordances. If the promise of participatory audiences lies with writer-reader exchanges of texts, images, videos, and other digital discourse, then establishing forums is a writerly adaptation to keep this potential for exchange possible while retaining control as the owner of one's own labor and craft. While forums are not a new phenomenon to digital discourse—with scholarship dating back over three decades—the ease of IPI templates makes the creation of purpose-specific forums and user-initiated forums common and advantageous for writers (as well as everyday users). The act of creating a forum for the overt purpose of moving audience participation away from one's writing is a particularly salient move that has no print analogues, because print texts do not contain any audience text directly on the initial ("original") writing that all audience members, across time and geography, can read.

Writers I studied were not *necessarily* invested in monitoring the created forums. They were more invested in managing the participation that was *closer*, quite literally, to their own writing. Comments that could have a negative impact on a writer's digital *ethos* were something to be minimized. Since a digital *ethos* can be shaped in a matter of moments, vitriolic audience responses need to be placed away from a writer's text, even if the forums were adjacent to text via hyperlink.

Rationales for forum creation were heterogeneous, but the primary reason given was to generate the appearance of being open to comments. As several journalists told me, they wanted to "offload comments" to another site for one of three reasons: first, to give readers opportunities to vent; second, to deescalate vitriol; and third, simply to avoid the obligation to read the comments. Bloggers tended to ask readers to respond on their public Facebook page, with many reporting that comments were "nicer" and "better" when commenters had to be associated with an identity. Forum creation, in general, functioned to alleviate a need to respond to comments and cull through the vitriol.

With respect to the actual production of forums, participants created forums in two ways, each with a nuanced purpose that macromanaged their writerly identity. First, and most often, participants produced a forum associated with their personal brand, such as a publicly accessible Facebook page or a forum on a personal website (Grimes, Monroe, and Armstrong all did this). Second, but less frequently, if writers were part of a larger community, then they moved the comment section to a preexisting forum related to the community. These two strategies accompanied each other; if both were possible and writers decided forum creation was necessary, then writers engaged in both acts. While I say more about branding in the conclusion of this chapter, for now I note that forum creation helped writers manage participation to give the impression of actively managing response. With a dedicated forum, readers could imagine themselves being read by "the writer." In fact, nine writers told me they wanted to project the image that they were reading the comments, despite only skimming them haphazardly. Forum creation ultimately allowed writers to project an *ethos* of care for their readers, even if that *ethos* was simply a projection.

My participants explicitly recommended this strategy to burgeoning writers who *already* receive comments, because comments and other types of participation may hinder novices and those who are not embedded in the consistent, intense nature of digital update culture. Such a viewpoint is backed up by a statistical tendency for comments to be uncivil (Chen and Lu 2017; Coe, Kenski, and Rains 2014; Kenski, Coe, and Rains 2017; Rowe 2015a, 2015b). In other words, establishing forums is a solution to the empirical evidence of the debasing nature of comments, something writers trying to garner audiences readily encounter. The writers I studied already had participation, which means they had inculcated a necessity to respond.

Indirect Management: Monitoring, Curating, and Controlling the Conversation

I now turn to indirect management. In addition to indirect, these strategies can be defined as "midlevel." I use three basic terms—*monitoring*, *curating*, and *controlling*—to describe these indirect ways writers reported responding to audiences (table 4.1). These terms are meant to capture the overall effort, on the part of digital writers, to corral readers while not directly forcing them to participate in certain ways or, alternatively, pandering to them.

Participants used *growing* (redditors), *monitoring* (reviewers), *curating* (journalists), and *controlling* (across all groups) as the four main verbs to describe the activities listed in table 4.1. Participants paired the word *conversation*, as I mention earlier, with these verbs. They saw themselves growing, monitoring, curating, and controlling conversations among commenters. If participatory audiences are expected to respond in update culture, then it appears that initial writers see themselves as engaging in conversation and corralling those conversations, often to their own ends. Despite participants reporting a desire to "continue the conversation" through comments and other forums of exchange, they wanted to have a particular type of conversation with characteristics that suited their aims.

While attempting to inculcate a specific kind of exchange is not surprising, it's notable because it recognizes the limits of digital discourse

Table 4.1. Terms and the accompanying behaviors observed or reported

Term	Definition
Monitoring	Reading comments Deciding whether comments violate rules Checking notifications of a specific template Observing the progress of digital exchanges for "healthy conversations" Asking in the writer's (initial) text for comments
Growing/ Curating	Mediating conflicts between commenters Developing ad hoc procedures for situations not accounted for in rules or guidelines Posing questions and initiating or instigating exchanges Clarifying exchanges between commenters, including identifying comments that are out of date, answering questions, and notifying commenters of information already present Helping commenters navigate the layout of the template (unfolding nested conversations, for example) Quoting and paraphrasing commenters
Controlling	Removing comments and commenters Asking questions to reorient comment exchanges Identifying certain comments as ideal or not ideal Tagging certain commenters to ensure exchanges Moving comments to a different venue

as democratic potential. Namely, if writers already interact with their audiences, then they already have built an *ethos* of credibility and, to a limited extent, a brand. This *ethos* and brand, in turn, become prioritized over the desires of participatory audiences. In the context of this project's methodology—that is, interviewing and observing individual writers—the comments from their perspective are not simply about exchanging ideas. The comments serve a different end: to enhance and build a writer's brand and reach. Indirect management of audience participation thus serves to assist writers, not readers. Of course, sometimes writers cannot be subtle and nuanced—they must directly manage their readers, especially the trolls.

Direct Management: Fighting Back and Battling the Trolls

Up to this point, I've avoided focusing too extensively on vitriolic comments, primarily because I've tried to foreground what writers do with their comments. Due to this focus, trolling comments haven't received detailed attention for two reasons. First, the writers I studied tended to ignore or delete trolling comments and accounts (if possible). Every single writer mentioned ignoring trolls in some way. The most frequent answer to my query, "How do you deal with trolls or bad comments?" was simply ignoring or deleting them. Many writers also told me that receiving vitriolic comments at least means one is being read. The common refrain I heard could be paraphrased *if you have haters, at least you have an audience*. Second, and more in line with the focus of this chapter, participants discussed at length macromanagement and indirect management more often than they did their trolling comments.

It became apparent to me that *trolling* is a catch-all term that exists along a spectrum ranging from "being an asshole" (many redditors) or "demented" (Rosa Kennedy) to trying to get a response through playfulness. Others scholars who have studied trolling and aggressive online behavior, including in reddit (Massanari 2015, 2017), 4chan's /b/ board (Manivannan 2014; Sparby 2017), and flaming language in online courses (McKee 2002) have also demonstrated the flexibility of this term. On reddit, trolling tended to be more playful, although numerous redditors, including AndrewSmith1986 and Kijafa, told me about threats commenters made to them. Reviewers tended to encounter loyal customers who took offense to their reviews; in this sense, trolling on Amazon tended to be less about a reviewer's identity and more about a relationship to a commodity. Journalists tended to experience the most hurtful and personalized attacks, almost all of which were mentioned as being on Twitter. Bloggers tended to rebuke trolls the most, which I attribute to protecting their personal space (the blog).

Taking on trolls typically occurred after macromanagement and indirect management failed. Once these strategies failed, writers were left to research and then take action, typically through either (1) direct confrontation or (2) reporting. Direct management involves a sense of power and ability to take action that not all writers can exert, especially novice and marginalized writers. As many of my participants noted, new and marginalized writers are in positions that lack such agency.

Three exchanges help illustrate ways writers directly confronted trolls. Bretty, a highly ranked Amazon reviewer, offered an excellent description of direct confrontation. In what follows, Bretty lays out an approach that isn't generalizable to all writers I studied. However, when participants did confront trolls, they tended to mimic Bretty's approach. We had the following exchange:

GALLAGHER: Do you ever respond to comments about your reviews?

BRETTY: Yeah, usually.

GALLAGHER: How so? What's that like for you?

BRETTY: It's a good question. I've got a sense of humor and I do take the piss out of people. If somebody puts something particularly stupid, I will probably be quite sarcastic back. If someone puts on "A great review. Thank you very much." Then I'll usually say, "oh, thanks for the comment." If they have a view they put on, I'm quite happy to engage in a debate. If someone might say, "I just think you're completely wrong. You're an idiot," I'd be sarcastic on that one. I'd say, "No, I disagree with your view because I thought XY." I would have no problem having a minor debate in the comments about why they liked it or I didn't. I don't always think I'm right.

GALLAGHER: Do you ever have to deal with really bad comments? Or trolls? Could you tell me a little bit more about that phrase "take the piss out of them." I'm being academic here.

BRETTY: Take the piss out of them. Laugh at them.

Bretty here demonstrates a keen level (and embrace) of sarcasm that many participants mentioned. If writers chose not to ignore trolls (ignoring trolls is obviously the most common strategy reported in this entire book), then they draw on the power of tone to battle trolls. This tone is often sarcasm or irony.

Bretty's perspective was shared by many other writers, including Max Patrick Schlienger, who was known as the top-ten redditor RamsesThePigeon. Schlienger told me, "The best way to deal with trolls is to not deal with them at all. Ignoring them is perhaps the best first reaction. But I've found that they can also be great fodder for entertainment if you're willing to make yourself the butt of the joke." He went on to tell me, "There was a comment that was close to a euphemism. So I was able to feign ignorance and play along with what they were saying, misinterpret what they were saying." Schlienger then pointed me to this exchange, which appears in in figure 5.1. Although the troll deleted the comments (probably because the troll felt defeated), Schlienger's comments remain, along with the voting system that illustrates Schlienger "won" the battle with the troll due to upvotes. Of this exchange, Schlienger said,

> Of course, they responded back and they tried to clarify while still being vitriolic and I just kept playing dumb. And the thing is, one thing I think people forget, is when you're writing on a public forum like reddit, you're not just writing back and forth to the person who is trolling you or even engaging you in a positive conversation, you're writing for anyone that might come along. And so, if I cast myself as a character, and that character is okay with being the butt of a joke, then people [watching the comment exchange] tend to respond positively to it. Because they respond positively to the content, they respond positively to me. And that makes the aggressor, the troll, just seem like a troll.

Schlienger reiterates textual attention (chapter 4) but from an unsuccessful perspective. He explicitly discusses how responding, reading, and

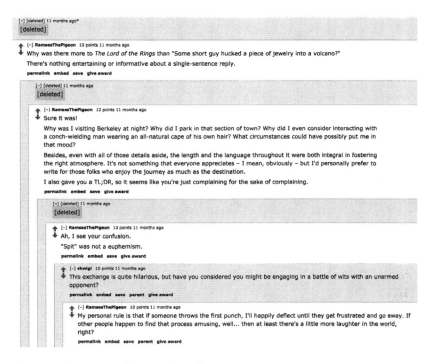

Figure 5.1. Comment exchange with a troll

monitoring comments involves other people outside the exchange between the troll and the initial writer.

Kijafa, a top-twenty-five redditor, had a similar take on contending with trolls. As he told me,

> It's hard to tell sometimes the difference between trolls and people [who] are genuinely angry people . . . people are genuinely angry in disagreeing with what you say vehemently but actually trying to engage you. What I find with trolls is the best way to, if you can do it, is play along where you just kind of throw jokes at them and uh just show that they're not getting to you. If you play along, and they realize that you realize they're messing with you and you are just having fun with them, they'll either get bored or, well, they'll usually get bored and do something else. Or the easiest way is to not engage them. . . . And sometimes the other commenters will address them for you.

When dealing with the kind of troll that is more playful, the objective became, for Schlienger and Kijafa, to beat the troll to the punch, thereby reducing the power of the troll.

Alternatively, trolls can be disregarded in hopes of larger community intervention. Dealing with trolls means considering how the wider communities and publics are reading that exchange, which other redditors, including Kijafa, Way_Fairer, DevasoHouse, and DiegoJones4, mentioned during interviews. In fact, I found that directly confronting trolls involved paying attention and considering how those outside the exchange will perceive that thread. The journalists I interviewed called this "broadcasting," which is when a writer retweets a vitriolic message on Twitter, often with a sarcastic comment, to show that she (and on Twitter, it's mostly "she") is following the potential harassment and claims agency.

Schlienger's and Kijafa's approaches offer us insight into a keen level of effort necessary to take on trolls even for those in positions of standing—Schlienger was consistently ranked as a top-ten redditor and Kijafa in the top twenty-five. While not all writers and users encounter trolls or want to take on trolls, developing a process for fighting trolls may be important for writers in an era of digital content production, something Schlienger's and Kijafa's accounts offer us. The recountings Schlienger and Kijafa offered attest to the level of time, patience, and persistence needed to combat trolls. They could not simply attack the troll; analysis of the troll's various comments and an attempt to combat types of commenting behavior were necessary. Of course, not all writers can or will go the lengths these participants did (and do) to counter the trolls. And this brings me to the second strategy, direct management.

Direct management involves appealing to a different authority, typically some corporate entity, and often necessitates detailing violation of rules and guidelines. This strategy often applies to writers who can't necessarily take on trolls as easily as Schlienger did or who lack the ability to confront the trolls, whether the writers are marginalized people or lack the access to confront their trolls. The reviewer Sheila Thomas recounted her efforts to take on trolls when I asked her about abusive comments.

> GALLAGHER: Do you ever have to deal with trolls or people who make rude or caustic comments?
>
> THOMAS: Yeah. I used to review products on a daily basis, and there were people who used to comment on my reviews. The same exact person commented like 20 times on 20 of my reviews, the same person, same comments, saying like, "Who knows if your reviews are true? You get the free products, you're probably just lying every time," whatever, and I'm like, "What is going on here?" I was so shocked. I'm like, "Excuse me?" First of all, that's not a nice thing to say. And second of all it's like, "Who are they to say that to me?" I don't want people to see that, because it's like I know what I am and I know that I'm being honest with my reviews. I don't want people to think that some

random person that's writing on my reviews, "Oh, are you really telling the truth? Are you lying? You get free stuff, of course you're going
to say everything is good." There was two times that I had to actually
call Amazon and I told them about it, and they were like, "Oh, we'll
look into it," whatever, and there was no issues. That person, all of
their comments were removed, so it was good.

GALLAGHER: That's helpful to know.

THOMAS: Yeah, no, but it was actually really hurtful when they wrote that.
I'm like, "What's going on here?" I don't want people to think that
I'm lying and stuff like that. I didn't even know that Amazon could
remove [comments]. I called [Amazon] and they're like, "Yeah, sure,
we'll look into it," and a few days later I got an email saying, "We're
really sorry. We really appreciate your reviews and everything. We
hope this never happens again. If it does, definitely call us and let
us know. We'll take care of this." I was like, "Wow, they'll take care of
that." I feel like I'm a part of a good community.

I quote this exchange at length because Thomas did not consider herself a top-level reviewer, despite her ranking at the time of our interview
(top one hundred). Thomas's self-perception helps offer context here:
she did not view herself as having the power to combat trolls, nor do
reviewers have the option to delete the responses to their reviews. While
she told me she was aware of Amazon's reviewing guidelines, she recalled these guidelines are generally meant for reviewers and wasn't sure
whether they applied to commenters. (As both she and I learned when
I helped her research it, they do.) Ultimately, she reached out to the
Amazon corporation and reported the abuse. The abuse was, fortunately
for Thomas, identified properly and subsequently deleted. Although
Thomas's situation may not happen for every user of social media, notably on Twitter or Facebook with respect to marginalized peoples, digital
writers may be at a distinct advantage when reporting abuse and vitriol.
Because digital writers are perceived as having text that they own, despite
corporations' terms of service frequently contradicting such a perspective, they may benefit from higher rates of report than users who are not
perceived as writers or producers of text.

In this section, I've drawn on the experiences of writers who directly
managed their writing and trolls. By offering these accounts, I aim to
illustrate that writers combat abusive audience participation in direct
ways that echo how speakers must counter bellicose listeners by taking
them on or appealing to a moderator. While all the management strategies I present up to this point fuse oral and written models of communication, direct management most closely resembles speakers contending
with listeners. The significance here is that writers who directly aim

to manage their audiences may need to shift their self-perceived roles from writer to speaker. The last and most specific management strategy, responsive management, however, takes us back to the idea of a writer-reader relationship.

Responsive Management: Ignoring, Deleting, Correcting, Updating

Responsive management, unlike macro, indirect, and direct textual management, is the most specific and common strategy writers reported. The four responsive-management techniques include ignoring, deleting, correcting, and updating. These strategies were common. Save for ignoring, responsive management thus offers a complementary counter-perspective to Laquintano's (2016) findings in *Mass Authorship and the Rise of Self-Publishing*. He observes,

> The authors [in this study] experimented freely with pricing and para-texts, but they did not make revisions to stories to increase sales. A number of new media practitioners have experimented with "versioning," or updating and modifying a text in response to different factors, as a form of digital cultural production. . . . This practice was almost entirely absent from the ways authors experimented with texts. Changing a text typically happened only if it had been entirely unread, in which case the author had the freedom to "unpublish" it in order to revise or rework the story. In isolated cases, authors uploaded new versions of their texts to correct typographical errors, but this was mostly unnecessary, since they had employed professional editors. (105)

While Laquintano notes that most of novelists and ebook writers (poker manuals) in his study do not engage in versioning or unpublishing, the writers I studied engaged in versioning. They did so not to increase profits or book sales; neither is applicable to my participants. Rather, these writers paid attention to comments and their audiences, thereby taking a different approach to the mutability of their texts. Texts in these IPI environments were, and are, expected to change. This expectation of change—even if it is not fully realized—creates an acceptability of versioning. Deleting, correcting, and updating fall directly into the category of versioning. In order for these to take place, the most common strategy in this entire study is used: ignoring comments.

Every writer I talked with, quite expectedly, discussed the art of ignoring comments. By "art," I mean how participants did not *avoid* comments. All participants *read* comments, as noted in previous chapters. In keeping with textual attention, participants read some comments more carefully than others. With respect to this chapter and textual management, participants processed comments in some form or another and then decided not to respond. All of them told me that not responding to comments was a learned experience. They had not adjusted to this type of response, were not formally trained for it, and did not believe responding was a primary tactic. Because it reflects participants' emic perspectives, I foreground ignoring as a management strategy. The practice of reading and then ignoring certain comments functions as a counterpart to textual attention. If textual attention served to keep readers on topic and served the purpose of civic engagement, then ignoring was a way to discourage off-topic commenting and defuse possible trolling. My participants had three broad categories of comments they ignored: overly positive, not helpful, and insincere. These categories are based on their perceptions.

First, participants ignored the "thanking" comments or "effusive praise." While positive comments were "nice" and participants enjoyed receiving them, positive comments that did not extend an exchange lacked purpose from the perspective of my participants. Matt Grimes articulated this emblematic experience well. He told me, "Only two [types of comments] exist for the most part: [either] agreeable, congratulations, and warmth or 'you're an idiot.' Not much of an in-between."

Second, participants ignored comments they perceived as not helpful. Grimes, for instance, told me he ignored comments that "pontificated without questions, which are most comments." Christy McKenzie described this as "comment-splaining," which is a riff on mansplaining. Every participant, independently of each other, told me most comments are for other commenters, an approach that cuts across all platforms. Participants believed commenters write for other commenters or for themselves. Lola Upton, a well-known journalist, told me that although comments are often authentic, regardless of whether they're good or bad, most commenters are "after attention." Rosa Kennedy, another journalist, echoed this sentiment by telling me some commenters just "want a microphone."

Third, participants ignored "insincere comments" or comments that did not seem genuine to the participant. Amazon reviewers embodied this strategy most often because they often received questions about their reviews. They noted that repeated similar questions were often insincere. Questions about the reviewer's identity and intentions were also seen as insincere. While reviewers did not use the term, they often described suffering ad hominem attacks.

Perception of a comment's tone was key for ignoring comments. Many commenters asked questions, but participants needed to decide which questions were real statements, sarcastic questions, or rhetorical questions. With respect to commenters who pose false or insincere questions, Kennedy labeled this type of commenter a "concern troll." I inquired about this term and was told, "[Concern trolls] act as though they're really worried but really trying to plant doubts." She elaborated on concern trolls as a category of commenter: "I had to figure out who was an anarchist and who was a real commenter and who was a concern troll." Concern trolls, often men but not always, try to insert themselves into a conversation for the opportunity to explain, despite the expertise of female journalists—that is, to mansplain to these women writers.

Once participants ignored certain comments, they were thereby able to identify which comments generally deserved some attention, that is, textual attention. On some occasions, these comments led writers to make changes to their initial text, including deleting, correcting, or updating the initial text. While these responsive revisions did not occur with every text or comment, they did occur often enough for participants to recall specific moments of change. Many recalled feeling burned out from the need to make such changes. Laquintano (2016) found this sentiment as well.

> When the authors marketed their ebooks, they often promised revisions, and they championed the flexibility of the ebook as a virtue. However, the feedback that propelled these revisions—its volume, ubiquity, and speed—often threatened to exhaust the resources of the author and his desire to continually revise the text. . . . Revisions often stalled, in some cases because an author's developing skill eventually outstripped his ability or desire to update the ebook. (177)

Laquintano notes the affective nature of versioning and updating, which my findings confirm. The writers I studied, however, tended not to make wide-scale changes as a result of what commenters said, as was the case with Laquintano's participants, who were writing books.

One of the reviewers I interviewed provided insight into the distinction between book writers and the everyday writers I interviewed.

GALLAGHER: You mentioned updating your reviews. Can you tell me a bit more about that, like how often?

AR2: Yeah, usually, to be honest, I'm not updating my reviews if you are speaking about books. If we are speaking about, for example, the electronics or things like that, then I will try to give products some time because you know, when you start using, most of the products would seem, first day, or 2, or 3, or a week, would seem cool and interesting, especially if this is something which you have not used previously. After some time, when you spend some more time, then probably you will observe some things which could be better, some

> things which could be improved. In that case I'm updating. I'm really
> trying to be as much honest as possible.

This top-rated reviewer, who chose to remain anonymous, offers some
clarity for why Amazon reviewers may update their reviews: the reviewed
products age (poorly or well).

Crucial to this updating is that the writers I studied weren't producing a novel-based story or ebook but everyday writing. They were writing,
but the environments in which they wrote—IPI contexts—inculcated a
quick, rapid type of writing. Participants recalled making smaller, more
incremental changes to their writing, which is why I use *deleting, correcting,
and updating* rather than the term *revision*. Participants mentioned deleting and correcting in response to comments, as well as the act of issuing
a "correction" or "update"; participants used relevant comments to help
them edit. If a comment pointed out a spelling error, factual error, or
usage error, then participants changed their texts to account for the comment. This kind of editing was very common with journalists and redditors, and bloggers reported doing it to some extent. While this strategy is
similar to what print writers encounter, it is different due to *who* offers the
editorial feedback. Participatory audiences become the source of editorial
feedback, although only for objective concerns with writing, such as gram-
matical errors or factual inaccuracies, as described by all participants.

Correcting and updating was occurred frequently, likely due to the
pressure of writing quickly in IPI environments. The digital journalists
spoke most explicitly about this, although redditors often mentioned
editing their work in response to a commenter. Lola Upton said she
"dives into comments when something is factually inaccurate or the
reader misconstrued what [she] wrote." Upton told me that "commenters are so focused on their reaction to a small word or phrase" they
do not finish reading. The only time Rosa Kennedy edited her work in
response to a comment was "to make notations about updates." Kennedy
told me she left these comments up out of respect to the commenter.
Skinner updated her work to issue a clarification statement based on
comments or to correct "a minor typo." She was "not required to dis-
close" that she corrected minor typos. Grimes echoed Kennedy's and
Skinner's perspectives in that he didn't change his work in any major
way. When I asked him about any pieces he'd edited or changed based
on comments, he said, "Not unless someone has pointed out an error,
spelling, or something like that." He mentioned he "would update the
original post" to indicate a change was made. While he wouldn't change
his articles in any significant way, he did state, "I'll add information but

won't change." Tracy Monroe, the *Forbes* journalist, made updates in terms of spelling and information "objective in nature." Overall, the frequency of correcting and updating, based on comments, provides evidence that participatory audiences exert influence on the way writers revisit and revise their texts, however minor that role may be.

In this sense, the texts are moments of exchange—change occurs not only around the texts but also in the texts *themselves*. Texts in IPI environments are literally encounters between writer and the reader-as-writer. In turn, the initial writer becomes a reader. To redescribe it a bit, the writer and audiences are engaged in a back and forth, an exchange that replicates orality in a ghostly echo. Responsive management, although specific, provides the most compelling evidence for viewing digital writing, in IPI environments, as talking in and through text.

ASPIRATIONAL BRANDING

The trajectory of this chapter moves from general to specific management techniques, with responsive management being what I see as the narrowest scope of textual management. As I conclude this chapter, an important feature hovering in the background of textual management is that as writers engage in a continuous process of call and response with their readers—that is, engage in textual attention—writers are also engaging in other activities not always visible in the texts themselves. These processes occur explicitly sometimes, although more often they occur implicitly. These processes also occur both synchronously and asynchronously. Writers fielded questions, responses, and feedback in ways that echo a speaker managing their audience, with the crucial caveat that digital writers manage multiple forums, social media accounts, and numerous texts, old and new.

From this perspective, textual management helps frame digital writers as engaging in what I call *aspirational branding*. *Aspirational branding* is my term for the professional activities of writers who lack the institutional or organizational apparatus for generating publicity, media, and advertising. Aspirational branding adds some texture and detail to my argument that writers turn to oral activities during the afterlife of their digital texts.

To extend my overall argument at the conclusion of these data chapters, I contend that the afterlife of digital writing requires seeing orality and written modes of communication as intimately related, due the precarious nature of digital labor. To be read and to be read *widely*, a clear goal of digital writers, means to become one's own social media manager, publicist, advertiser, circulator, editor, acquisitions editor, content moderator, and production assistant. All these positions are overlaid on each other, emergent and iterative.

Communication scholar and media researcher Brooke Duffy has described a similar phenomenon[1] in *(Not) Getting Paid to Do What You Love: Gender, Social Media, and Aspirational Work* (2017). In an exemplary study of social media influencers, such as fashion bloggers, vloggers, and instagrammers, Duffy notes the "telling disparity between the upper echelons of social media fame and the lower cadres of content producers" (188). Those influencers at the bottom and even in the middle are caught in an aspirational *ethos* (12–44). Duffy uses the term *aspirational* to describe *ethos*, consumption, and labor in order to "highlight the incentive future reward for present-day productive activities" (7). As is true for other stratified vocations, we only hear about the most successful of social media influencers or, in the context of my book, writers. The difficult, exhausting, time-consuming labor is often edited away, leaving only the beautiful decorum of Instagram or the rage of Twitter from the most successful of these influencers and writers. The lesser-known writers, like the ones in this book, are left to aspire toward these incommensurate, manicured examples.

Brooke Duffy's (2017) framework helps encapsulate, identify, and crystallize the affective labor present in aspirational branding. Writers need to build personas, as other researchers have found (Ledbetter 2014). Writers cultivate and rework their own image and *ethos*, repeatedly. Sometimes, due to their digital presences, these personas even hurt participants' chances of landing other jobs. Two of my more well-known participants, Heather Armstrong and Penelope Trunk, blogged extensively about these experiences, sometimes to their own detriment. Many of the redditors were only willing to be interviewed when I told them they could use their screennames rather than their real names. Writers in this book provided services and entertainment to their audiences, in the form of textual attention (chapter 4) and the managing practices in this chapter. My participants, like those in Duffy's study, were "compelled to invest their energy and human capital in building their affective networks. From engaging with followers and reciprocating feedback to formal networking and informal schmoozing, relationship-building activities were articulated as work" (79).

While my participants were not engaged in the extensive diversity of social media platforms Brooke Duffy's (2017) informants were, due in part to their positions as writers, they did engage parallel forms of *work*. The bloggers I studied most closely synced up with the kind of affective networking Duffy describes. But other participants, even those who did not yearn to be paid for their writing, echoed a sentiment related to affective networks. The Amazon reviewers were engaged in customer service not only by writing reviews but also by answering questions on their reviews. Many of them voiced their frustration with Amazon's policies because they knew the monetary value of the service they provided wage free. To add a more complicated layer of irony, reviews left on Amazon's site are technically considered the property of Amazon and not of those who write the reviews. The journalists discussed not having the protection of an editorial board or the infrastructure to provide them with a stable wage. The redditors, while not engaged deeply with monetary incentives, were highly engaged with relationship building in an effort to expand the reach of their reddit accounts; they wanted to accrue karma and know that they were being read widely. Even though the redditors were the least interested in seeing their writing as labor, they valued metrics and wanted to "start some big shit" (StickleyMan). For these reasons, aspirational branding rather than aspirational labor seems apropos of what everyday digital writers seem to be doing. It's work, and they recognize this fact; many redditors in my study called karma-whoring "grinding." Reviewers often remarked about the exhaustion of trying to write numerous reviews.

But what digital writers are doing is often hidden in today's social media climate. Managing audiences is not the extra effort to be a successful writer. Managing audiences is *integral* to twenty-first-century writing. Digital writers manage their audiences in an effort to develop a better writerly brand because they aren't afforded the kinds of protections, services, and support previous generations of writers had (or are purported to have had). Aspirational branding thus integrates the work of managing into digital writing to avoid seeing digital writing, as well as writing more generally, as something devoid of labor. Digital writing is neither quick nor easy. Digital writing is a grinding, time-consuming activity. And managing an audience is a hard, affective, laborious endeavor.

6

ETHICS IN UPDATE CULTURE

If the afterlife of digital writing involves timing, attention, and management, then what are the ethical implications of looking at these strategies? Structurally, this chapter thus wrestles with two questions. First, what are the negative effects and costs of update culture? The costs of update culture provide us with insight into the way the strategies presented, that is, timing, attention, and management, can be viewed as having ethical implications in two ways: mitigating being "always on" and reducing feelings of economic exploitation. Second, how are we to determine what is ethical? Here, I turn to virtue ethics as a useful ethical paradigm. Rather than rules or outcomes, habits or virtues might function to help guide our normative decision-making processes. I emphasize that searching for writers and their habits helps provide us with *contingent yet normative ethical frameworks*. In doing so, I reformulate the strategies of textual timing, attention, and management into corresponding ethical counterparts of consistency, persistence, and patience. After laying out these ethical habits as virtues, I discuss them as *digital communication virtues* that enable effective writing in update culture.

THE COST OF UPDATE CULTURE

Before I turn directly to ethics, I contextualize the intense world of update culture, an intensity many readers of *Update Culture and the Afterlife of Digital Writing* are aware of. I want to dispel overly positive interpretations of participatory audiences and update culture generally. Update culture has taken a toll on my participants, some more than others. Three Amazon reviewers reported having trouble with their marriages due to the amount of time they spent writing reviews. In my follow-up interviews, these three reviewers reported reducing the amount of time they spent reviewing to spend more time with their spouses and children. Alternatively, the journalist Tracy Monroe wrote anywhere between nine at night and three in the morning, the only time she could find due to taking care of her children and other jobs that

DOI: 10.7330/9781607329749.c006

paid her a living wage. Redditors described feeling as if they sometimes were pandering to the "hivemind." Other redditors told me that once they accrued their karma, they became much less interested in karma. Instead, they were more interested in having a genuine and sincere exchange. Update culture, because of the companies that produce coercive and sleek templates, ultimately can have negative effects upon digital writers.

These effects coalesce around the feeling of economic exploitation, a theme that emerged as I conducted follow-up interviews. All writers except the redditors reported some feeling of economic exploitation. Even some of the redditors, though, felt a touch of economic exploitation if they were community (subreddit) moderators; reddit was making money from the labor of their content moderation. This resentment makes sense: these writers were content producers and personally generated attention around that content—yet they saw very little return economically. Two reviewers, Jason Rob and Mike W, crystallized this feeling of exploitation.

Jason Rob became disillusioned with reviewing because Amazon changed the rules of reviewing, a change that inadvertently created a subculture of unethical reviewing. Chee Chew, writing on *The Amazon Blog*, reported on October 3, 2016, that Amazon had eliminated incentivized reviews, meaning reviewers would be required to purchase the product or receive it from the official Vine program I discuss in chapter 3. As Rob told me, this policy made reviews even more unreliable and problematic. He said during our follow-up interview,

> But in spite of that new rule, sellers are still asking people to buy a product and then they will reimburse you by PayPal, so therefore they circumvent the policy and they still get a verified review, which is really what they want, a verified purchase review. Makes it look legitimate, but in fact, it's no more legitimate than if they had just given you the product for free, and you had to put a disclaimer. So, actually by creating that "no incentivized reviews" policy, Amazon has created a huge subculture of even more dishonest reviews, because now there's no way to track it at all.

He then told me that he was fed up with Amazon and its exploitation.

> So, whereas I was highly motivated to review lots of things, now I could care less, and my reviews are much shorter. I still will spend time reviewing something that I'm truly interested in. But as far as anything else, I just don't even put forth the effort. And why should I, because it's finally dawned on me that the only one benefiting here is Amazon.
>
> And I've developed such a distaste for Amazon now, I even go out of my way not to buy stuff from Amazon for various reasons. Not the least of which is they're frequently not the lowest price anymore. I can go to

walmart.com and get things a lot cheaper, sometimes more than 50% cheaper in some cases.

Rob's disillusionment led him to creating YouTube videos, even managing to get a free gym membership through savvy negotiating. Though Rob continued to review here and there, his dissatisfaction with the reviewing process, and as a customer, magnified his feelings of economic exploitation.

If Rob was disillusioned, then Mike W was downright angry at the policy change and turned to only reviewing books. Mike W noted, like Rob, that Amazon seemed to eliminate older reviews that had accumulated numerous "helpful votes." He reflected on this dissatisfaction.

> So essentially, they rendered me invisible and there's some good reasons for it because there were a lot of crappy reviewers that were just shills. But for someone like me who really put a lot of time into it and I sold, I can't prove it, but I know I made them thousands and thousands and thousands of dollars just on the Fire TV Stick and the HTC Six tablet. I would love to know what I made and I wish there was a way to quantify it, but it just feels like a lot of disrespect and so I've essentially stopped contributing there.

In fact, Mike W was bothered so much by this review disappearing that after our second interview, he wrote Amazon and managed to have the highly ranked Fire TV Stick review reinstated. Nevertheless, Mike W's reflection here crystallizes the anger and annoyance at having one's writing and other content subject to the whims of a global company.

Rob and Mike W exhibited emblematic feelings of exploitation by massive, global corporations that provide free and easy-to-use templates with the goal of exploiting users for free labor. These examples, I hope, demonstrate that update culture creates the potential for negative effects embedded in attention or information. And writers must cope with these effects, something that textual timing and textual management facilitate.

TIMING, ATTENTION, AND MANAGEMENT AS COPING MECHANISMS

In my estimation as an observer, textual timing and textual management function—in addition to being two strategies of digital writing's afterlife—as ethical coping mechanisms for the situations I describe above, perhaps even in response to the time-intensive and emotionally intensive strategy of textual attention. Timing certainly helped writers develop ways to "turn off" or "unplug," two terms that came up repeatedly in interviews, especially with reviewers, bloggers, and journalists.

Whether writers fused *kairos* and *chronos* or considered the interface and algorithm, some sense of a qualitative-quantitative approach to time helped writers avoid being "always on." Management is quite literally a coping strategy, most often to deal with trolls while not turning off the engaged readers.

In addition to helping writers unplug, all three strategies helped writers consolidate power to themselves as they engaged in *aspirational branding* (see chapter 5). The platforms they used, platforms that provided them templates with which to write, placed a burden upon these writers that historically has not been faced by individual writers. I see timing, attention, and management as ethical responses when coping with the negative aspects of an unpaid information economy. In such an economy, writers are expected to write for little to no compensation and must balance this uncompensated labor with their home lives, such as being careful not to ignore their families or writing into the wee hours of the morning. Writers' attention is pulled in numerous directions by various, often competing, audiences, including machine audiences, such as algorithms and bots.

For this reason, I fault none of the writers I studied for trying to get clicks or pandering. Writing online is a brutal affair—for my participants as well as other everyday writers, including ourselves and students. It is associated with unpaid writing and content production, such as video production. Many of the writers I interviewed also had YouTube channels they were hoping to monetize. This writing and content production requires strange and uneven hours that can cause familial strife. I would not judge my participants for giving out good reviews for free products or shilling products on their blog posts or writing clickbait headlines or dropping native advertising into their posts.

But I found that many of the writers I studied were fiercely ethical. They had internal standards—most likely because it was *their* brand at stake and not a company's or a platform's. The reviewers, for instance, often expressed annoyance that novitiate reviewers did not pay attention to the community guidelines (see my discussion of the concept of helpfulness in chapter 3). They wanted people to write not humorous or entertaining reviews but instead helpful reviews, which could in turn would accrue helpful votes. While I largely attribute this effort to the reviewers' privileged positions as top-tier reviewers, the reviewers were concerned with *good reviewing* in general. They considered themselves writers and responsible shoppers. In other words, the reviewers liked to read reviews themselves and used reviews to help them buy products; all the reviewers I interviewed reported reading reviews to determine which products to buy. They were not only part of the reviewing community but also had individual motivation for their reviews to *be written well.*

The journalists, bloggers, and redditors adopted similar roles of ethical commitment to a broader community (their participatory audiences) while retaining commitment to their individual voices and viewpoints. Such a tension for these writers often did not pose too much of a problem because they were not paid and thus did not need to pander to the crowds or undercut their personal viewpoints.

Before I continue on to ethics explicitly, I note that not all my participants had such agency. These were the parenting bloggers Heather Armstrong and Penelope Trunk, notably because they had successfully monetized their brands. Both reported to me that they rarely felt they had the time to write because their aspirational branding had turned to paid branding. The associated burdens that come with paid branding place pressures on writer-sponsorship relationships.

In particular, Heather Armstrong, one of the few participants who managed to get paid for some of her writing, left the blogosphere because sponsored posts put too much pressure on both her content and family. In an interview with the *Guardian*, Armstrong said, "What happened over the last couple of years is the brands have been given a lot more say and a lot more control than they did when I was starting out" (Dean, September 15, 2015). Armstrong went on to comment, "Writing stories around [products] is torturous. You're basically writing copy for a brand, is what you're doing." This type of pandering and coercion spilled into Armstrong's interactions with her readers; in fact, she told me during an interview that, because her blog had "developed into a community," she had to address this issue with her readers. She told me, with respect to paid or sponsored posts, "I needed to talk [in a blog post] about the way my writing works. That I need to get paid for this." I bring up Armstrong's case because I believe once those engaged in aspirational branding are paid, ethics becomes murky. While this issue is largely outside the scope of this book, more research should be conducted to distinguish the writing strategies of those who are paid for their digital writing from the writing strategies of those who are not.

THE VIRTUES OF DIGITAL WRITING'S AFTERLIFE

I now address ethics directly through the claim that my participants demonstrated ethical habits for contending with update culture. Because digital writing and digital rhetoric are contingent, they disrupt *normative* ways of producing texts and interacting in such environments. Ways we *should* write or *ought* to act, which are normative claims, are seemingly lost because contexts change and are quickly forgotten. The contingent nature of digital writing raises ethical aspects, such as pandering to algorithms, related to the practices and strategies I document in this book. Notably, what kinds of digital virtues observed in these participants are worthy of emulation?

As I use the term, *virtues* are based on the ethical framework of virtue ethics. Rather than offering rules (deontology) or outcomes (consequentialism), virtue ethics offers dispositional characteristics or virtues as its ethical framework. In classical Aristotelian ethics, this framework emphasizes habits or virtues that will lead to *eudaimonia*. Certain kinds of people, namely, exemplars, illustrate these qualities. Exemplars are people who take action, make choices, and have a sense of proper motivation with respect to a particular disposition. The advantage of this paradigm is its inordinate flexibility; that is, people exhibit a diversity of virtues while offering a normative way of acting. In this sense, it is counterintuitively a contingent normative framework. Virtue ethics is thusly concerned with the following sorts of questions: "What kind of person do I want to be? How should I live my life? What does it mean to be a good person?" (J. Duffy 2017, 230). Rather than atomistic behaviors, virtues ethics frames character traits as worthy of emulation.

A *normative, contingent ethical framework* in the afterlife of digital writing would thus need to account for specific situations and be flexible enough to be mutable from context to context, flexibility virtue ethics makes possible. Important here is that exemplars are not static or worthy of emulation monolithically. Exemplars may change their behaviors based on a deep understanding of context and audience—another reason virtue ethics holds promise for rhetoricians. Exemplars are not generalizable ethical agents; they are ethical with respect to a particular virtue. For instance, a brave exemplar might not be a temperate exemplar or vice versa. Exemplars are human and may make mistakes from time to time (like all of us). A virtue-ethics framework, as Shannon Vallor (2010) puts it, is "flexible enough to accommodate itself to the changing particulars of our technological situation, yet broad enough to allow us to draw conclusions that are of general interest and normative significance" (158). Virtue ethics, as a paradigm, allows us to make normative, contingent decisions based not on rules or outcomes but on *habits and dispositions* (J. Duffy 2014, 2017; Holmes and Colton 2018). That is, the sources of our normative contingent framework are people, an idea other ethicists have forwarded (Korsgaard 1996).

Virtue ethics provides a useful frame for digital writing and rhetoric because it frames the habits of writers, not outcomes or rules, as guides for ethical engagement in the (digital) world. An epistemology of change, like the one established throughout this book, asks us to move beyond specific platforms, codes, or algorithms and toward the people on those platforms—identifying habits along the way. And to be controversial, machines are not ethical so long as the word *ethics* implies a framework for human behavior. Algorithms are not ethical any more than a parabolic equation is ethical. But people are—algorithm programmers are certainly ethical (or not). Hence, I have focused on a case-study methodology and highlighted the people behind the writing we so frequently encounter on the internet.

So, you may ask yourself, are the participants in this book exemplars? Are they ethical? Before I answer, it's important to remember that our ethical habits and dispositions can take a "knock," according to virtue ethicist Rosalind Hursthouse (1993, 103). Put another way, ethical people, even exemplars, are not *always* ethical. We make mistakes and have our lapses. A particular virtue or habit, along with the relative reliability of that virtue or habit, is what makes one an exemplar. For instance, one can be courageous (a virtue) but not necessarily patient (another virtue). Likewise, what courage looks like depends on a host of factors embedded within a community (*polis* according to the ancient Greeks). Exemplars therefore embody a characteristic worth modeling within a community that values the embodiment of that characteristic.

My answer, then, is that the participants in this book demonstrated ethical habits, even if their content sometimes was not ethical. They engaged in digital virtues worthy of emulation. Specifically, the strategies of textual timing, attention, and management corresponded to the habits of consistency, persistence, and patience with respect to content production. These digital writing dispositions, habits, or virtues are ethical. To be clear, the content of participants who were exemplars was not necessarily worthy of emulation across all contexts and purposes (and I believe they would not frame themselves as worthy of emulation generally). However, these habits of consistency, persistence, and patience are useful for achieving the goals of being read as well as for knowing what to do as a writer *after* delivery and *during* circulation. These habits are powerful for helping a writer become widely read and do so in sustainable ways that still offer respect to and for participatory audiences.

Crucially, the habits of consistency, persistence, and patience are mundane habits easy to know and crucial to digital writing but difficult to enact. As mundane, and possibly overlooked, habits, I refocus

Holmes's argument in *The Rhetoric of Videogames as Embodied Practice: Procedural Habits* (2017). Holmes writes, "Rhetoric and composition studies continues to have difficulty in addressing the presence of mundane habit-shaping design elements or genres that often function rhetorically at levels of nonconscious behavior reinforcement" (254). While Holmes's argument is couched in the mundane and overlooked affordances of videogames, his broader argument is for attending to the mundane facets of digital writing and rhetoric rather than the more notable, memorable, or distinctive moments of persuasion. Consistency, persistence, and patience are three such habits that echo such ordinariness and tedium but focus on writers and not videogame users. Moreover, these are the emic habits and language of my participants. Thus, rather than scaffolding with theory, I have scaffolded ethics with the habits of and evidence from my participants, thereby building an empirical ethical framework contingent enough to function across platforms but still be based on the habits of digital writers. These habits still have utility for individual writers but are adaptable to various types of situations and contexts on the internet.

CONSISTENCY

Consistency is the habit participants not only demonstrated in their writing but also advocated in their explicit advice to aspirational reviewers, redditors, bloggers, or journalists. They advised novices to write consistently. By consistency, I mean participants advised writing with regularity at specific times of day or on specific days of the week. Their ideal type of writing occurred with stability and constancy. For them, writing with predetermined deadlines on a consistent basis was better than writing longer pieces, ones audiences might simply skim, published at random increments. Journalists, for instance, advised students to write so content would be published or released on expected days, such as Mondays and Thursdays. Reviewers advised establishing particular times of the day to review and focusing solely on writing during these times. Redditors told me that novice redditors should log onto the site consistently, observing interactions carefully. Bloggers told me that publishing shorter pieces more often was better than publishing longer content inconsistently. Broadly, it seemed to be better to have no website or web presence at all than one that was inconsistent.

While consistency is useful for all three strategies I present in this book—and I personally believe it is a critically important habit for writing even outside IPI environments—consistency speaks most directly to textual timing. To time one's texts in update culture, via *kairos-chronos* fusion, interface time, or algorithmic time, requires consistency. In fact, many participants said it was important to "stay on top" (a phrase used independently by participants during interviews) of various audience responses. They recounted stories of monitoring news cycles and various comment threads. They also told me anecdotes about needing to establish routines or practices that enabled them to become successful at their respective endeavors. In other words, effective digital timing requires the habit of consistency.

PERSISTENCE

In terms of textual attention, participants advocated persistence, or the action of repeating a task. They understood they would need to repeat many tasks, including acknowledging other comments, something I saw frequently when writers engaged in the various practices of textual attention. Redditors read through their comments, looking for commenters who were genuinely engaged, even if the commenters were not simply parroting back similar points of view. Journalists expressed a sincere desire to continue the conversation, which might be due to their commitment to democratic exchange. Continuing conversations required them to engage in message exchanges they had had before. Bloggers loved comments, even if, as Kelly Salasin described, the comments "can be a bit repetitive" or, in her typical understated demeanor, "not nice." Penelope Trunk told me commenters couldn't "throw anything at" her that she "hadn't seen before." Reviewers dealt with receiving or buying products they'd used many times before. Many of them remarked about the repetition of reviewing low-quality kitchen gadgets and how they owned multiple travel battery packs and salad spinners. The reviewers also could talk at length about the types of comments they received and how they often had links bookmarked to various instructions, demonstrating a savvy persistence for engaging textual attention. Redditors wanted to instigate large conversations, even if that meant dealing with numerous repetitive responses from users who did not see initial replies.

Participants ultimately understood that part of their role as digital writers was repeating claims and persisting through that repetition. Comments and other types of participatory response can scale up quickly in IPI environments. As a result, participants found themselves effective identifiers of patterns. Through a sea of comments, many of which they'd experienced before, participants learned the value of persistence.

PATIENCE

Patience, though recommended implicitly by participants, was the habit that came up least explicitly. Patience might be considered a deliberateness or an ability to accept or tolerate. In this case, that toleration involved comments from a broad range of readers, some of whom could be harassing or violent. Patience was more something participants seemed to embody rather than mention during our interviews.

To this end, patience corresponds to all strategies but most strongly to textual management. To manage participatory audiences, whether recalcitrant trolls or positive readers, requires patience, something I observed in terms of both texts and tone. I noticed participants developed a "thick skin," a phrase used across the various groups of writers in this project. Participants advised having a "thick skin," especially during the early phases of their writerly activities. The women I interviewed, so often the target of harassment, mentioned tolerating a certain level of agonism so long as it did not rise to the level of harassment or explicit vitriol.

In terms of patience, journalists advised tolerating snarky comments if those comments were genuinely engaged, such as asking a real question even if it was couched in cantankerous language. Redditors advised novice redditors to learn the language and patterns of particular subreddits so novices could more easily identify which language to tolerate and which language was out of the norm for a particular community. Bloggers found themselves resisting the urge to delete comments that simply disagreed with them but were not threatening. Reviewers negotiated with various forms of disagreement over what constituted a five-, four-, three-, two-, or one-star review. Reviewers also tolerated personal opinions about reviews of books, television shows, and other types of entertainment. A habit of patience helped participants manage the *scale* of participatory response. The frequency and rapidity of response in digital environments are not typically encountered in print writing. Thus, for digital writers, managing that response is crucial, as I argue in chapter 5.

CODA: DIGITAL COMMUNICATION VIRTUES

Together, consistency, persistence, and patience form what I call *digital communication virtues*. Digital communication virtues are part of a broader category of virtue ethics, which has received periodic attention in writing studies, including more recent work about pedagogy (J. Duffy 2014, 2017, 2018), technology and social media (Holmes and Colton

2018), and moral character in the teaching of writing (Spigelman 2001). Virtue ethics is relevant here because the framework helps writing studies researchers and theorists shift normative ethics away from rules or outcomes and toward dispositions.

Digital communication virtues are communication practices digital writers use to contend with various types of information communication technologies (ICTs). Vallor (2016) discusses what might be labeled *communication virtues* in the context of ICTs. She writes, "The new communication habits enabled and fostered by ICTs are shaping how we define the truth, when and how often we tell it, when we expect to be told it, where and in whom we expect to find it, how we package it, how we verify it, and what we do with it and are willing to have done with it" (121). As I see it, consistency, persistence, and patience are communication virtues for contending with the way ICTs shape our discourse, specifically IPI templates and the environments they produce. These virtues function as ethical ways to contend with (and resist) the emerging habits of social media platforms equipped with such templates and their affordances. Such a view is in line with Vallor's insistence that we need digital sources of normativity: "As traditional norms, standards, and habits of appropriate disclosure crack under the weight of radical changes in information and communication practices, it is essential that we consider what norms, standards, and habits will replace them" (122). Consistency, persistence, and patience are just such norms and habits writers need to develop so they can deal with what happens after they deliver a text to the internet, share and circulate content on social media, and monitor their participatory audiences who consume that content. In short, these virtues help contend with and attend to the afterlife of digital writing and rhetoric. While I do not argue that these virtues are standards, they are also habits that can help guide writers to develop standards on a contingent basis because these habits provide a type of normativity for how to write and produce content. And these sources of normativity are the habits developed by writers who have been successful within their respective communities.

These digital communication virtues are thus useful ways for grappling with the afterlife of digital writing and rhetoric. For instance, undergirding the habit of consistency is an assumption that writers will produce multiple texts and need to engage in ongoing content production. Undergirding persistence is an implicit need for ongoing iteration that does not take long breaks. Writing yields texts, but those texts require that writers revisit and revise them even after the texts have been delivered or published. Similarly, undergirding patience is repeated engagement with a text. Undergirding all three is the idea that a text may be finished but digital writing is not finished. Writers do not necessarily let their writing speak for itself, which is a clear distinction from, for instance, literary fiction or academic publication. The writer matters, and a digital writer typically gets to clarify *intention*. These foundational shifts ask us to rethink our pedagogical and epistemological approaches to digital writing and rhetoric, issues to which I now turn.

7

LEARNING AND PEDAGOGY IN UPDATE CULTURE

What kinds of learning frameworks can we take away from the strategies of timing, attention, and management? The strategies presented in this book are useful for those writers who have audiences, as well as for those who do *not* have audience participation. That is, I believe these strategies are useful beyond writing that already has a digital presence and receives audience comments. In this chapter, I focus on how these strategies are useful to novice writers. To make my argument, I discuss the concept of inadvertent attention through the case study of Amanda Gailey (real name). Second, I narrow my focus to address pedagogical strategies aimed at engaging digital writing and rhetoric. With respect to teaching and pedagogy, these strategies help us rethink and reconceptualize how to "consider your audience" in a networked digital world.

INADVERTENT ATTENTION AND THE CASE OF AMANDA GAILEY

While timing, attention, and management are useful for digital writers with interactive audiences, they are also useful for those who write online and share their work on various social media platforms but who do not *yet* have large audiences. In this latter context, the utility of timing, attention, and management can be found in the possibility of receiving *inadvertent attention*. By inadvertent attention, I mean receiving hostile audience response, including but not limited to acerbic trolling, harassment, death threats, sexualized violence, misogynistic comments, and racist vitriol. Inadvertent attention describes the way an innocuous piece of discourse, such as written content, a video, a GIF, or an emoji, can go viral and draw the ire of threatening commenters, something Massanari has written about with respect to researchers becoming the target of online harassment (2018). I argue that textual timing, attention, and management are powerful strategies writers can use—and, according to my participants, *do* use—when contending with inadvertent attention.

DOI: 10.7330/9781607329749.c007

194 of 2,446 people found the following review helpful

⭐☆☆☆☆ **Magpul feeds on death**, June 15, 2014

By A. Gailey

Verified Purchase (What's this?)

This review is from: **Magpul Industries iPhone 5 Bump Case (Wireless Phone Accessory)**

I foolishly ordered this phone case before I realized that this is the company that made the 30-round magazine Adam Lanza used to slaughter 20 kids and six adults at Sandy Hook. They have fought gun reform tooth and nail, trying to militarize America's streets, and led the recall effort against Colorado senators who actually tried to do something after their fellow citizens were gunned down in a theater there. Some shoppers are happy to hand their money over to the death industry but I am not. Back it goes to Amazon. I won't feed this country's scourge.

Figure 7.1. Amanda Gailey's review of Magpul's phone case

A case study of inadvertent attention provides context to this concept, as well as illustrates the deleterious effects of negative commenting. Amanda Gailey, a faculty member at the University of Nebraska at Lincoln, posted to Amazon the cell-phone case review shown in figure 7.1. It's important to note Gailey is not a top-tier reviewer; I found her through contact with one of my participants from my earlier work.

From the screenshot in figure 7.1, we can see that thousands of people decided her review was unhelpful because it evaluated not the product's quality but the manufacturer of the product (Magpul produces guns as well as cell-phone cases). Unlike many of my participants, she was not reviewing with the express aim of rising in the Amazon review rankings. However, as with many top reviewers, Gailey's purpose was still to be helpful. I asked her about her purpose in writing the review.

GALLAGHER: Could you tell me about your purpose in writing the review?

GAILEY: Yea . . . it would not occur to me to write a product review for just any product that I disagreed with. That just seems a little weird to me. There are just too many. The reason I wrote the review was because I bought the phone case not knowing about the manufacturer. . . . I got a new phone and a new phone case after looking around a little bit online. I didn't even pay attention to who the manufacturer was. I just paid attention to the fact that it had fine reviews and would do the job. I put the case on my phone when it arrived a couple of days later. . . . My husband ended up liking the phone case. So he looked [the phone case] up to see if it had maybe other colors or something like that. . . . He said something like "I don't know if I should tell you this, but I just discovered that the company that made your phone case . . . this is a side line for them and their main business is gun accessories." And I was like "Oh what!?" And I was kind of thinking, you know, how bad is it? I wanted to know what kind of business they are and what exactly they're doing. So I looked them up and I found out, "Oh god, they're Magpul." I mean this isn't like they also occasionally do something with guns. They actually make high-capacity magazines. They made the high-capacity magazines used at Sandy Hook. And then they are really vile active lobbyists.

Gailey went on to tell me about her motivation for the review.

> I'm not sure if everyone and their brother has a Magpul case, but they sell a decent number of them on Amazon. And so if you're not in that mode, and you're just searching for phone cases, you might end up buying something where your money is going to an industry that you don't really want to support. So that was my motivation.

After writing the review, Gailey experienced a decisive backlash. She told me that numerous comments (which I haven't included in this book because they're vitriolic) threatened her, ranging from violence to targeted harassment. She reflected, "I anticipated down the line that there would probably be some downvotes [unhelpful votes] or some nasty comments. But I didn't plan on following the responses to the review."

After a few weeks of initially writing the review, Gailey went back and revisited the responses (the afterlife of her review). What she found horrified her.

> Something made me think about the review again. I can't remember what. It might be someone left a nasty comment. I went over to Amazon and looked at it. I hadn't been following the comments so when I went there, I realized that somebody sounded the alarm. And they're all coming [to my review] to post and it was freaky for a couple of hours. I was not sure what to make of it. Some of the comments were really violent. At one point, they were posting the physical location of my office. They posted my personal email address. I was eventually able to track down the causal chain here: Someone had found my review and posted it to the wall of Magpul. There were no comments on that post, but the next day, there was this guy named Dan Cannon [who] wrote a post about it on guns.com. And I believe that he was tipped off by Magpul to do that. There were a bunch of comments [on Cannon's post]. That's what caused the first kind of wave. It was what caught the attention of the gun's rights people. And then it got picked up by an AR15 [a website] forum. [AR15] went to my Facebook page and found a picture of me on vacation holding a turtle and photoshopped it into a bunch of different memes. It just went from there.

While Gailey considers gun-control activism part of her identity, the negative wave of reception was so powerful that it drew the attention of *Politico* (Valentine 2014). As *Politico* reporter Matt Valentine wrote,

> Gailey knew that she was weighing in on a controversial issue. "I anticipated some negative comments and down votes," she says. But she never expected her brief product review to trigger the massive digital harassment campaign that followed. "I got concerned when I saw comments about beating my head in with a sledgehammer."

Gailey's case, certainly not unique, provides us with an exigence, that is, a situation that demands a response of some sort. Rather than letting the comments deter her or her cause, she continued fighting back and working for gun control. Since she first wrote the Amazon review (June 2014), our first interview (March 2015), and our final interview (February 2018), she has continually confronted the gun lobbyists, notably the National Rifle Association (NRA). For her efforts, she has been spotlighted on the neo-Nazi website Breitbart and other websites that shill for the NRA. Her picture has been posted to Breitbart, and her reviews on ratemyprofessor.com have been vandalized.

She has fought back against the gun-lobbyist swarms. She advised anyone who receives threats due to the important work they do:

> If you feel like you're getting swarmed or targeted because of something that you actually are proud to have done or said, then get out in front of it and own it, because the kind of cowering or hoping the storm passes is actually sending the kind of . . . I guess it's the digital equivalent of fear pheromones or something that they want.

For Gailey, standing up against digital bullies and trolls is crucial because it can make them go away. Gailey has even gone on Fox News, but her appearance caused little fanfare because they were expecting a meek faculty member, not a driven gun-control activist.

Important, Gailey did not ignore the trolls or the comments. Very clearly, she read them. In the past, digital writers such as Gailey might have simply ignored the comments, as was the advice to users at the dawn of social media: "Don't read the comments." But this advice ignores the very essence of social media, IPI environments, and the goal of many digital writers. After all, if a vital goal of being a writer is to be read, then reading responses is a natural behavior.

We've seen these strategies with younger people too, notably those who have grown up with social media and whose childhoods are inundated with templated digital environments (Millennials and Generation Z). Take, for example, the social media activism of students after the shootings at Stoneman Douglas High School in Parkland, Florida (spring 2018). Students created social media accounts and were immediately the subject of propaganda campaigns, disinformation acts, and outright harassment. But they did not shy away from these acts. Instead, they continued timing their tweets, attending to (and giving attention to) their supporters, and managing their social media feeds and identities—large-scale examples of the three strategies I present in this book. They broadcasted the harassment they received, circulating the vitriol to their publics and garnering even more support.

The Stoneman Douglas student-activists, along with Gailey, show us that digital writing requires contending with inadvertent attention in some way. It is my hope that timing, attention, and management are useful tropes for describing the heterogeneous activities digital writers initiate after they initially write or publish on the internet. To be clear, I think these strategies are useful for those who already have audiences. But I also believe they are useful for casual everyday writers and social media users who may suddenly find themselves victims of targeted digital campaigns, especially those who identify as women and as members of other minority groups.

Rather than encouraging writers to steer away from social media, and perhaps avoid the comments altogether, I argue for a more nuanced approach. Some comments can be useful to recirculate or "signal boost" (perhaps showing off one's digital support). Other more deleterious harassing comments can be deleted, if possible. Moreover, vitriolic comments might be spotlighted to create more content—thereby frustrating trolls who cannot receive the "lulz." Of course, these claims are contextualized, and decisions must be made on a case-by-case basis. Nevertheless, timing, attention, and management can assist writers with the tough, emotionally taxing afterlife of digital writing.

To transition into more concrete pedagogy, I want to briefly mention that I've already instituted these practices of digital writing's afterlife in my own pedagogy. Like many other teachers whose pedagogies are digital, I often have students write blogs, compose videos for YouTube, and produce content for various social media platforms. Several student projects have inadvertently gone viral. One student even had a brief documentary made about his blog documenting the bathroom graffiti on our campus. The video received thousands of views and the student received "fan" messages on his personal Facebook account. For reasons such as this, it's important to consider what happens to writing, especially student writing, after publication and during that writing's afterlife. There are many things writers do with digital writing after it's on the internet. We must help students recognize this afterlife of writing. And we need to include these features in our own digital pedagogies.

INTO THE CLASSROOM

In addition to helping writers who inadvertently receive unwanted attention, the strategies of timing, attention, and management can help teachers of digital writing widen the scope of our pedagogies. This section, then, accounts for the ongoing change inherent when teaching digital writing and rhetoric in IPI environments. Broadly, I encourage a pedagogy that directly addresses and accounts for the afterlife that digital writing necessarily entails. We can begin doing so by starting with our own foundational assumptions about writing.

A pedagogy that addresses the afterlife of digital writing values the entire process of writing, including *all* the labor and time involved in attending to writing after it is published or put on the internet. Such a move requires researchers, practitioners, and teachers of writing to uncleave writing and speaking, as well as listening and reading. In doing so, we need not only to teach students how to write but also what they are expected to do with their writing after they've written. To echo Paul Prior (1998), we need to represent, account, and teach the richly diverse semiotic activity users engage in when they inscribe in and on interactive and participatory internet environments.

I wish to intensify this claim: people are doing quite a bit of work after they write a text, and we need to document, describe, and teach these heterogeneous activities. After all, in terms of the participants I've studied, writing cannot be finished in the sense of having written. Sometimes a single text may be finished, but finishing isn't what writing means. Our pedagogies need to account for writing that never ends and the activities that writing calls for once it's on the internet. More colloquially, we need pedagogies, teaching strategies, and more studies about what writers do after their writing has "gone to press" or is "forthcoming" or "published."

To elaborate on what an afterlife pedagogy entails, I briefly reframe the data chapters with a pedagogical focus. Textual timing helps us move away from concrete due dates and "forgetting" about the text afterward. Digital writing asks us to think about when to publish and when to share our writing. Rather than establishing due dates for texts, we might ask students to consider consistency. Active, ongoing production may account better than due dates can for the production processes of digital update culture and social media. Textual attention assumes participatory audiences: humans, machines, bots, algorithms, and other things can read, interact, and participate with a text or other act of discourse. Giving attention to, as well as inculcating, audience interactions implies that writers need to learn to interact through and with text. They need continuously emergent social skills that are contextualized to specific templates. Textual management is meant to describe the diverse labor of monitoring one's writing and discourse associated with the frequency, scale, and speed of digital culture. Managing writing and participatory audiences requires developing various managerial models and mechanisms for writing.

An obvious avenue teachers of writing can take is to build relationships among writing studies, media studies, and communication studies.

More generally, those who study writing in its various forms might assemble collaborative pedagogies with communication scholars, especially those engaged in empirical work. These collaborations should be mutually advantageous, for not only can writing studies scholarship benefit from theories of speech and media communication but media communication and speech programs can benefit from writing studies scholarship.

Of all the constructs that may be most helpful here, considering audiences, both human and machine, might best be configured as an ongoing *process* that does not end and that involves the rhetorical canons (invention, style, arrangement, delivery, and memory). Rather than a group of people or demographic that is prefigured to exist, I suggest audience might be a concept used during the entire lifespan of writing—before, during, and *after* production, as well as in the midst of circulation. Developing audience awareness as an emergent process has several pedagogical implications. Our teaching approaches need to frame audience consideration across production, distribution, and circulation processes, as well as describe how these are intersecting nonlinear and recursive processes—like all writing processes. If we teach writing in digital contexts, either through blogging or through alternatives such as social media platforms, then we ought to adjust our audience approaches to account for these contexts. In these instances, we could ask students to consider audience not only before they write but also after they write. We can ask students to consider how their audience(s) changes, why these changes happen, and what factors are out of students' control.

To push on this, with respect to participatory audiences and their comments, we might ask students to manage their audiences and writing. As students manage their texts, they might ask themselves, Do I want to update older texts based on comments, new information, or other texts I've subsequently written? Students might also attend to the emotional impact of such audiences and comments. We might ask our students to consider the following questions: How do you ignore hurtful or irrelevant comments? What is the emotional impact of these comments? What issues of identity are at play here? How might gender, race, sexuality, and class shape whether one attends to comments or not? As these questions suggest, considering audience as an ongoing process aids in our consideration of where audience fits into larger theories of digital writing and digital rhetoric. It can help students think not only about their announced readers, eventual readers, and invisible audiences but also about the writer they will be next week, next month, and next year—or simply after the next comment they read. The participation afforded on the internet, often through comments but not always, opens up these possibilities for invigorated theories, practices, and methods of writing that account for the afterlife of digital writing.

CODA: THE LABOR OF THE AFTERLIFE

Pedagogically, my argument in this book can be articulated as follows: there is an entire composing process that happens after a digital text is created and we, as instructors, need to account for this process.[1] We need to account in our pedagogies for this afterlife, perhaps even challenging conventional understanding of due dates and semester structures that inhibit seeing how digital writing circulates when freed from institutional time constraints. More practically, however, we need to value the labor this afterlife demands. Having students engage in digital writing and social media strategies requires an intense time commitment that can command students' attention at strange hours of the day and unexpected days of the week—holidays too. Students may need to engage audiences frequently and at the audience's behest. Managing digital writing requires students to think not only about the claims of their own arguments but also about the reception of those arguments, including the way arguments may need to be altered across digital platforms and venues.

We need to develop assignments that account for the timing, attention, and management involved when students engage in digital writing, including the affective engagement of responding to audiences. While I do not have easy solutions, a useful strategy I have developed is to ask students to keep a log of the all the ways they engage audiences, including articulating timing and management strategies. The afterlife of digital writing thus raises our collective awareness that writers now *regularly* engage and involve audiences. Students are aware of this and expect to attend (and tend) to their audiences. Writing instructors need to articulate the work that writers do after they publish. Administratively, we should argue for this labor to be recognized as a valuable part of digital writing instruction and curricula.

In order to advocate for such inclusions, we need to continue resisting pernicious metaphors about writers composing in isolation. Digital writing, at least, is a highly social and fluid activity. Many of my participants reported that they wanted to engage readers and have conversations. If we attend to the afterlife of digital writing, we can better see that writers and audiences are having conversations with each other. To be a writer in this milieu means to figure out ways to keep the helpful conversations going. The strategies of timing, attention, and management can help continue these conversations.

8
AN EPISTEMOLOGY OF CHANGE

Through the chapters about textual timing, attention, and management, I endeavor to show digital writing has an afterlife that cannot be contained by a single text, video, image, or moment of discourse, even if we account for the various processes, activities, iterations, drafts, and revisions that go into producing the text. Moreover, my use of the term *afterlife* pushes our notions of writing to postpublication, that is, *after* delivery and *during* circulation. This book thus opens up theories of writing processes to consider what writers do after delivery and during circulation.

In a writerly afterlife, digital writers still engage in complex writing activities. They write carefully and make time to compose. They revise often and, interestingly, update their work when participatory audiences offer effective enough feedback (and templates enable the writing to be literally updatable and editable). Writers in this study were highly social, constantly rereading their texts in light of what readers wrote, as well as in response to the accumulation of ambient affordances.

Yet, digital writers who consider their participatory audiences and commenters engage in a broad range of activities we might not normally associate with writing. Digital writers manage their content while taking on the work of editors, publishers, and marketers. They time their writing with savvy acuity, based on qualitative experiences and quantitative abstractions of those experiences. Specifically, digital writers on the internet can be described as entrepreneurs, perhaps even vertically integrated companies, who contend with the speed, scale, and frequency of social media and rapid content creation. They deploy oral types of communication practices because the circulation of their writing is so fast that traditional descriptions and metaphors associated with writing cannot fully capture or contain it.

Moreover, because writers are attuned to the speeds, accelerations, and circulations of update culture, they understand that the afterlife of writing is as important as the initial writing, drafting, delivery, and publication. The afterlife is all about figuring out what to do with writing

DOI: 10.7330/9781607329749.c008

after it's written. For these reasons, the afterlife of writing may look like the activities of a company but with a key distinction: there is no company. The writers have become the firms, doing the work of multiple people and filling multiple roles, becoming website moderators, customer-service representatives, text curators, social media managers, multimodal producers, and advertising agents.

This chapter therefore argues that the afterlife of digital writing involves activities that fuse written and oral modes, expanding a writer's brand. From my observations and interviews, this fusion has its origins in self-motivated entrepreneurial drive, one that exists due the lure of being *read widely*. This chapter subsequently lays out an epistemology of digital writing's afterlife. In doing so, I tease out the ideas of *fluidity* and *change* as ways to study digital writing and its afterlife. I conclude with remarks about the intersection of this epistemology and the methods required to study such change.

The afterlife of digital writing expands our understanding of what writing can be and what responsibilities fall upon writers. Writers, depending on what they're doing in the life cycle of their content, become speakers, managers, and agents. The strategies of timing, attention, and management provide evidence that writing is contingent in digital environments, and especially so in IPI environments. This contingency, change itself, can be understood as a guiding epistemology.

AN EPISTEMOLOGY OF CHANGE IN UPDATE CULTURE

Change, then, is what buttresses the implications in this chapter. As the chapters about textual timing, attention, and management make clear, writing in IPI environments is inherently fluid, like conversations and oral exchanges. In update culture, changes in writing can happen rapidly, at scale, and without warning (or documentation). In update culture, the constant need to rethink and update writing in IPI environments blurs distinctions between writing and talking because we *talk with text*. The increased fluidity, echoing Zygmunt Bauman's *Liquid Modernity* (2000), between writing and talking has an epistemological implication: the subjects and objects of written and oral exchanges are in a state of flux. Digital writing is inordinately changeable—even if the subjects and objects don't change, we know they *can*, as recent theories of planned obsolescence have shown us (Fitzpatrick 2011). And we *expect* this change. While this is nothing new given the rise of late-stage capitalist postmodern theory in the 1980s and 1990s, I have tried to push beyond fluidity as a conclusion and instead frame fluidity as a given. With respect to writing and rhetoric in IPI environments, what thus happens when fluidity is a given?

My answer, in sum, is that, with respect to IPI environments, we need analytical categories that fuse writing and orality. Writing and orality need to be put back together in deeply interconnected ways, and we need to develop language that captures this connection. But this connection is not exactly a replication of Walter Ong's secondary orality (1991, 133–36), because radio and podcasting have made orality readily available in our mobile, networked world. Rather, the real-time feedback and response of audiences to digital writing answers Plato's fears about the author of a written document not being present and accountable in face-to-face dialectic. I have opted to fuse terms (i.e., *textual timing, textual attention, textual management*), rather than create neologisms because my participants discussed their activities through a fused language. Participants coupled writing and orality, putting these approaches together as they wrote (and write) digitally. Thus, as I have attempted to show, the writers in my study turned to fusions of oral and written tropes, describing their actions, habits, and dispositions through both types. They slid back and forth between the logics of writing and orality during our interviews, demonstrating that these are simply metaphors for deeply related activities.

This fusion thus frames digital writing, specifically IPI writing, as inherently participatory. When participatory audiences are a given, that is, when they are a foundation and not a finding, the elements of communication, including writer, audience, text, medium, and context, take on a different relationship: they become a forward-moving process that nevertheless relies upon previous instantiations of writing, as well as writers and audiences. What was written or spoken prior accretes over the course of time, while new information is always ready to be introduced. In IPI environments, written texts can accrue, which is unlike talking. Unlike print writing, though, the texts in these environments can change, often without evidence or signaling of such changes.

Change then is part of being a writer in these environments. Creating texts that can last but are not expected to last is a feature I observed across my case study participants. The knowledge writers produce in these environments, though collected by corporations such as Google, Facebook, and Twitter, is not necessarily unstable but *is* updatable. Reframing writing as something that can and will be updated offers us a way to think differently about written discourse: digital writing changes. Digital writing is an activity that moves across, into, and through various digital platforms and devices in an attempt to communicate.

LIMITS AND FUTURE AREAS OF RESEARCH

My claims in this book, and about update culture's general epistemology of change, are couched in template rhetoric. This limits the scope of my work and claims. I do not want to create a general theory of digital writing, because any grand narrative is doomed ultimately to failure. Instead, I hope other scholars will poke weaknesses in my template argument, as well as extend it, because this defines the *scope* of my study. If some scholars take up this book—both its strengths and weaknesses—then I can update template rhetoric accordingly, drawing on the responses of my audiences.

At this point, however, I push a bit beyond the scope of my case studies to consider broader cultural and technological trends. In my research, I examined a recent variant of digital texts, those mediated by internet templates. As I note in chapter 2, these templates give rise to the expectation of rapid and updatable texts. More specifically, I study what writers do after an initial text is completed and the heterogeneous strategies they employ to guide their multifaceted postproduction process (which is itself a production process). The concept of update culture, then, facilitates writing beyond an initial text—the afterlife of digital writing.

This afterlife of writing is now, I think, everywhere. Everyday writers must attend to the afterlife of their writing. Without attending to the afterlife of writing, digital or not, we cannot fully account for the textured and diverse processes of delivery, circulation, iteration, and revision writing entails. Writing on the internet is somewhat like tossing a bottle into the digital ocean and monitoring the ocean to see what the tide brings in. With this book, then, I endeavor to connect the various dispersed activities of digital writing, even the ones we don't expect or want writers to take on.

Update culture is only increasing in intensity, and template design is increasingly easy to use. With the speeds and scales of the internet and social media, digital writing and writers will continue to close the perceived gap between writing and orality. From a broad perspective, this project means to heal a larger rift and put something together: talking and writing. By using textual timing, attention, and management, we can see that talking, writing, reading, and listening are becoming closer, rejoining one another. In this project, such talking/writing/reading/listening is meant to increase writers' ability to be read widely and commented upon frequently.

I therefore want to pose four future areas of research I believe this book opens up. First, researchers might investigate the economic role of responding to comments and participatory audiences. Comments have an economic value in terms of audience attention, as points of data, in an information economy. Up to this point in *Update Culture*, I have largely bracketed this economic role because I have focused on how individual writers consider their comments and not how comments shape the economics of writers' labor. Second, how do organizations and groups of people contend with comments? While I have examined this question with respect to individuals, studying organizations across contexts would complement the findings of this book. Studying comment moderators who work for organizations, such as the *New York Times*, Facebook, and Twitter, can help shed light on how organizations contend with comments. Third, although it is outside the scope of this book, adding the perspective of commenters—why, how, in what ways commenters write—to this research can help answer the following question: how is writing becoming more exchangeable, interactive, and fluid on the internet? Finally, how are machines beginning to function as audiences and not simply tools? On the internet, algorithms and bots can now write and read texts in ways their designers did not intend. Future research about participatory audiences could investigate how machines are becoming audiences.

DOCUMENTING AN EPISTEMOLOGY OF CHANGE

I now turn to a self-critical implication of this epistemology: documenting writing practices and strategies in update culture. The problem of change in update culture presents methodological issues. With respect to visual digital rhetoric, Gries points to, and attempts to resolve, some of these issues with the approach she labels "iconographic tracking" (2013, 2015). While Gries's new materialist approach tends to occlude human beings, who often circulate images, iconographic tracking nevertheless opens up methods of digital rhetoric research by attempting to account for an image across contexts and through its iterative process. It's a methodological attempt to describe an epistemology of change. Instead of attempting to coin my own term, I want simply to offer the idea of recording and observing change as integral to digital writing and rhetoric.

As digital researchers, we need to frame change as part of writing. While most scholars who study writing understand that writing is a process as well as a product, a crucial implication of this study is that digital texts *themselves* are sites of change. The document, product, and "thing" are dynamic. For example, when I interviewed people, they changed their texts during and after my questioning. While this may have happened with other writers in prior media, the writing my participants changed was the actual final product audiences see and participate with. Not only are texts produced and processed in nonlinear and recursive ways but the texts *themselves* evolve over the course of time and context, accumulating responses and conversations as they develop.

The historical differences are related to, as I mention in the introduction, speed, scale, and geography. The site of writing is now interactive, built on IPI templates designed for speedy exchange of text. These templates, and the devices in which they're integrated, allow for text to be exchanged at extraordinarily high rates. People from around the world can exchange texts at speeds never before seen with writing.

To document change, I believe screen captures and screenshots must be integrated in and throughout digital writing and rhetoric projects. During interviews, researchers should record the actions of their participants on the screen because participants can edit and update texts in response to research questions immediately. Frustrating at times for me, participants changed their text without any evidence of the change. Interfaces also changed over the course of the project, with new ambient affordances arising and older ones fading into the dustbin of digital history. I began thus to document changes through screenshots and screen captures. I do not, however, view these types of evidence as individuated research objects. Rather, taking a series of them describes rich contexts so researchers can better frame the lifespan of a text or other types of activity (in my case, that which is entered into an IPI template).

This approach has three opportunities and two drawbacks. The first opportunity of this method is that writing and rhetoric researchers will have more evidence. Second, they can trace change not only in terms of words but also interface design. Interfaces have a major impact on writers and therefore should be accounted for in terms of visual design. Third, researchers can use the evidence when returning to participants at a later date, reminding the participants of the changes they made.

The drawbacks are structural and may be difficult to overcome. First, writing research is so embedded in print journals that to fill articles (or books) with screenshots and screen captures is not practically, economically, socially, or theoretically acceptable yet. Digital writing and rhetoric research is still dominated by the written word, at least in terms of scholarly publication. While electronic and digital journals are beginning to be more acceptable for scholars, it is imperative that researchers find suitable alternatives in order to instigate publication changes. Second, and more theoretically, screenshots and screen captures can reify and homogenize writing as static, monolithic pieces of evidence. I've fallen into this trap more than a few times throughout this book. Videos of on-screen changes can help us lessen this problem, but that brings us back to the first drawback. By tracking change, I hope to push the study of writing beyond text and inscribed discourse and toward seeing writing as something fluid and changeable.

Appendix A
HOW THIS BOOK CAME TO BE

I officially interviewed the first writer for this project in 2013 and concluded my interviews in 2018. Unofficially, this project began in my 2006 graduate seminars, when I interviewed underground Philadelphia rappers who posted music to Myspace pages and then monitored the reception of their tunes. Over the course of this extended decade, I've learned that digital writing has simply become writing. Online and offline distinctions have become murky at best, especially with the advent of augmented reality, wearable technologies, and mobile media. The trepidation about reading comments and putting one's work online seems to have faded. Anger and frustration appear to have replaced fear of reading the comments. The writers I interviewed in 2017 and 2018 were more aware of not being paid to produce content than they were at the start of this project; that is, they were aware of their own digital exploitation, an issue writing studies must address in the coming years.

Over the course of this entire project, many writers expressed misgivings about excessive social media use. From the beginning to the end of the project, writers were figuratively and literally exhausted, weary of becoming victims of a digital mob mentality while recognizing simultaneously they were often part of the mob (a paradox participants were deeply reflective about). While I dislike generalizing, I largely believe the writers I studied had become accustomed to comments and had developed an expectation of them, regardless of whether the comments were positive or negative.

In the course of reading this book, then, readers may wonder what I, as a researcher who has sought to synthesize seemingly disparate case studies, think about digital comments and participatory audiences. Do I condemn the comments? To be direct, I have found that comments are exceedingly off topic and statistically skew negative in terms of sentiment analysis. In this sense, I condemn the comments. However, as my participants reminded me, insightful comments exist, sometimes at a surprising rate. As Tracy Monroe told me, "For every ten comments I read, one or two contains insight. There are gems." A record of even

DOI: 10.7330/9781607329749.c009

awful comments remains a record of how everyday readers respond to people they perceive as writers. Recording how people react to comments and audience reception is important because it helps to dredge the afterlife of digital writing, thereby making overlooked, ignored, and seemingly unimportant steps visible.

In the remaining part of this appendix, then, I want to enact the philosophy undergirding this book. I describe how this book came to be in the real, lived sense of the researcher. I want to make the steps of this project visible to my readers in a way that echoes Prior's epic appendix in *Writing/ Disciplinarity* (1998). I've long admired Paul's work; he is a colleague of mine, but his work also figured prominently in my early work in graduate school. In echoing Paul's own appendix, I start with steps I believe are not always clean, clear, or neat, as well as recognizing that research processes are nonlinear, recursive, and iterative—sometimes not productively.

As I note, this project's origins and motivations grew from my 2006 UMass Amherst seminars with Anne Herrington (research methods) and Donna LeCourt (emerging technologies). I'd planned to come to graduate school to become the "best Willa Cather scholar in the world" (a quotation literally included in my graduate-school application). But all the literature courses were full because I was too ignorant to realize I should enroll in graduate courses before I came to campus. Thus, I enrolled in Anne's and Donna's courses, setting off my trajectory in writing studies. These scholars also became members of my dissertation committee.

While I was taking these courses in the fall of 2006, Facebook had become popular on college campuses. Myspace was already massive and popular. I found social networking websites interesting because they changed rapidly. I could check profiles and read people's updates of their pictures, About Me sections, and favorite quotes—the last of which was a quirky activity popular from about 2004 to 2007. I chose to write a paper about underground rappers in Philadelphia who kept Myspace profiles. Philadelphia was (and remains) my hometown, and I knew the rappers from working with them as we pulled overnight shifts at a grocery store. These rappers used Myspace as a way to circulate their music without much cost. They used Facebook to a lesser extent because Facebook was largely a college website in 2006. I found the rappers functioned as their own audience for their Myspace pages. They were prosumers, although I did not know of this term at the time. (LeCourt did, but she let my lack of background knowledge slide.) The rappers paid attention to their connections on Myspace, that is, their "friends," often talking during my interviews with them about how they fused all those friends into a personalized demographic.

Over the next three years, I took a variety of courses and left this project on hold. During coursework, I worked a lot at a grocery store and saw the importance of blogging and digital writing. At one point, a coworker created a blog to discuss all the recipes he created from the grocery store's specialty items. Once I received my master's degree, I got hired as an adjunct at Quinsigamond Community College (QCC), where I saw the rise of smartphones make writing more mobile and able to circulate at faster speeds. Spring 2010 was the first time I saw a student reading on her phone. I saw students writing entire paragraphs as text messages, and I wrote an article about emoticons (Gallagher 2012).

I bring up my experiences at QCC, where I worked from 2009 to 2013, because audience awareness is an important skill community college students desire. Students at community colleges, due to the marginalized status some of them experience during high school, want the power that comes with being able to flexibly *consider the audience*. This powerful phrase was the driving force behind my dissertation, *Interactive Audience and the Internet* (2014). I was—and still am—attracted to the idea of audience because learning to adjust your language to an audience makes you more persuasive. Audience awareness is about powerful control and agency.

My dissertation investigated the ways three writers—StickleyMan, Tracey Monroe, and Kelly Salasin—considered their audiences. I chose them because they were willing and because they seemed to have a lot of attention via comments. I worked on this project from 2011 to 2014. I recommend reading the full methodology of the dissertation for why I chose these participants. However, to summarize, each writer in the dissertation had a different relationship with the audience: Salasin was totally in charge of her public blog, Monroe ran a closed Facebook group, and StickleyMan ran a public forum.

I met with several other graduate students while I thought through my dissertation: Emma Howes, Linh Dich, Christian Pulver, Sarah Finn, Chris DiBiase, and Leslie Bradshaw. We met at LeCourt's house, at coffee shops, and at each other's houses or apartments while thinking about our research. We bounced ideas off each other. I bring this up because I realized during these meetings that writing is often refined, careful talking. Orality and literacy aren't the same, but they are closely related—something I now realize pointed me in the direction of this book. These informal conversations, like the informal practices of an athlete, prepared me for writing a dissertation, as well as helped me realize the importance of participatory audiences.

Along the way, I met my spouse. While this detail may not seem important, my spouse, an engineer, was hired at the University of

Illinois, Urbana-Champaign. I was hired as a trailing spouse in the spring of 2014. During my job visit, Spencer Schaffner (a highly ranked Amazon reviewer himself but not a participant in this book) made an innocuous comment about studying Amazon reviewers because they receive a lot of comments. Based upon Schaffner's comment and feedback from other colleagues, I began to rethink my project. What exactly were some larger findings that might be turned into a book? This question was largely motivated by a desire to dramatically expand my pool of participants in order to write a book for tenure.

I wrestled with this question during the 2014–15 academic year, constantly reading new articles and books but spinning my wheels until I realized my project's larger contribution: writers were doing a lot of stuff *after* they wrote. It was during this academic year that I found circulation studies and realized my dissertation and current work could contribute to this bourgeoning area of writing studies because, for all the benefits of the process movement, the process seemed to stop at what might be described loosely as *publication*. I made this discovery as I wrote an article for *Written Communication* (2015a). In rereading the transcribed interviews from my dissertation, I realized each writer was trying to "continue the conversation," a phrase each of the writers used without my prompting. Writers, I found, were doing a lot of activities after they initially wrote to keep that conversation going.

In the winter of 2015, having realized my work was really about what people do in response to their comments—that is, what happens after delivery—I applied for IRB approval from my university. As non-tenure-track faculty, I had to get special approval just to apply. Thankfully, my department head, Michael Rothberg, approved. Schaffner gave me advice about the application: write it in such a way that any digital writer can be a participant so long as they consider the comments they receive. I then began conducting interviews and reading participants' writing in February 2015. I contacted the top one hundred Amazon reviewers based on rankings (www.amazon.com/review/top-reviewers). With the help of those I contacted for my dissertation, I found numerous bloggers and journalists from a snowball sample. Tracy Monroe helped me find many journalists. I found the top-level redditors by contacting them based upon their accrued karma, using the website karmalb.com. After sending out numerous emails and messages, I interviewed everyone who was willing, and I conducted follow-up interviews with anyone willing. I conducted interviews over my personal phone or video-chat account, using my own minutes and tools in order to protect the identities of participants. When I interviewed participants, I tried to give them the freedom to share as much as they were willing, and I tried to create a jovial, humorous atmosphere because they were volunteering for free. I read between ten and twenty of their most recent texts, as well as all the comments on those texts, before I initially interviewed them and using those texts as my initial documents (and I quickly realized those digital artifacts were mutable). Reading their work helped me build context and provide jokes about ridiculous comments they'd received. I found this technique to be helpful because it built an interpersonal connection with people who were essentially strangers.

As I interviewed, and after the interviews were conducted, I went back and forth between my previous work and my new information (transcripts, participants' texts, etc.). I found that much had changed since my dissertation because I was no longer focused on the participants in isolation but on the connections between them. As I performed axial coding (Strauss and Corbin 1998) again and again, breaking apart tagged codes from my dissertation and relating this older information to my newer information, one large theme remained across all case studies: writers were definitely managing their texts as the texts circulated. That was clear, and in fact, many of these concepts of textual management were anticipated in my dissertation, although they were not categorized as such.

Timing and attention were a bit different. Timing I came across accidentally. When I asked participants about advice for my students, they recommended writing recently and consistently. They frequently advised writing every day or creating an expectation for when the audience could access new content (every Tuesday, for instance). They mentioned considering when to deliver writing based on what the audience is doing, such as writing and delivering at lunchtime or directly after work because people often check their phones at these times. Once I aggregated all the mentions related to timing, I realized I could theme a data chapter around timing because print texts, unlike speeches, do not strongly emphasize temporality. This was my opening gambit for the chapter on timing: digital texts do indeed have a temporality to them, at least according to my participants. The element of temporality prompted me to investigate scholarship about *kairos*, which in turn led me to *chronos* via Smith's (1969) work, which I cite in chapter 2. I subsequently realized my participants thought of timing in terms of both *kairos* and *chronos*.

The chapter on textual attention is perhaps the most radical departure from my previous work because it represents a dramatic rethinking of the concept textual listening from my dissertation. Previously

(Gallagher 2015a), I largely believed listening was an excellent metaphor to use because (1) my participants used the language of listening when describing reading comments and (2) it was a concept left over from my dissertation. However, I was too influenced by my participants' perspectives.

Steve Holmes, a colleague and friend, read an early draft of this chapter in September 2017 and repeatedly asked why it wasn't focused on attention. The word *attention* littered the chapter, he noted. Holmes asked why I was trying to frame the activity as listening when it clearly wasn't related to hearing at all. After Holmes's comments, I realized I was trying to perform too many mental gymnastics about why listening wasn't actually listening (it seems preposterous now that I've typed it out). Following Holmes's advice, I pursued the concept of attention, which was not terribly difficult, because that concept was largely already in place. I simply needed to address it explicitly and draw on scholarship about attention.

While these are the data chapters of the book, the theoretical frame derives from my ongoing work about templates and typography. Templates, as I mention in chapter 2, get the afterlife of digital writing off the ground quite literally. Print writing can't be updated so audiences who already have that text can see updates. Digital writing can be. Print writing is hard to circulate across time and space. Digital writing is not. Templates enable circulation. I mention this because I did not initially see this connection. But I asked myself, Why is what happens after delivery and during circulation important and relevant now? My answer was that writers could engage in lots of activities after delivery and during circulation. As such, templates are perhaps my attempt at a generalizable theory of social media, although I would not call it a coherent theory. It's simply an attempt to describe how writing has become flexible, agile, and updatable.

Appendix B
INITIAL INTERVIEW QUESTIONS FOR REVIEWERS, JOURNALISTS, AND BLOGGERS

What are your goals when you write, post, or create online texts?

What brings you to the internet? What are your goals for turning to the internet?

What is the purpose of the site [specific to the participant] in general? What is the writing supposed to look like on this site?

What is your purpose for maintaining the sites that you do, continuing to update them? How does this relate to your original, stated purpose?

Why did you choose this particular site or digital space for your writing? What drew you to it? How has the site's formatting been influential for your online writings and postings?

How has the site's formatting or layout altered your writings and postings? In what ways has the layout and formatting been useful or not useful?

How have other users of the site influenced the way you write or post?

Please describe your ideal audience. Do you ever encounter this ideal audience? Can you describe your reaction when you encounter this audience?

What kind of audiences are you trying to avoid?

When you don't encounter your ideal audience, what are some strategies you use to get them to read your texts? How do you react to an audience that isn't ideal?

How important is your audience when writing initially?

Does the audience ever interfere with your writing goals?

How important is audience feedback for what you write in the future?

How important is audience feedback or participation?

How often do you revise your writing based on audience feedback?

I teach digital writing to college students. Do you have any advice for my students?

DOI: 10.7330/9781607329749.c010

Appendix C
INITIAL INTERVIEW QUESTIONS
FOR REDDITORS

Could you describe yourself a bit? The only real information I could use is an age or age range and general location (North America, Northeast, etc.). I'm also interested in how much you write in your daily life outside of reddit.

What brought you to reddit?

When do you think are the best and worst times to post on reddit? Why?

Have you ever had to deal with trolls? How do you contend with them?

What do you consider your most successful posts? How would you define these posts?

Could you tell me a little bit about the hivemind and your views of it?

Who do you consider your audience when writing on reddit?

Why do you think you became successful at reddit?

What would you say you're "known for" on reddit?

What advice do you have for people who "want to break into reddit"? This might be students or novices.

DOI: 10.7330/9781607329749.c011

Appendix D
FOLLOW-UP INTERVIEW QUESTIONS

Please note that questions were adjusted to particular writers and their platforms, as well as to their answers from our first interview. I also used their guidance about what texts to discuss. I also asked specific follow-up questions.

In general, what is your reaction when people post or comment on your online writings? Can you describe this process for responding? What makes you decide not to respond?

Do commenters (secondary writers) ever post, discuss, or converse about your texts with each other? How do you react to this conversation? Describe your process for joining this conversation. If not, describe your rationale for not joining this conversation.

Do you ever revise your posts or writings based on your audience's comments or responses? How do their posts, comments, writings, or interaction shape your future posts or writings?

Are there any consistent commenters? Do you have a special, unique, or different sort of relationship with these consistent commenters?

What kind of situation do you encourage or not encourage to create participation and garner attention?

In what ways do you ever comment or post on your own writings? What is your purpose for commenting or not?

What is your reaction when there aren't any commenters (secondary writers)? How do you adjust your text, if you do?

In what ways does your audience(s) shape your future posts?

If there are any privacy settings, what is your rationale for setting them the way you do?

In what ways do you circulate your writing? In what ways does your audience circulate your writing? How do you know or not know?

How does the layout and design encourage or not encourage the circulation of your texts?

In what way does circulation intersect with your writing goals?

DOI: 10.7330/9781607329749.c012

NOTES

INTRODUCTION: UPDATE CULTURE

1. This case study, of the blogger Kelly Salasin, largely informs much of what is written in this book because her case formed a basis for my dissertation. To read more about Salasin's case, see Gallagher (2018).

2. Ann Blakeslee (2001) and Deborah Brandt (1990) have observed that what happens after a text is published or distributed is significant to how the writing process occurs. Blakeslee observes that physicists sought to pique interest in their findings before publication in an effort to have those findings more widely accepted after publication (27).

3. Walter Ong's (1991) idea of secondary orality is useful here. If Ong's argument that secondary orality is "a more deliberate and self-conscious orality, based permanently on the use of writing and print," then update culture is a type of communicative decorum that signals an inversion of secondary orality. Namely, in update culture, we expect writing to act like orality, including the multitasking and constant presence of an audience that print and literate cultures do not necessarily emphasize (136).

CHAPTER 2: TEMPLATE RHETORIC

1. Historically, we know the internet did not take off until the World Wide Web (the web) went visual for everyday users. The web did not grow in popularity until the graphical web browser, Mosaic, was introduced in 1993 by a team of students and professionals from the University of Illinois at Urbana-Champaign. (The leaders of this team were Marc Andreessen and Eric Bina.) This historical anecdote shows that structures in form users of the internet, and communicative activities are largely reactive to broad structural forces and forms.

2. See Richard Lanham's *The Electronic Word* (1993) as well as Collin Brooke's *Lingua Fracta* (2007). I also echo Martin Heidegger's presence-at-hand, or readiness-to-hand, argument.

3. Wendy Chun makes a similar connection between interface and ideology in *Programmed Visions* (2011, 66).

CHAPTER 4: TEXTUAL ATTENTION

1. Barbara Biesecker (1989) saw the origin of rhetorical discourse as both in a situation and in the rhetor, which she takes up through the Derridean concept of différance.

CHAPTER 5: TEXTUAL MANAGEMENT

1. Brandt (2014) has used vocational aspiration to denote "a growing awareness of how writing is associated with occupations and life work" (14).

CHAPTER 7: LEARNING AND PEDAGOGY IN UPDATE CULTURE

1. John Trimbur (2000) has addressed a similar issue of print circulation in terms of material conditions and the artificial separation of the rhetorical canons of delivery and memory from invention, style, and arrangement (189).

REFERENCES

"About Top Contributors." Amazon.com. Accessed October 18, 2019. https://www
.amazon.com/gp/help/customer/display.html?nodeId=202076130.

Arola, Kristin L. 2010. "The Design of Web 2.0: The Rise of the Template, The Fall of
Design." *Computers and Composition* 27 (1): 4–14. https://doi.org/10.1016/j.compcom
.2009.11.004.

Barnes, Renee. 2015. "Understanding the Affective Investment Produced through Commenting on Australian Alternative Journalism Website New Matilda." *New Media &
Society* 17 (5): 810–26. https://doi.org/10.1177/1461444813511039.

Bauman, Zygmunt. 2000. *Liquid Modernity*. Malden, MA: Polity. https://doi.org/10.2307
/3089803.

Beck, Estee. 2016. "A Theory of Persuasive Computer Algorithms for Rhetorical Code
Studies." *Enculturation* 23.

Beer, David. 2016. *Metric Power*. New York: Palgrave Macmillan. https://doi.org/10.1057
/978-1-137-55649-3.

Biesecker, Barbara A. 1989. "Rethinking the Rhetorical Situation from within the The-
matic of Différance." *Philosophy and Rhetoric* 22 (2): 110–31.

Bitzer, Lloyd F. 1968. "The Rhetorical Situation." *Philosophy and Rhetoric* 1 (1): 1–14.
https://doi.org/10.1007/s13398-014-0173-7.2.

Blair, Ann. 2011. *Too Much to Know: Managing Scholarly Information before the Modern Age*. New
Haven, CT: Yale University Press.

Blakeslee, Ann M. 2001. *Interacting with Audiences: Social Influences on the Production of Scientific Writing*. Mahwah, NJ: Erlbaum. https://doi.org/10.1177/1050651902250949.

Bogost, Ian. 2007. *Persuasive Games: The Expressive Power of Videogames*. Cambridge: MIT
Press.

Bolter, Jay David, and Richard Grusin. 2000. *Remediation: Understanding New Media*. Cambridge, MA: MIT Press.

boyd, danah. 2014. *It's Complicated: The Social Lives of Networked Teens*. New Haven, CT: Yale
University Press.

Brandt, Deborah. 1990. *Literacy as Involvement: The Acts of Writers, Readers, and Texts*. Carbondale: Southern Illinois University Press.

Brandt, Deborah. 2014. *The Rise of Writing: Redefining Mass Literacy*. Cambridge: Cambridge
University Press.

Brock, Kevin, and Dawn Shepherd. 2016. "Understanding How Algorithms Work Per-
suasively through the Procedural Enthymeme." *Computers and Composition* 42: 17–27.
https://doi.org/10.1016/j.compcom.2016.08.007.

Brooke, Collin Gifford. 2009. *Lingua Fracta: Towards a Rhetoric of New Media*. Cresskill, NJ:
Hampton.

Brooker, Phillip, Julie Barnett, John Vines, Shaun Lawson, Tom Feltwell, and Kiel Long.
2017. "Doing Stigma: Online Commenting around Weight-Related News Media." *New
Media & Society*. https://doi.org/10.1177/1461444817744790.

Brown, James J. Jr. 2012. "Composition in the Dromosphere." *Computers and Composition* 29
(1): 79–91. https://doi.org/10.1016/j.compcom.2012.01.004.

Brown, James J. Jr. 2015. *Ethical Programs: Hospitality and the Rhetorics of Software*. Ann Arbor:
University of Michigan Press.

DOI: 10.7330/9781607329749.c013

Burton, Katelyn L. 2015. "Eternal or Ephemera? The Myth of Permanence in Online Writing." *Computers and Composition* 38: 57–67. https://doi.org/10.1016/j.compcom .2015.09.010.

Canter, Lily. 2013. "The Misconception of Online Comment Threads." *Journalism Practice* 7 (5): 604–19. https://doi.org/10.1080/17512786.2012.740172.

Carnegie, Teena A. M. 2009. "Interface as Exordium: The Rhetoric of Interactivity." *Computers and Composition* 26 (3): 164–73.

Carr, Nicholas. 2010. *The Shallows: What the Internet Is Doing to Our Brains.* New York: W. W. Norton.

Chaput, Catherine. 2010. "Rhetorical Circulation in Late Capitalism: Neoliberalism and the Overdetermination of Affective Energy." *Philosophy and Rhetoric* 43 (1): 1–25. https://doi.org/10.1353/par.0.0047.

Chen, Gina Masullo, and Shuning Lu. 2017. "Online Political Discourse: Exploring Differences in Effects of Civil and Uncivil Disagreement in News Website Comments." *Journal of Broadcasting & Electronic Media* 61 (1): 108–25. https://doi.org/10.1080/08838151 .2016.1273922.

Chevalier, Judith A., and Dina Mayzlin. 2006. "The Effect of Word of Mouth on Sales: Online Book Reviews." *Journal of Marketing Research* 43 (3): 345–54. https://doi.org/10 .1509/jmkr.43.3.345.

Chun, Wendy Hui Kyong. 2011. *Programmed Visions: Software and Memory.* Cambridge: MIT Press.

Chun, Wendy Hui Kyong. 2016. *Updating to Remain the Same: Habitual New Media.* Cambridge: MIT Press.

Citton, Yves. 2017. *The Ecology of Attention.* Cambridge: Polity.

Coe, Kevin, Kate Kenski, and Stephen A. Rains. 2014. "Online and Uncivil? Patterns and Determinants of Incivility in Newspaper Website Comments." *Journal of Communication* 64: 658–79. https://doi.org/10.1111/jcom.12104.

Coe, Richard M. 1975. "Eco-Logic for the Composition Classroom." *College Composition and Communication* 26 (3): 232–37.

"Community Guidelines." Amazon.com. Accessed October 18, 2019. https://www.amazon .com/gp/help/customer/display.html?nodeId=201929730.

Cooper, Marilyn M. 1986. "The Ecology of Writing." *College English* 48 (4): 364–75. https:// doi.org/10.2307/377264.

Cunningham, Carolyn Michelle. 2012. *Social Networking and Impression Management: Self Presentation in the Digital Age.* Lanham, MD: Lexington Books.

Dagenais, John. 1994. *The Ethics of Reading in Manuscript Culture: Glossing the* Libro de buen amor. Princeton, NJ: Princeton University Press.

Dashti, Ali A., Ali A. Al-Kandari, and Hamed H. Al-Abdullah. 2015. "The Influence of Sectarian and Tribal Discourse in Newspapers Readers' Online Comments about Freedom of Expression, Censorship, and National Unity in Kuwait." *Telematics and Informatics* 32 (2): 245–53. https://doi.org/10.1016/j.tele.2014.08.007.

Dean, Jodi. 2005. "Communicative Capitalism: Circulation and the Foreclosure of Politics." *Cultural Politics* 1 (1): 51–74. https://doi.org/10.2752/174321905778054845.

DeLuca, Katherine. 2018. "Shared Passions, Shared Compositions: Online Fandom Communities and Affinity Groups as Sites for Public Writing Pedagogy." *Computers and Composition* 47: 75–92. https://doi.org/10.1016/j.compcom.2017.12.003.

Dingo, Rebecca. 2012. *Networking Arguments: Rhetoric, Transnational Feminism, and Public Policy Writing.* Pittsburgh: University of Pittsburgh Press.

Dobrin, Sidney. 2011. *Postcomposition.* Carbondale: Southern Illinois University Press.

Dubisar, Abby M., and Jason Palmeri. 2010. "Palin / Pathos / Peter Griffin: Political Video Remix and Composition Pedagogy." *Computers and Composition* 27 (2): 77–93. https:// doi.org/10.1016/j.compcom.2010.03.004.

Duffy, Brooke Erin. 2017. *(Not) Getting Paid to Do What You Love: Gender, Social Media, and Aspirational Work.* New Haven, CT: Yale University Press.

Duffy, John. 2014. "Ethical Dispositions: A Discourse for Rhetoric and Composition." *JAC* 34 (1–2): 209–37.

Duffy, John. 2017. "The Good Writer: Virtue Ethics and the Teaching of Writing." *College English* 79 (3): 229–50.

Duffy, John. 2018. *Provocations of Virtue: Rhetoric, Ethics, and the Teaching of Writing.* Logan: Utah State University Press.

Edbauer, Jenny. 2005. "Unframing Models of Public Distribution: From Rhetorical Situation to Rhetorical Ecologies." *Rhetoric Society Quarterly* 35 (4): 5–24.

Edwards, Dustin. 2018. "Circulation Gatekeepers: Unbundling the Platform Politics of YouTube's Content ID." *Computers and Composition* 47: 61–74. https://doi.org/10.1016/j.compcom.2017.12.001.

Edwards, Dustin. 2017. "On Circulatory Encounters: The Case for Tactical Rhetorics." *Enculturation.* http://enculturation.net/circulatory_encounters.

Enoch, Jessica, and Jean Bessette. 2013. "Meaningful Engagements: Feminist Historiography and the Digital Humanities." *College Composition and Communication* 64 (4): 634–60.

Eyman, Douglas. 2015. *Digital Rhetoric: Theory, Method, Practice.* Ann Arbor: University of Michigan Press. http://dx.doi.org/10.3998/dh.13030181.0001.001.

Fitzpatrick, Kathleen. 2011. *Planned Obsolescence: Publishing, Technology, and the Future of the Academy.* New York: New York University Press.

Gallagher, John R. 2012. "The Emotion for Opening the Text Message." *Transformations: The Journal of Inclusive Scholarship* 22 (2): 36–43.

Gallagher, John R. 2014. "Interactive Audience and the Internet." PhD diss., University of Massachusetts.

Gallagher, John R. 2015a. "Five Strategies Internet Writers Use to 'Continue the Conversation.'" *Written Communication* 32 (4): 396–425. https://doi.org/10.1177/0741088315601006.

Gallagher, John R. 2015b. "The Rhetorical Template." *Computers and Composition* 35 (1): 1–11. https://doi.org/10.1016/j.compcom.2014.12.003.

Gallagher, John R. 2017. "Challenging the Monetized Template." *Enculturation* 24. http://enculturation.net/challenging_the_monetized_template.

Gallagher, John R. 2018. "Considering the Comments: Theorizing Online Audiences as Emergent Processes." *Computers and Composition* 48: 34–48.

Gallagher, John R., and Steve Holmes. 2019. "Empty Templates: The Ethical Habits of Empty State Pages." *Technical Communication Quarterly* 28 (3): 271–83. https://doi.org/10.1080/10572252.2018.1564367.

Galloway, Alexander R. 2012. *The Interface Effect.* Cambridge: Polity.

Goffman, Erving. 1959. *The Presentation of Self in Everyday Life.* Edinburgh: University of Edinburgh.

Gries, Laurie. 2013. "Iconographic Tracking: A Digital Research Method for Visual Rhetoric and Circulation Studies." *Computers and Composition* 30 (4): 332–48. https://doi.org/10.1016/j.compcom.2013.10.006.

Gries, Laurie. 2015. *Still Life with Rhetoric: A New Materialist Approach for Visual Rhetorics.* Logan: Utah State University Press.

Gries, Laurie, and Collin Gifford Brooke. 2018. *Circulation, Writing, and Rhetoric.* Logan: Utah State University Press.

Gurak, Laura J. 2003. *Cyberliteracy: Navigating the Internet with Awareness.* New Haven, CT: Yale University Press.

Hallinan, Blake, and Ted Striphas. 2016. "Recommended for You: The Netflix Prize and the Production of Algorithmic Culture." *New Media & Society* 18 (1): 117–37. https://doi.org/10.1177/1461444814538646.

Hariman, Robert. 1992. "Decorum, Power, and the Courtly Style." *Quarterly Journal of Speech* 78 (2): 149–72. https://doi.org/10.1080/00335639209383987.

Harvey, David. 1989. *The Condition of Postmodernity: An Enquiry into the Origins of Cultural Change.* Hoboken, NJ: Blackwell.

Hawhee, Debra. 2004. *Bodily Arts: Rhetoric and Athletics in Ancient Greece.* Austin: University of Texas Press.

Holmes, Steve. 2014. "Rhetorical Allegorithms in Bitcoin." *Enculturation* 18. http://www.enculturation.net/rhetoricalallegorithms.

Holmes, Steve. 2017. *The Rhetoric of Videogames as Embodied Practice: Procedural Habits.* New York: Routledge.

Holmes, Steve, and Jared Colton. 2018. *Rhetoric, Technology, and the Virtues.* Logan: Utah State University Press.

Hookway, Branden. 2014. *Interface.* Cambridge: MIT Press.

Horn, Nicholas M. Van, Aaron Beveridge, and Sean Morey. 2016. "Attention Ecology: Trend Circulation and the Virality Threshold." *Digital Humanities Quarterly* 10 (4). http://www.digitalhumanities.org/dhq/vol/10/4/000271/000271.html.

Hursthouse, Rosalind. 1999. *On Virtue Ethics.* Oxford: Oxford University Press.

Jackson, H. J. 2001. *Marginalia: Readers Writing in Books.* New Haven, CT: Yale University Press.

Jaques, Elliott. 1982. *The Form of Time.* New York: Crane Russak.

Jenkins, Henry. 2008. *Convergence Culture: Where Old and New Media Collide.* Rev. ed. New York: New York University Press.

Jenkins, Henry. 2013. *Spreadable Media: Creating Value and Meaning in a Networked Culture.* New York: New York University Press.

Johnson-Eilola, Johndan. 1995. "Accumulation, Circulation, Association: Economies of Information in Online Spaces." *IEEE Transactions on Professional Communication* 38 (4): 228–38. https://doi.org/10.1109/47.475594.

Johnson-Eilola, Johndan. 1997. *Nostalgic Angels: Rearticulating Hypertext Writing.* Santa Barbara: Praeger.

Jung, Julie. 2014. "Systems Rhetoric: A Dynamic Coupling of Explanation and Description." *Enculturation* 17. http://enculturation.net/systems-rhetoric.

Kareklas, Ioannis, Darrel D. Muehling, and T. J. Weber. 2015. "Reexamining Health Messages in the Digital Age: A Fresh Look at Source Credibility Effects." *Journal of Advertising* 44 (2): 88–104. https://doi.org/10.1080/00913367.2015.1018461.

Kennedy, Krista. 2016. *Textual Curation: Authorship, Agency, and Technology in Wikipedia and Chambers's Cyclopædia.* Columbia: University of South Carolina Press.

Kenski, Kate, Kevin Coe, and Stephen A. Rains. 2017. "Perceptions of Uncivil Discourse Online: An Examination of Types and Predictors." *Communication Research,* 1–20. https://doi.org/10.1177/0093650217699933.

Kinneavy, James. 1986. "*Kairos*: A Neglected Concept in Classical Rhetoric." In *Rhetoric and Praxis,* edited by Jean Dietz Moss, 79–105. Washington, DC: Catholic University of America Press.

Kirschenbaum, Matthew. 2016. *Track Changes: A Literary History of Word Processing.* Cambridge, MA: Harvard University Press.

Kjeldsen, Jens E. 2016. "Studying Rhetorical Audiences: A Call for Qualitative Reception Studies in Argumentation and Rhetoric." *Informal Logic* 36 (2): 136–58.

Korsgaard, Christine. 1996. *The Sources of Normativity.* Cambridge: Cambridge University Press.

Lacey, Kate. 2013. *Listening Publics: The Politics and Experience of Listening in the Media Age.* Cambridge: Polity.

Lanham, Richard. 1993. *The Electronic Word.* Chicago: University of Chicago Press.

Lanham, Richard. 2006. *The Economics of Attention: Style and Substance in the Age of Information.* Chicago: University of Chicago Press.

Laquintano, Tim. 2010. "Sustained Authorship: Digital Writing, Self-Publishing, and the Ebook." *Written Communication* 27 (4): 469–93. https://doi.org/10.1177/074108831037 7863.

Laquintano, Timothy. 2016. *Mass Authorship and the Rise of Self-Publishing.* Iowa City: University of Iowa Press.

Laquintano, Tim, and Annette Vee. 2017. "How Automated Writing Systems Affect the Circulation of Political Information Online." *Literacy in Composition Studies* 5 (2): 43–62.

LeCourt, Donna. 2017. "Habermasochism: The Promise of Cyberpublics in an Information Economy." In *Economies of Writing: Revaluations in Rhetoric and Composition,* edited by Bruce Horner, 225–37. Logan: Utah State University Press. https://doi.org/10 .7330/9781607325239.c015.

Ledbetter, Lehua. 2014. "The Business of Feminism: Rhetorics of Identity in YouTube's Beauty Community." PhD diss., Michigan State University.

Len-Rios, Maria E., M. Bhandari, and Y. S. Medvedeva. 2014. "Deliberation of the Scientific Evidence for Breastfeeding: Online Comments as Social Representations." *Science Communication* 36 (6): 778–801. https://doi.org/10.1177/1075547014556195.

Lipari, Lisbeth. 2010. "Listening, Thinking, Being." *Communication Theory* 20 (3): 348–62. https://doi.org/10.1111/j.1468-2885.2010.01366.x.

Loke, Jaime. 2012. "Public Expressions of Private Sentiments: Unveiling the Pulse of Racial Tolerance through Online News Readers' Comments." *Howard Journal of Communications* 23 (3): 235–52. https://doi.org/10.1080/10646175.2012.695643.

Losh, Elizabeth. 2009. *Virtualpolitik: An Electronic History of Government Media-Making in a Time of War, Scandal, Disaster, Miscommunication, and Mistakes.* Cambridge: MIT Press.

Madden, Mary. 2014. "Public Perceptions of Privacy and Security in the Post-Snowden Era." Pew Research Center. https://www.pewinternet.org/2014/11/12/public-privacy -perceptions/.

Malinen, Sanna. 2015. "Understanding User Participation in Online Communities: A Systematic Literature Review of Empirical Studies." *Computers in Human Behavior* 46 (May): 228–38. https://doi.org/10.1016/j.chb.2015.01.004.

Manivannan, Vyshali. 2014. "Tits or GTFO: The Logics of Misogyny on 4chan's Random—/B/." *Fibreculture Journal* 22. http://twentytwo.fibreculturejournal.org/fcj -158-tits-or-gtfo-the-logics-of-misogyny-on-4chans-random-b/.

Manovich, Lev. 2002. *The Language of New Media.* Reprint ed. Cambridge: MIT Press.

Marchionni, Doreen. 2015. "Online Story Commenting: An Experimental Test of Conversational Journalism and Trust." *Journalism Practice* 9 (2): 230–49. https://doi.org/10 .1080/17512786.2014.938943.

Massanari, Adrienne L. 2015. *Participatory Culture, Community, and Play: Learning from reddit.* New York: Peter Lang.

Massanari, Adrienne. 2017. "#Gamergate and The Fappening: How reddit's Algorithm, Governance, and Culture Support Toxic Technocultures." *New Media and Society* 19 (3): 329–46. https://doi.org/10.1177/1461444815608807.

Massanari, Adrienne L. 2018. "Rethinking Research Ethics, Power, and the Risk of Visibility in the Era of the 'Alt-Right' Gaze." *Social Media + Society* 4 (2): 1–9. https://doi.org /10.1177/2056305118768302.

Matheson, Calum. 2014. "Procedural Rhetoric beyond Persuasion: First Strike and the Compulsion to Repeat." *Games and Culture* 10 (5): 1–18. https://doi.org/10.1177/155 5412014565642.

Mays, Chris. 2015. "From 'Flows' to 'Excess': On Stability, Stubbornness, and Blockage in Rhetorical Ecologies." *Enculturation* 19. http://enculturation.net/from-flows-to-excess.

McKee, Heidi. 2002. "'YOUR VIEWS SHOWED TRUE IGNORANCE!!!': (Mis)Communication in an Online Interracial Discussion Forum." *Computers and Composition* 19 (4): 411–34. https://doi.org/10.1016/S8755-4615(02)00143-3.

McLuhan, Marshall. 1962. *The Gutenberg Galaxy: The Making of Typographic Man.* Toronto: University of Toronto Press.

Molinari, Deana L. 2004. "The Role of Social Comments in Problem-Solving Groups in an Online Class." *American Journal of Distance Education* 18 (2): 89–101. https://doi.org/10.1207/s15389286ajde1802.

Morey, Sean. 2015. *Rhetorical Delivery and Digital Technologies: Networks, Affect, Electracy.* New York: Routledge.

Moss-Racusin, Corinne A., Aneta K. Molenda, and Charlotte R. Cramer. 2015. "Can Evidence Impact Attitudes? Public Reactions to Evidence of Gender Bias in STEM Fields." *Psychology of Women Quarterly* 39 (2): 194–209. https://doi.org/10.1177/0361684314565777.

Muckelbauer, John. 2008. *The Future of Invention: Rhetoric, Postmodernism, and the Problem of Change.* Albany: SUNY Press.

Mueller, Derek N. 2018. *Network Sense: Methods for Visualizing a Discipline.* Louisville: University Press of Colorado.

Mueller, Robert S. 2018. "Internet Research Agency Indictment." https://www.justice.gov/file/1035477/download.

Nahon, Karine, and Jeff Hemsley. 2013. *Going Viral.* Cambridge: Polity.

Norman, Donald. 1988. *The Psychology of Everyday Things.* New York: Basic Books.

Ong, Walter J. 1991. *Orality and Literacy: The Technologizing of the Word.* 3rd ed. New York: Routledge.

O'Reilly, Tim. 2005. "What Is Web 2.0? Design Patterns and Business Models for the Next Generation." http://oreilly.com/web2/archive/what-is-web-20.html.

O'Sullivan, Donie. 2018. "How the Russians Did It." CNN. http://money.cnn.com/2018/02/16/media/internet-research-agency-mueller-indictment/index.html.

Palmer, Philip S. 2014. "'The Progress of Thy Glorious Book': Material Reading and the Play of Paratext in *Coryats Crudities* (1611)." *Renaissance Studies* 28 (3): 336–55. https://doi.org/10.1111/rest.12013.

Pangallo, Matteo A. 2017. *Playwriting Playgoers in Shakespeare's Theater.* Philadelphia: University of Pennsylvania Press.

Perelman, Chaim, and Lucie Olbrechts-Tyteca. 1969. *The New Rhetoric: A Treatise on Argumentation.* Notre Dame, IN: University of Notre Dame Press.

Pfister, Damien Smith. 2014. *Networked Media, Networked Rhetorics: Attention and Deliberation in the Early Blogosphere.* University Park: Penn State University Press.

Pflugfelder, Ehren Helmut. 2017. "reddit's 'Explain like I'm Five': Technical Descriptions in the Wild." *Technical Communication Quarterly* 26 (1): 25–41. https://doi.org/10.1080/10572252.2016.1257741.

Phillips, Whitney. 2015. *This Is Why We Can't Have Nice Things: Mapping the Relationship between Online Trolling and Mainstream Culture.* Cambridge: MIT Press.

Porter, James E. 2009. "Recovering Delivery for Digital Rhetoric." *Computers and Composition* 26 (4): 207–24. https://doi.org/10.1016/j.compcom.2009.09.004.

Potts, Liza, Melissa Beattie, Emily Dallaire, Katie Grimes, and Kelly Turner. 2018. *Participatory Memory: Fandom Experiences across Time and Space.* Intermezzo. http://intermezzo.enculturation.net/06-potts-et-al.htm.

Powers, Devon. 2015. "First! Cultural Circulation in the Age of Recursivity." *New Media & Society* 19 (2): 165–80. https://doi.org/10.1177/1461444815600280.

Prior, Paul. 1998. *Writing/Disciplinarity: A Sociohistoric Account of Literate Activity in the Academy.* New York: Routledge.

Prior, Paul, Janine Solberg, Patrick Berry, Hannah Bellwoar, Bill Chewning, Karen J. Lunsford, Liz Rohan, Kevin Roozen, Mary P. Sheridan-Rabideau, Jody Shipka, Derek Van Ittersum, and Joyce Walker. 2007. "Re-situating and Re-mediating the Canons: A Cultural-Historical Remapping of Rhetorical Activity." *Kairos: A Journal of Rhetoric, Tech-*

nology, and Pedagogy 11 (7). http://*kairos*.technorhetoric.net/11.3/binder.html?topoi /prior-et-al/mapping/index.html.

Ratcliffe, Krista. 2006. *Rhetorical Listening: Identification, Gender, Whiteness.* Carbondale: Southern Illinois University Press.

Reader, Bill. 2012. "Free Press vs. Free Speech? The Rhetoric of 'Civility' in Regards to Anonymous Online Comments." *Journalism and Mass Communication Quarterly* 89 (3): 495–513.

Reagle, Joseph Michael. 2010. *Good Faith Collaboration.* Cambridge: MIT Press.

Reagle, Joseph M. 2015. *Reading the Comments: Likers, Haters, and Manipulators at the Bottom of the Web.* Cambridge: MIT Press.

Rice, Jeff. 2016. "Digital Outragicity." *Enculturation* 23. http://enculturation.net/digital _outragicity.

Rice, Jeff. 2017. "Circulated Epideictic: The Technical Image and Digital Consensus." *Philosophy & Rhetoric* 50 (3): 272–91.

Rickert, Thomas. 2013. *Ambient Rhetoric: The Attunement of Rhetorical Being.* Pittsburgh: University of Pittsburgh Press.

Ridolfo, Jim. 2012. "Rhetorical Delivery as Strategy: Rebuilding the Fifth Canon from Practitioner Stories." *Rhetoric Review* 31 (2): 117–29. https://doi.org/10.1080/07350198 .2012.652034.

Ridolfo, Jim. 2013. "Delivering Textual Diaspora: Building Digital Cultural Repositories as Rhetoric Research." *College English* 76 (2): 136–51.

Ridolfo, Jim. 2015. *Digital Samaritans: Rhetorical Delivery and Engagement in the Digital Humanities.* Ann Arbor: University of Michigan Press.

Ridolfo, Jim, and Dànielle Nicole DeVoss. 2009. "Composing for Recomposition: Rhetorical Velocity and Delivery." *Kairos: A Journal of Rhetoric, Technology, and Pedagogy* 13 (2). http://*kairos*.technorhetoric.net/13.2/topoi/ridolfo_devoss/velocity.html.

Rivers, Nathaniel. 2016. "Paying Attention with Cache." *Enculturation* 23. http:// enculturation.net/paying-attention.

Rivers, Nathaniel A., and Ryan P. Weber. 2011. "Ecological, Pedagogical, Public Rhetoric." *College Composition and Communication* 63 (2): 187–218.

Rowe, Ian. 2015a. "Civility 2.0: A Comparative Analysis of Incivility in Online Political Discussion." *Information, Communication & Society* 18 (2): 121–38. https://doi.org/10.1080 /1369118X.2014.940365.

Rowe, Ian. 2015b. "Deliberation 2.0: Comparing the Deliberative Quality of Online News User Comments across Platforms." *Journal of Broadcasting & Electronic Media* 59 (4): 539–55. https://doi.org/10.1080/08838151.2015.1093482.

Santana, Arthur D. 2013. "Virtuous or Vitriolic: The Effect of Anonymity on Civility in Online Newspaper Reader Comment Boards." *Journalism Practice* 8 (1): 18–33. https:// doi.org/10.1080/17512786.2013.813194.

Santana, Arthur D. 2016. "Controlling the Conversation: The Availability of Commenting Forums in Online Newspapers." *Journalism Studies* 17 (2): 141–58. https://doi.org/10 .1080/1461670X.2014.972076.

Selfe, Cynthia L., and Richard J. Selfe. 1994. "The Politics of the Interface: Power and Its Exercise in Electronic Contact Zones." *College Composition and Communication* 45 (4): 480–504. https://doi.org/10.2307/358761.

Sheridan, David M., Jim Ridolfo, and Anthony J. Michel. 2012. *The Available Means of Persuasion: Mapping a Theory and Pedagogy of Multimodal Public Rhetoric.* Anderson, SC: Parlor.

Sherman, William H. 2008. *Used Books: Marking Readers in Renaissance England.* Philadelphia: University of Pennsylvania Press.

Simonson, Peter. 2014. "Reinventing Invention, Again." *Rhetoric Society Quarterly* 44 (4): 299–322. https://doi.org/10.1080/02773945.2014.938862.

Smith, Craig R., and Scott Lybarger. 1996. "Bitzer's Model Reconstructed." *Communication Quarterly* 44 (2): 197–213. https://doi.org/10.1080/01463379609370010.

Smith, John E. 1969. "Time, Times, and the 'Right' Time: *Chronos* and *Kairos.*" *The Monist* 53 (1): 1–13.

Smith, John E. 1986. "Time and Qualitative Time." *Review of Metaphysics* 40 (1): 3–16.

Solberg, Janine. 2012. "Googling the Archive: Digital Tools and the Practice of History." *Advances in the History of Rhetoric* 15 (1): 53–76. https://doi.org/10.1080/15362426.2012.657052.

Sparby, Erika M. 2017. "Digital Social Media and Aggression: Memetic Rhetoric in 4chan's Collective Identity." *Computers and Composition* 45: 85–97. https://doi.org/10.1016/j.compcom.2017.06.006.

Spigelman, Candace. 2001. "What Role Virtue?" *JAC* 21 (2): 321–48.

Spinuzzi, Clay. 2015. *All Edge: Inside the New Workplace Networks.* Chicago: University of Chicago Press.

Springer, Nina, Ines Engelmann, and Christian Pfaffinger. 2015. "User Comments: Motives and Inhibitors to Write and Read." *Information, Communication & Society* 18 (7): 798–815. https://doi.org/10.1080/1369118X.2014.997268.

Stanfill, Mel. 2015. "The Interface as Discourse: The Production of Norms through Web Design." *New Media & Society* 17 (7): 1059–74. https://doi.org/10.1177/1461444814520873.

Strauss, Anselm, and Juliet Corbin. 1998. *Basics of Qualitative Research: Techniques and Procedures for Developing Grounded Theory.* 2nd ed. Thousand Oaks, CA: SAGE.

Sung, Kang Hoon, and Moon J. Lee. 2015. "Do Online Comments Influence the Public's Attitudes toward an Organization? Effects of Online Comments Based on Individuals' Prior Attitudes." *Journal of Psychology* 149 (4): 325–38. https://doi.org/10.1080/00223980.2013.879847.

Syverson, Margaret A. 1999. *The Wealth of Reality: An Ecology of Composition.* Carbondale: Southern Illinois University Press.

Tarsa, Rebecca. 2015. "Upvoting the Exordium: Literacy Practices of the Digital Interface." *College English* 78 (1): 12–34.

"Terms of Service." Forbes.com. Accessed October 18, 2019. https://www.forbes.com/terms-and-conditions/#16bc5f83193f.

Thompson, Kathryn. 2014. "'No One Cares, Apostolate': What Social Cheating Reveals." *Games and Culture* 9 (6): 491–502. https://doi.org/10.1177/1555412014552521.

Tiersma, Peter M. 2010. *Parchment, Paper, Pixels: Law and the Technologies of Communication.* Chicago: University of Chicago Press.

Trimbur, John. 2000. "Composition and the Circulation of Writing." *College Composition and Communication* 52 (2): 188–219.

Turkle, Sherry. 2011. *Alone Together: Why We Expect More from Technology and Less from Each Other.* New York: Basic Books.

Ürper Çatalbaş, Dilruba, and Tolga Çevikel. 2016. "Editorial Policies, Journalistic Output, and Reader Comments." *Journalism Studies* 17 (2): 159–76. https://doi.org/10.1080/1461670X.2014.969491.

Valentine, Matt. 2014. "The Gunfight in Cyberspace." *Politico,* December 2014. https://www.politico.com/magazine/story/2014/12/gunfight-activists-online-113236.

Vallor, Shannon. 2010. "Social Networking Technology and the Virtues." *Ethics and Information Technology* 12 (2): 157–70. https://doi.org/10.1007/s10676-009-9202-1.

Vallor, Shannon. 2016. *Technology and the Virtues: A Philosophical Guide to a Future Worth Wanting.* Oxford: Oxford University Press.

Vatz, Richard E. 1973. "The Myth of the Rhetorical Situation." *Philosophy and Rhetoric* 6 (3): 154–61.

Warnick, Barbara, and David S. Heineman. 2012. *Rhetoric Online: The Politics of New Media.* 2nd ed. New York: Peter Lang.

Welch, Kathleen. 1999. *Electric Rhetoric: Classic Rhetoric, Oralism, and a New Literacy.* Cambridge, MA: MIT Press.

"What Is Amazon Vine?" Amazon.com. Accessed October 18, 2019. https://www.amazon.com/gp/vine/help.

Wuebben, Daniel. 2016. "Getting Likes, Going Viral, and the Intersections between Popularity Metrics and Digital Composition." *Computers and Composition* 42: 66–79. https://doi.org/10.1016/j.compcom.2016.08.004.

Yancey, Kathleen Blake. 2004. "Made Not Only in Words: Composition in a New Key." *College Composition and Communication* 56 (2): 297–328.

Ziegele, Marc, Timo Breiner, and Oliver Quiring. 2014. "What Creates Interactivity in Online News Discussions? An Exploratory Analysis of Discussion Factors in User Comments on News Items." *Journal of Communication* 64 (6): 1111–38. https://doi.org/10.1111/jcom.12123.

ABOUT THE AUTHOR

JOHN R. GALLAGHER is an assistant professor of English and writing studies at the University of Illinois, Urbana-Champaign. Gallagher has been published in *Written Communication, Computers and Composition, Enculturation, Technical Communication Quarterly, Rhetoric Review,* and *Transformations.* Gallagher focuses on template rhetoric and the way online writers contend with their participatory audiences. He is currently working on a manuscript tentatively titled *Machine Audiences.*

INDEX

ABL. *See* Anonymous Blogger
accuracy, 21, 30
acta diurna populi Romani, 11
adhocracies, all-edge, 104–5
ad hominem attacks, 129
affordances, ambient, 45–47, 85
afterlife, 4; in digital writing, 11, 39, 44, 151, 152, 156–57, 159
algorithms, 5, 20, 141, 160; power of, 69–70; timing and display of, 15, 50–51, 70–73, 76
All Edge (Spinuzzi), 104
all-edge adhocracies, 104–5
Amazon: exploitation by, 136–37; template used by, 18
Amazon reviewers, 20, 21, 71, 73, 89, 101, 105, 121, 134, 135, 142, 166, 169; descriptions of, 28–30(table); exploitation of, 136–37; guidelines for, 113, 118; inadvertent responses to, 148–50; motivations of, 138–39; responses by, 90, 91–92, 114–15; template timing, 65–66, 67–69; timing of writing, 58, 60–62, 63; updating by, 130–31; and Vine program, 66–67
Ambient Rhetoric (Rickert), 45, 51–52
AndrewSmith1986, 22, 54, 59, 113, 123
anonymity, 19
Anonymous Blogger (ABL), 25(table)
Anonymous reviewer 1 (AR1), 30(table), 60, 63, 70, 86
Anonymous reviewer 2 (AR2), 30(table), 60, 68, 130–31
application programming interfaces (APIs), 9
Armstrong, Heather, 25(table), 74, 102, 104, 133, 139; on algorithmic timing, 70, 72–73; on reader comments, 88, 89
Arola, Kristen, 33
AR1. *See* Anonymous reviewer 1
AR2. *See* Anonymous reviewer 2
AskReddit, 54, 55; threads in, 93–96
aspirational branding, 102, 132–34, 138, 139
attending, 79, 80
attention, and listening scholarship, 78–79; reflexive, 81–82. *See also* textual attention

audiences, 8, 15, 18, 56, 75, 165; attention to, 77–78, 83–85; comments from, 86–87, 163–64; forums, 119–21; maintaining/expanding, 132–33; managing, 113–16; as ongoing process, 153–54; participatory, 10, 12, 131; rules and guidelines for, 117–19; sincere responses to, 90–93; text changes and, 3–4; textual attention, 79–80; and textual management, 103–4; and timing of writing, 59–60; and writers, 9, 20, 33–34
automation, 70
Available Means of Persuasion, The (Sheridan, Ridolfo, and Michel), 50

backstage activities, 103
Barthes, Roland, 7
Bauman, Zygmunt, *Liquid Modernity,* 157
/b/board, 123
behavior: rules and guidelines, 40–41, 116–18; trolling, 122–24
bias, researcher, 30–31
Bickford, Susan, 80
Bitzer, Lloyd, 5, 86; "The Rhetorical Situation," 52, 98
Blair, Ann, *Too Much to Know,* 11–12
bloggers, 3, 20, 21, 25(table), 30, 102, 105, 120, 123, 139, 169; algorithms, 69, 71–72; on reader comments, 88–89; rules and guidelines, 113, 117; timing of writing, 58, 137; work habits, 142, 144; writing experience, 74–75
blog posts, 3, 39
Bodily Arts (Hawhee), 51
bots, 5, 71, 160
boyd, danah, 108
Bradshaw, Leslie, 165
branding, aspirational, 15, 102, 132–34
Brandt, Deborah, *The Rise of Writing,* 14
Breitbart, 150
Bretty, 29(table); confronting trolls, 123–24
broadcasting, confronting trolls, 126
Brooke, Collin, 62; *Circulation, Writing, and Rhetoric,* 4; *Lingua Fracta,* 55
Brown, James, Jr., *Ethical Programs,* 7, 41, 103
Burton, Katelyn, 8

Valentine, Matt, 149
Vatz, Richard, "The Myth of the Rhetorical Situation," 98
versioning, 128
Vine program, 66–67, 136
violence, threats of, 116
virality, 52–53
Virtualpolitik (Losh), 55
virtue ethics, 140–41, 145
virtues, 16, 140; digital communication, 144–46
voices, community, 80

Warner, Michael, 86
Warnick, Barbara, *Rhetoric Online*, 32–33, 56–57
Way_Fairer (Scott Steffens), 22(table), 91, 115, 126; on timing of writing, 59, 64
web design, 33
websites, 117
Web 2.0, 18. *See also* interactive and participatory internet
web users, writing and, 56–57

What you see is what you get (WYSIWYG) programs, 34–35
Winston, Sandy, 29(table)
women, 130; internal frames, 115–16; rules and guidelines, 117–18
word processing, 34–35
WordPress, 18
writers, 103; and algorithms, 69–70; in all-edge adhocracies, 104–5; aspirational branding, 132–33; and audiences, 9, 33–34, 83–84; ethics of, 138–39, 141–42; and participant forums, 119–21; purposes of, 100–102; sincere responses by, 90–93; style, 20, 21; textual attention by, 79–80, 85–90, 93–97; work habits of, 142–44. *See also* digital writing, writers
Writing/Disciplinarity, 164
writing police, 15
WYSIWYG. *See* What you see is what you get

Yancey, Kathleen Blake, 33
YouTube videos, 62, 137, 138